The Imprisonment of Women

The Imprisonment of Women

Russell P. Dobash
R. Emerson Dobash
Sue Gutteridge

Basil Blackwell

© Russell P. Dobash, R. Emerson Dobash and Sue Gutteridge 1986

First published 1986

Basil Blackwell Ltd
108 Cowley Road, Oxford OX4 1JF, UK

Basil Blackwell Inc.
432 Park Avenue South, Suite 1503,
New York, NY 10016, USA

British Library Cataloguing in Publication Data
Dobash, Russell P.
  The imprisonment of women.
  1.Women prisoners
  I. Title II. Dobash, R. Emerson
  III. Gutteridge, Sue
  365'.43   HV8738

  ISBN 0-631-14318-1
  ISBN 0-631-14319-X Pbk

Library of Congress Cataloging in Publication Data
Dobash, Russell.
  The imprisonment of women.
  Bibliography: p.
  Includes index.
  1. Women prisoners—Great Britain—History.
  2. Female offenders— Great Britain— History.
  3. Prison psychology—History. 4. Reformatories for women—
  Great Britain—History. I. Dobash, R. Emerson.
  II. Gutteridge, Sue. III. Title.
  HV9644.D63 1986   365'.43'0941   86–3544

  ISBN 0-631-14318-1
  ISBN 0-631-14319-X (pbk. : alk. paper)

Typeset by Alan Sutton Publishing Limited, Gloucester
Printed in Great Britain by Billing and Sons Ltd, Worcester

Contents

28747

List of Plates

Acknowledgements

We should like to thank a number of people who assisted in the creation of *The Imprisonment of Women*. Initial inspiration for one of us came some years ago in discussions with Bud Pfuhl and Peter Garabedian at Arizona State University. Both created what became a long-standing interest in crime and imprisonment which led first to research in American penal institutions and then to work in British prisons.

The book benefited from discussions with Pat McLaughlin and Sarah Nelson, and Pat McLaughlin and Julia Bard commented on various sections. We are indebted to the published work of Michel Foucault for many theoretical ideas, and we benefited from discussion with him in which some important issues were clarified.

Eleanor Bruce performed her usual competent job of creating a polished manuscript, aided in the final stages by Rachel Haigh. We thank both of them for their patience as we worked through several drafts.

The Carnegie Trust for Scotland partially supported the research at Cornton Vale, and the SSRC (ESRC) supported research on men's prisons which indirectly aided this work. Finally, we would like to thank the staff and prisoners at Cornton Vale who gave their time to talk to us about prison and imprisonment. We would like to note that details of particular examples have been changed and fictitious names have been used throughout.

Plate 1 is reproduced from L. Jewitt, 'Scolds and how they cured them in the good old times', *The Reliquary* (October, 1860). Plates 2–10 are taken from Henry Mayhew and John Binney, *The Criminal Prisons of London and Scenes of Prison Life* (Griffin, Bohn and Co., London, 1862), reprinted by Frank Cass in 1968 and reproduced here by permission of Frank Cass & Co. Ltd. Plates 11 and 12 were kindly supplied by the Hertfordshire Constabulary. We would especially like to thank Inspector Partridge for his assistance. The plates were expertly photographed by Frank Nowikoski of Braco.

1

The Imprisonment of Women in Britain and the United States

The imprisonment of women in Britain and the United States today reflects the end product of a process that has its roots in early nineteenth-century British prisons. Confining women and men in prisons, asylums and workhouses was thought to be the best way of dealing with many of the problems that beset society including social unrest and crime. A prison was meant to be a world that would lead to physical discipline and moral transformation. From the very beginning, women in prison were treated differently from men, considered more morally depraved and corrupt and in need of special, closer forms of control and confinement. They became a pariah class, separate and distinct from the ideal, chaste and morally correct women of the Victorian era and this continues even today. In this book we will focus on the development of prisons for women from their early creation and expansion to the present. We will consider the nature of various prison regimes that have developed not only to control, punish or to reform prisoners but also to support the operation of the prison itself. Such regimes have been shaped by an early emphasis on work and religion and now by a focus on therapeutic interventions. With the development of each new regime something of the old has usually remained, resulting in a composite of over a hundred years of experimentation blended into routines that shape the daily life of the prisoner and the prison. Images of the nature of criminal women and theories about the causes of their crimes have been a source of intense debate and have often informed the development of unique responses to them. The fear, disgust and outrage revealed in these ideas help explain the kinds of regimes that were developed to deal with criminal women. It is our aim to examine this complex of prison regimes and images of the women who are closely confined within them in order to chart the development of women's prisons from the nineteenth century to the present.

1

Today, women confined in the jails and prisons of Britain and the United States are usually poor and, in America, disproportionately black. Their offences are rarely vicious, dangerous or highly profitable. They are usually there for petty thefts, often shoplifting, public order offences, such as public drunkenness, breach of the peace and, unique to women, for offences related to prostitution.[1] Recent commentators and the mass media would have us believe that there has been an extraordinary increase in the criminal activities of women and that they are increasingly involved in heinous crimes and acts of terrorism and violence.[2] The evidence for such a trend is very slim indeed. Certainly, recent reports for England and Wales indicate that the rate of crime and incarceration for women has been increasing in the past two decades but there is no similar increase for Scotland.[3] Despite this increase, and it is not phenomenal, research also indicates that the type of crimes committed is not changing. Most crimes of women arise from their circumstances within wider society. For example, 90 per cent of welfare fraud in America involves the Aid to Dependent Children programme and 70 per cent of the offenders are women.[4] Such patterns are, of course, subsequently reflected in rates of imprisonment.

Women constitute about three to four per cent of the prison and jail populations in Britain and the United States in any given year. In 1984 the daily average prison population of the whole of England and Wales was 42,295 men and women.[5] Women made up 3.5 per cent (1,473) of the population, and this represents a considerable increase over previous years. From a low point of 841 women in 1965, the population has nearly doubled. From 1970 to 1975 the rate of increase was 23 per cent and from 1975 to 1980 it was 24 per cent, when the daily average reached a peak of 1,516.[6] Interestingly, the numbers in 1982 (1,326) and 1983 (1,390) were well below this peak. One of the major reasons for this increase has been the tendency of the courts to place women in prison on remand prior to their court appearance; most of whom eventually receive outright discharges or non-custodial sentences.[7] In 1960 women on remand awaiting trial represented only five per cent of the population, in 1970 nearly ten per cent and today almost 16. The other major reason is failure to pay fines. Of those received into prison to serve sentences in 1984, nearly 40 per cent were for fine default.[8]

There is a crisis of overcrowding in the British prison system which is containing far greater numbers than it was designed for, but that crisis began at least three decades ago with the build-up of the prison population. Since 1955 the population of men has doubled, but the extraordinary increases actually occurred in the 1960s. Despite this rise in the imprisonment of men and women during the last two decades, the proportion of women to the overall prison population has not changed dramatically, declining from 1950 when women represented 5.4 per cent of the daily average population to the 3.5 per cent of today. Despite the changes in the proportion of women to men, the overall increase in the prison population in general means that there are certainly more women in prison today than there were 20 years ago. However their numbers are still small and they continue to comprise a small proportion of the average population. Daily averages do not, of course, tell the whole story. In any given year a much greater number of women pass through prison and jails, particularly since many are there awaiting trial or serving short sentences. For example, in 1977, 7,000 women were actually processed through the prisons in England and Wales[9] while the number of prisoners held on any given day was obviously much smaller.

There are of course many more women in American prisons and jails than in Britain, an obvious reflection of the greater population base. In the early 1970s the daily average population of women in the United States was around 6,000 in state and federal prisons. As in Britain, women represented approximately three per cent of the overall prison population.[10] In California in 1972 women made up almost four per cent of the prison population.[11] However, it is important to point out that prisons in North America are organized and administered on a number of different levels, unlike British prisons which are centrally administered. This means that the above statistics only pertain to prisons and not to local city and county jails in which most women and men are held. The most recent statistics for a twelve-month period in 1982–83 indicate that the average daily jail population in the United States was 227,500. Of this number approximately seven per cent, 15,925, were adult women.[12] These data also indicate that there has been a sharp rise in the numbers of both women and men in jails in the United States and the rate of increase has been higher for women. Since 1978 the number of men has increased by 40 per cent while the number of women has increased by 65 per cent.[13]

The conditions experienced by women in prison vary greatly. In the United States they vary from state to state and most importantly relative to type of institutions. American city and county jails are notoriously overcrowded, understaffed and often characterized by inadequate facilities. On first impression, the prisons for women appear quite different from short-term jails. An historical legacy of paternalism and therapeutic ideals initially expressed through the building of reformatories in the late nineteenth and early twentieth century means that many look like 'a small college campus'. Forbidding prison walls, fortress-like entrances and cell blocks have been replaced by cottage-style accommodation, low or non-existent perimeter fencing and dormitory-style sleeping arrangements. Not all women's prisons are built like this, but various nationwide surveys indicate that this is the norm.[14]

British institutions for women are less diverse, ranging from closed, maximum security facilities such as the women's wing at Durham to more open conditions at prisons such as Askham Grange. There are now twelve establishments imprisoning women throughout Britain. In England and Wales there are eight closed prisons and three open prisons for adult women.[15] In Scotland, with its separate penal system, there is only one institution for women, Cornton Vale. It is intended to hold women over sixteen years of age convicted of all sorts of offences from the most petty to the most serious. Although some of the open prisons in England are in old country houses, the reformatory ideal with an emphasis on agrarian self-sufficiency and cottage-style living patterns never took hold in Britain even in the two newest prisons for women, the rebuilt Holloway in London and Cornton Vale.

Although prisons for women are often the more up-to-date institutions in the penal system, this does not necessarily mean that women are imprisoned in the best conditions. Indeed, men with trivial offences might be held under conditions of relaxed or moderate security. By contrast, women who commit trivial offences, which accounts for most women prisoners, are often held in one institution equipped with maximum security arrangements deemed necessary for the very few who have committed more serious offences. Surveys of womens' institutions in the United States also indicate that they are usually in remote areas and offer fewer medical, educational and vocational facilities than prisons for men.[16] An American prison official, Velimesis, concluded after a thorough examination of the facilities and programmes available to women that therapeutic concerns, such as attempts to help women 'develop empathy, maturity, unselfishness, [and] warmth' appeared wide-spread whereas vocational programmes were non-existent or filled with 'mediocrity and irrelevance'.[17] She concluded, 'most job training is a farce.' This is in spite of the fact that most women who leave prison will be working and are often the sole wage-earner in their household. Nor should it be assumed that the existence of facilities means that they can be used by the prisoners. Recent reports from Holloway indicate that British women are usually denied the use of facilities often because of staff shortages. Holloway has become the focal point for concerns and protests about the living conditions experienced by women in British prisons. In any given year this prison receives into custody approximately 50 per cent of the women passing through the English prison system. It is often overcrowded and the conditions experienced by women in the psychiatric wing have been described as appalling.

Even if we accept the official account that prisons for women are well equipped, we have to go beyond physical conditions and ask additional questions about the arrangments for imprisoned women. While not denying that brightly painted buildings and the existence of gardens make an important difference in physical conditions, they do not necessarily reflect the personal relationships and styles of conduct that constitute the nature of daily life within such a physical setting. The nature of the regimes in prison, their operation and the relationships between staff and prisoners may be just as repressive in the campus- or cottage-style prison as those in the traditional-style cell blocks or tiered galleries. After a recent study of Bedford Hills, a women's reformatory in New York which looks like a private college, Jim Fox concluded that the underlying atmosphere was one of 'intense hostility, frustrations and anger'.[18]

Despite the conditions in these prisons and the significant number of women passing through them, little systematic research exists on the nature of the experience of the women confined in them. Until recently, most of the contemporary research on the experiences of confinement has been from North America. The bulk of this research was conducted in the 1960s and was primarily oriented to providing accounts of how women and men coped with prison rather than with the nature of prisons or the process of imprisonment. As one would expect, these works represented the assumptions of the social sciences of that period. Liberal researchers of the time were rightly concerned about the impact of imprisonment on prisoners. How did they experience the 'pains of imprisonment', what were the forms of collective and individual adaptation, and most importantly how could penal regimes be changed to reduce the deprivations of confinement? According to the accepted orthodoxy of the period, prisoners, especially men, coped with imprisonment through the adoption of a virulent anti-social, anti-staff subculture. This subcultural adaptation was seen as an impediment to rehabilitation, and if, following the logic of the argument, the pains of imprisonment were reduced, one of the important impediments to rehabilitation, the inmate subculture, would also be reduced.

Similar assumptions, although often not articulated, underpinned the research on women in prison. American investigators such as Kassebaum and Ward, Giallombardo and Heffernan, reported alternative forms of adaptation in women's prisons.[19] Women did not develop virulent anti-staff norms. Rather, according to these investigators, they established various forms of family style and/or homosexual relationships as methods of coping with confinement. These researchers often concentrated on the sexual orientations of women, possibly a reflection of the prevalent theories about women's crime which stressed its bio-psychological and sexual basis. Much subsequent research has focussed on similar considerations about the nature of women prisoners and how they cope with prison life to the neglect of a great many issues about the prison itself, its regimes, policies, practices and orientations to those confined.

Until recently, contemporary British research on women in prison was dominated by bio-psychological perspectives about women and girls. They are more likely than male prisoners to be seen as low in intelligence, maladjusted, emotionally disturbed and in need of psychological and psychiatric intervention.[20] This literature is dominated by the work of a few researchers approved by the government, since it has been very difficult for academic researchers with alternative perspectives to breach the walls of Britain's prisons.[21] We will discuss the significance and impact of this perspective more fully in chapters 5 and 6, but it is important to point out that this approach is not some vestige of an earlier era predating contemporary feminist and critical analysis. It is still very much apparent. Recent work in this tradition has concluded, for example, that one group of women who commit frauds and forgeries is '. . . composed of dull and ill-educated women from large, poor families who illegally apply for every sort of sickness, unemployment, or special sort of public benefit, of which there is a vast variety today'.[22] Psychopathology, premenstrual tension and a variety of other 'physical and mental disorders' are thought to play a prominent role in the criminality of women and their subsequent response to imprisonment.

Some recent research on the imprisonment of women in Britain has certainly moved away from this preoccupation with the bio-psychological nature of women in confinement and towards a consideration of other issues.[23] There have also been some important and incisive biographical accounts of the imprisonment and criminality of women.[24] Nevertheless, much of this research concentrates on the nature of individual experiences within prison and continues to neglect wider issues.

Beginning in the early 1970s, especially with the work of Irwin and Cressey, social scientists were urged to expand their conceptions of imprisonment in order to include elements of the wider social world, especially the theft subculture, in order to explain how prisoners adapted to prison life.[25] According to these accounts, values, ideals and patterns of behaviour are imported into the prison from the wider society and these should be included in any analysis of prisons. An explanation such as this should have been obvious to social scientists, but their concern about and fascination with the inside had made it almost impossible to go beyond the gates to consider wider social forces. Yet the outcome of this new orientation has not been all that significant. Instead of looking at prison in relation to the outside world of political, economic and social activity or of turning their attention to the prison itself, its regimes, policies, practices and philosophies, this work was much more narrow and seemed simply to add another incremental dimension to the traditional studies of coping with life inside. Earlier research had concentrated on the way individuals experienced prison life, and this new orientation simply expanded this to include their background prior to coming into prison.[26] The focus of this conventional work on contemporary prison life remains primarily on adaptation, coping, and socialisation into the inmate subculture.

Conventional accounts of the history of imprisonment generally consider the creation of prisons in the early nineteenth century as an exceptional, unique and progressive development in the response to crime and deviance. Ann Smith has provided us with a useful, and indeed the only, statement of administrative developments from the late eighteenth century through to the 1950s.[27] According to her account, the history of the imprisonment of women can be seen as one of steady progress reaching its pinnacle in the therapeutic ideals of the present era. While proffering some mild rebukes to penal administrators she is primarily uncritical and straightforward. More recent histories usually tell a very different story. It was not until feminist historians and critical social scientists began to explore penal issues that explanations went beyond the conventional, reductionist and individual approaches that had dominated the literature of life inside contemporary prisons and beyond the conventional histories emphasizing administration and progressive development.

Critical approaches to prison history have played a significant role in the new investigations and interpretations of the rise of the modern system of criminal justice and imprisonment. Marxists, feminists and critical scholars have proposed new, revised histories. Some of these explanations rely heavily on economic factors, viewing changes in the modes of production and fluctuations in labour markets as the sole determinates of the forms and severity of criminal justice. They posit that during periods of economic expansion, when labour is in demand, progressive ideas and reactions to crime are more likely. Alternatively, during periods of depression, when there is an overabundance of labour, judicial and penal repression is more likely to be used as a means of punishing and absorbing the unemployed.[28] There is much to commend this argument, especially when one considers recent developments within the depressed economies of Western societies. Recent expansions in prison populations, extensions of severe sentences and proposed prison building schemes are all occurring in a depressed economic climate characterized by high rates of unemployment.

A fuller account of the history of imprisonment must also include a consideration of social, cultural and institutional patterns. The most important contributions to the new critical or revisionist accounts of the development of confinement have been made by three scholars, David Rothman, Michael Ignatieff, and most importantly for our analysis Michel Foucault.[29] Although these authors differ somewhat in their interpretations, they are all concerned with explaining the changes in responses to crime that emerged in the late eighteenth and early nineteenth century in the United States, Britain and France. Prior to this period, the target of responses to crime and disorder was punishment of the body. With the rise of industrial capitalism and the creation of the modern state responses began to be directed at altering and training the mind and the body of criminals, with work and discipline replacing whipping and hanging. The penitentiary was seen as a new strategy of power, a technology aimed at changing behaviour through religious exhortation and persuasion allied to routines of discipline. Foucault has argued that the penitentiary was the apex of the carceral society created in the nineteenth century. Prisons were 'positive' mechanisms, created to produce the willing subject, men and women who would not have to be compelled to labour but would willingly accept the demands of the new industrial order.

By the end of the nineteenth century new experts on crime and imprisonment began to offer novel interpretations of crime and medical and psychological methods of classifying and thus distributing prisoners within and across a range of institutions. These mechanisms were intended to ensure that the appropriate technology of correction was applied to the right sort of prisoner. Prison officials had long been concerned about separating the young from the old, men from women, and the 'hardened' criminal from the novice. Prison medical staff and psychologists promised more precise measurements of moral and psychological characteristics that would aid in classifying prisoners and thereby increase the chances of their regeneration.

Revisionists' accounts such as those of Foucault, Ignatieff and Rothman seldom if ever consider the possibility that patriarchal and gender-based assumptions might have played a role in the development of modern prisons. Were women sent to prison during the nineteenth century also seen as potential labour power to be transformed into disciplined workers, or did other sorts of assumptions dictate penal responses? If patriarchal assumptions were apparent, did they result in the creation of unique institutions for the punishment and reform of women and did prisons for women become the sites for the generation of new theories of the criminality of women?

Issues such as these have only recently come to the fore. Feminist scholars, such as Estelle Freedman and Nicole Rafter have begun to investigate the history of confinement of women in the United states. They have discovered that women imprisoned in nineteenth-century America often suffered unique forms of confinement because there were so few in the penal system and because of patriarchal assumptions about and responses to women.[30] In the first decades of nineteenth century America, women were predominantly confined in separate wings of prisons for men, usually provided with poorer living conditions and sometimes subjected to physical and sexual abuse by male warders. By the end of the century, wider social and ideological forces produced strong pressures to change the conditions of confinement for these women. Reformatories for women emerged in the context of increasing concern for the regulation of youth, public morals and domestic training. The American reformatory movement was the answer to the neglect and repression experienced by women. Reformatories were not built in every state. They spread primarily in the north and north-east. These institutions were the epitome of progressive ideals. According to their creators women would be diagnosed and assessed by a group of professionals who would then be able to apply the best individualized treatment.

These recent researches have revealed the importance of patriarchal assumptions and practices in determining the nature of the confinement of women in the nineteenth and early twentieth centuries. Official perceptions of the supposed malleability and innate maternal characteristics of women led to the creation of special institutions intended to train and rehabilitate them. Freedman argues that staff in women's reformatories acted in a benevolent and sisterly fashion towards their charges, in her words they were 'Their Sister's Keepers'. We would question the supposed 'sisterly' relationship between prison staff and prisoner based on our reading of the accounts of women in nineteenth century prisons in Britain and the United States. Other research, most notably the work of Rafter, has also challenged this general assumption. She found that with the creation of the modern women's reformatory in the 1870s a bifurcated system emerged, one branch included prisons and jails and the other reformatories. The prisons and jails housed most women and were definitely not based on the benevolent, sisterly and therapeutic ideals of the reformatories. The black and poor women who were sent to them experienced degrading, often appalling, conditions and treatment.

The work of Rafter, Freedman and others has made important and unique contributions to our understanding of imprisonment, exploring yet another issue about women that has long been 'hidden from history' and providing concrete material on the operation of a number of specific American institutions. In Britain, there has been no work of comparable size and scope on the critical history of women in prison. Most of the existing historical work has tended to be relatively uncritical biographies of prison reformers such as Elizabeth Fry and Mary Carpenter, or general overviews of legislative and administrative developments.[31] However, in the recent revisionist accounts of prisons in general, a few short historical accounts critically addressing the issues of women have begun to appear.[32] In addition to this lack of a critical historical analysis, there have also been very few attempts to investigate life inside contemporary British prisons for women. Recent work has certainly made a start in this area, though, as we indicated above, the work tends to remain at an individual level of analysis and much more needs to be done.

In writing *The Imprisonment of Women* we have several major purposes in mind. The first is to provide an account of the history of women in prison in Britain from the late eighteenth until the twentieth century. We do not seek to provide a comprehensive description of these developments, but are concerned with several major issues: how class and gender assumptions have shaped the imprisonment of women over time; the operation of regimes of punishment and discipline; the content of authoritative, official discourses on the criminality and imprisonment of women, and the way official conceptions and government policies have been translated into prison practices. This in turn must be considered in the overall context of women in society and relative to the criminality of women. While our main interest is in the imprisonment of women, we seek to contribute to an understanding of the criminality of women by exploring the socio-economic circumstances in which crimes have occurred in the past and continue to do so in the present. As part of this more comprehensive integrated approach, we are concerned to demonstrate where possible the way women react to their imprisonment, the ways they struggle against punishment and discipline and/or seek to cope with the deprivations of confinement. Much has been written about the importance of understanding the reactions of those subjected to penal regimes, especially by Foucault, but few concrete examples are offered.[33] This is possibly because it is very difficult to obtain evidence of past collective and individual struggles. We have, however, discovered some good historical evidence of the ways in which women did respond to the new technology of imprisonment.

Our historical analysis is meant to serve two main purposes: to present evidence where little or none has been widely available before, and to provide a background for understanding the development of the imprisonment of women today. Researchers usually fail to explore the relationship between historical patterns and contemporary forms of imprisonment. As Ignatieff has argued, historical research '. . . has not extended itself into the twentieth century'.[34] We have found clear links with the past in the current thinking about women prisoners and in the operation of British prisons. Most directly, the ideologies of doctors and psychologists in the late nineteenth century and early twentieth have been extremely important in shaping contemporary Home Office thinking on women in prison and in the creation of the New Holloway and Cornton Vale.

The contemporary aspects of our research begin with a demonstration of the way this thinking has had an important impact on British prisons today. We show how government bodies established to plan these new institutions were heavily influenced by psychiatric conceptions of the criminality of women which underpinned the creation of therapeutic regimes in Cornton Vale and the New Holloway. We then analyse the way therapeutic ideals espoused by penal experts have been translated into the organization of prison regimes and the daily lives of women prisoners. What we find is that these ideals have made some impact on the structure of prisons for women, generating art therapy, group work, and a proliferation of professional helpers. They have not, however, done much to alter contemporary prisons which are still basically geared to disciplining and punishing women, regardless of the rhetoric of rehabilitation and the existence of group work and counselling. We demonstrate the impact of this trend by showing how therapeutic assumptions and social and medical professionals have colluded with or acquiesced to traditional penal demands to tighten regulation and surveillance within prison and to ensure that women are closely confined and heavily scrutinized. Our detailed research into the operation of Cornton Vale provides considerable evidence of this pattern.

We then consider the daily lives of women while in prison and we find that, like their nineteenth-century counterparts, for the most part they work. According to official government pronouncements women work because it is part of the process of rehabilitation. We show how the work women do in prison has very little to do with providing skills for wage work and only pays lip service to training them to be better housewives. Work in prison is for the benefit of the institution: cleaning and producing goods for sale. Any training that occurs is mainly a secondary by-product of this process.

Relationships inside and outside the prison are also an important part of women's lives during their period of confinement. One of the most important relationships for their daily lives is the nature of their contact with prison officers. Penal regimes are operated by prison officers and administrative staff and it is impossible for prisoners to avoid their influence. Despite some contemporary views about breaking down these barriers and establishing therapeutic relationships, we found that in the main barriers continue to exist and staff are not seen as people to turn to for help, and there is little acceptance among the prisoners of the relevance of treatment as a solution to their problems within or outside prison. Following the concerns of past research, we also examine the relationships between women prisoners themselves and assess the way prison, in contradiction to penal ideals, actually impedes relationships with their children, family and friends. We found little evidence of the family or kin types of relationships reported in American research.

Women in Cornton Vale are best characterized as living in an atomized world in which any attempts to form friendships are deemed inappropriate and detrimental to good prison discipline. With very few exceptions, women experience a close form of individual confinement with few possibilities for developing alliances and friendships and maintaining significant contact with the outside world.

The research that forms the basis of this book is both historical and contemporary. In order to gather first-hand information about the operation of women's prisons we conducted intensive fieldwork at Cornton Vale, the only women's prison in Scotland. The research involved participant observation and interviews in all sections of the prisons over an eight-month period.

The first four months of fieldwork were spent just being in the prison. We spent time in the living units, at all the workplaces (kitchens, laundry and workshops), at the Health Centre, in the education block, in the administrative office, in the social work department, at the reception area for new prisoners, in the visiting hall, in the punishment blocks and in the staff canteen. We observed and sometimes experienced prison life from early morning till late at night, weekdays and weekends. This period was one of intense observation, and participation when it seemed appropriate, for example in the kitchens, workshops and laundry.

After this period of observation, we conducted interviews with fifty-nine women, half of the population.[35] They were selected to form as complete a cross-section as possible of the prison population in terms of prison regime and sentence length. At a preliminary meeting between the interviewer and the prisoner, she was asked if she would agree to be interviewed, and if so a future time was arranged for the interview. This approach allowed time for the woman to change her mind if she wished. We felt this method was extremely important within a prison context since prisoners are rarely allowed the opportuntiy to make their own decisions. Complete privacy during the interview and confidentiality were ensured. There were no refusals.

The interviews covered several major areas: experiences prior to sentencing, including remand and contact with courts and solicitors; past criminal and penal experiences; living arrangements and everyday experience of confinement; contact with and attitudes towards social work and medical professional staff; perceptions and experience of work inside and outside prisons; experiences of the system of punishment; contacts with friends and relatives both within and outside the prison and relationships with uniformed staff. The interviews were not tape recorded, but extensive notes were taken and written up immediately afterwards. Although the interviews involved systematic questions with the same topics covered in each interview, the style of the interviews was predominantly open-ended, allowing for plenty of elaboration and discussion. Each interview took an average of one hour but the range was from thirty minutes to four hours.

Information from the participant observations and interviews was supplemented by use of various prison records, including admission and discharge records, disciplinary records, punishment reports, social work and education records and official Government reports and statistics.[36] We were not interested in using these records to provide an alternative account of the women we interviewed, a technique sometimes used by other researchers, but to gather information about the creation of the prison itself as well as the operation of discipline, social work and education in the most modern women's prison in Britain.

The historical research allows us to show the continuities and discontinuities of British reactions to women in prison from the early nineteenth century to the present. Evidence about the operation of penal institutions in the past came from official reports and parliamentary papers, annual prison reports for Scotland from 1834 to the present, pamphlets and books from the period, and a few personal, first-hand accounts of crime and imprisonment.[37] While this has provided an unexpeced wealth of information about women in prison in the past, we are well aware of the need for additional work on this under-researched area, particularly localized work on specific prisons and their operation, and on issues such as education and the role of female staff.

In the following chapters we will use this evidence to examine the imprisonment of women from its early beginnings to its most modern form. We will begin by recounting the forms of punishment that predated the rise of systematic confinement and the penitentiary. For the most part, the story of the imprisonment of women is one of crimes that do not warrant the punishment. Over time, the woman prisoner has been transformed from evil to mad and responded to accordingly, with closer and closer forms of control and confinement reaching beyond her body and into her mind and emotions.

2

The Physical and Symbolic Punishment of Women

The prolonged confinement of women and men was an unusual punishment until the late sixteenth century. Physical and symbolic punishments, such as whipping, hanging and public ridicule, were the main methods used in pre-industrial societies. Some forms of confinement in nunneries, monasteries, castles and watch-towers did exist in the late middle ages, but it was only with the rise of mercantile capitalism that systematic confinement began to emerge. This did not receive immediate, widespread acceptance nor did it result in the wholesale rejection of traditional punishments. Rather, systematic imprisonment was first employed as an auxiliary to traditional punishments and it was not until the early nineteenth century that it was accepted as the most appropriate means of responding to crime and deviance.

In this chapter we will explore the background to the development and consolidation of systematic confinement by considering the nature of the physical and symbolic punishments in pre-industrial periods, the emergence in the sixteenth century of the first forms of systematic confinement in houses of correction established in England and Holland, crime and its punishment (hanging and transportation) in eighteenth-century Britain, and the subsequent deterioration of houses of correction and gaols during that time. This analysis will provide the necessary background for understanding the creation of modern penal institutions for women by establishing the differences between early methods of dealing with the crimes and deviance of women and the more systematic techniques of incarceration. Throughout this chapter, we will explore the way gender and class assumptions shaped these responses through the institutional and ideological patterns associated with patriarchy and early capitalism.

Physical and Symbolic Punishments in Pre-industrial Societies

The punishment of offenders prior to the sixteenth century primarily involved direct physical responses, such as banishment, ritualized punishments and public shamings.[1] These responses were not necessarily exacted through an organized legal and judicial system dictating explicit punishments for specific offences. Courts and legal proscriptions had a part to play, but just as important, the church and the community were responsible for discovering transgressions and punishing offenders. However, the most brutal and physical punishments were usually the rights of monarchs and judiciary, under whose power women and men might be subject to physical and capital punishments such as whipping, branding, boring of the ear, dismemberment of the body, hanging, burning to death and numerous other forms of direct, physical punishment and torture.[2] In some cases, punitive justice acted out the crime of the condemned when carrying out the execution. For example, in the eighteenth century, the execution of a French servant girl consisted of a re-enactment of the crime of murdering her mistress. She was condemned to be taken to the location of execution in a rubbish cart and a gibbet was to be erected

> . . . at the foot of which will be placed the same chair in which her mistress was sitting at the time of the murder; and having seated the criminal there, the executioner of the High Court will cut off her right hand, throw it in her presence into the fire, and, immediately afterwards, will strike her four blows with the cleaver with which she murdered the said mistress, the first and second on the head, the third on the left forearm and the fourth on the chest; this done, she will be hung and strangled on the gibbet until she is dead: and when two hours have elapsed her dead body will be removed and the head separated from it at the foot of the gibbet on the scaffold, with the same cleaver she used to murder her mistress, and the same head exhibited on a pole twenty feet high outside the gates of Cambrai, . . . and the rest of the body put in a sack, and buried near the pole at a depth of ten feet.[3]

In this theatrical and brutal manner, justice re-enacted the crime for those who watched, directly demonstrating the final reckoning of the evil-doer.

The case of a Dutch woman, Tryn Peters, aptly illustrates the variety of more usual punishments directed at offenders. She was executed in Amsterdam in 1617 after a long criminal career resulting in numerous physical and symbolic punishments. On eight occasions, she had 'stood on the place where evil-doers are punished, with a rope about her neck and attached to the gallows; four times [she] has been banished from Holland and Westfriesland for life under threat of hanging; five times branded and both her ears cut off by the hangman.'[4] After this litany of symbolic and physical punishments stretching over a period of eleven years she again committed a theft, 'together with a certain accomplice and in broad daylight, she entered a house, the door of which one had forgotten to shut and stole a woman's skirt, blouse and jacket, which were found among her things and restored to their owner.'[5] She was executed by strangulation for this offence.

Tryn Peters's case demonstrates both the type of offences for which women were usually punished and the variety of punishments used in pre-industrial societies. According to available records, women in the late middle ages were rarely perpetrators of violence. They usually committed minor thefts with accomplices and suffered a wide variety of punishments.[6] A woman might have had a longer criminal career if she was able to 'plead her belly'; a common plea that might prevent or, at least, delay execution. Because of pregnancy, women like Tryn Peters might 'merely' be subjected to symbolic punishments followed by mutilation and/or banishment. This leniency was for the sake of the foetus, since women were merely the vessels of the unborn soul. Such 'preferential' treatment also had another side. Women were often subjected to more severe punishments for the same offences as men.[7] During certain periods in the middle ages, women could be burned to death for adultery or for murdering a spouse, whereas adultery was sometimes not considered an offence for men and the murder of a wife might not result in any prosecution. If punished, the guilty husband would be subjected to hanging only and saved the greater agony of burning. This difference reflected women's subordinate position within the family, the state and the church.

The most noticeable example of this different treatment was for the offence of witchcraft. From the fourteenth until the seventeenth century, thousands of women and men were accused of witchcraft and executed. Estimates vary, but historical analysis of archival material reveals that 80 or 90 per cent of the offenders were women.[8] Often these women were older, independent, though relatively powerless, and some were knowledgeable in the ancient art of healing.[9] Various symbolic and materialist explanations have been offered for these witchcraft panics and the inevitable waves of executions. Yet, the fact that women were the main victims leads to the inescapable conclusion that ideals relating to the correct position of women in society were significant in providing direction for these panics. Older, isolated women threatened existing conceptions of females and the practices and skills of some of them clearly threatened the established church and/or the embryonic institution of medicine. Given the orthodox conception of women as dependent members of families, it is not surprising that those of the periphery of society often became scapegoats when economic, social and political change generated a climate of fear and concern. The waves of witchcraft persecutions that intermittently swept Europe, Britain and America constituted one technique for the powerful to demonstrate the power of the church, and sometimes the state, by exploiting the superstitions and fears of the populace. Women's bodies were the instruments for exorcising political and social evils, establishing the power of institutions, and for the symbolic marking of boundaries of appropriate female behaviour.

As brutal and widespread as these persecutions were, they represented only the most dramatic of a number of unique offences and punishments for which women were the primary targets. Mutilations, whipppings and executions, although not infrequent, occurred much less often that other forms of punishment and public shaming.

Well into the late eighteenth century, European and British communities used a number of direct physical punishments, such as the pillory and stocks, and symbolic chastisements, such as misrules and charivaris, to atttempt to control the behaviour of wayward members of the community. Charivaris and misrules were highly ritualized forms of shaming often directed at women and men who offended against patriarchal community order.[10] The primary offences against this order were perceived inversions of the 'natural' male hierarchy or public quarrels and accusations relating to family reputations. The punishments varied for men and women. Men, for example, might be subjected to a 'cuckold's court' or forced to ride backward on a donkey for allowing their wives to cuckold or dominate them. They might also provoke community sanction for overstepping the bounds of appropriate patriarchal domination, when, for example, they beat their wives to excess. It is important to note that it was only when a man grossly overstepped the bounds of appropriate chastisement by mutilation or by nearly killing his wife, that he might be sanctioned by the community through the performance of a misrule or a charivari.[11] When one analyses the chastisements directed at men for inversions or offences against the patriarchal order, it becomes clear that they were rare occurrences but when performed, were usually highly symbolic, and often frivolous affairs. By contrast, community chastisements directed at women were likely to be more physical, direct and serious.

Under a rigid patriarchal order, women were expected to be subservient to men in most spheres of life, especially within the home and church. This does not mean that they were always subservient, since women in pre-industrial Europe were sometimes economically independent, working in jobs such as brewers, innkeepers and bakers. Nevertheless, male dominance was perceived as the natural order and when women attempted to speak out against their husbands or other men within the community, including church leaders, they risked being defined as public nuisances, shrews, nags and viragos. 'Offences' of this nature could lead to condemnation and unique punishments such as the cucking and ducking stool which were used throughout Britain until the late eighteenth century as devices for restraining, punishing and silencing the 'common scold'. The ducking of women was often used by local magistrates and church leaders for 'restraining evil'. For example:

> Katherine Saunders, accused by the churchwardens of St Andrews for a common scold and slanderer of her neighbours was adjudged to the ducking stool.

> In Leeds in 1694, the Court of Sessions ruled that 'Anne, the wife of Phillip Saul, a person of lewd behaviour, be ducked for daily making strife and discord amongst her neighbours.'[12]

A more brutal and painful method of punishing the 'common scold' and sometimes prostitutes, was through the application of the scold's or gossip's bridle. The branks was an iron cage placed over the head, and most examples incorporated a spike or pointed wheel that was inserted into the offender's mouth in order to 'pin the tongue and silence the noisiest brawler.' This spiked cage was intended to punish women adjudged quarrelsome or not under the proper control of their husbands. The common form of administering this punishment was to fasten the branks to a woman and parade her through the village, sometime chaining her to a pillar for a period of time after the procession. In most cases women were released from the branks after a set period of time, though in some instances the duration of punishment was geared to behavioural reform, that is, the bridle was not removed until 'the evil-doer had repented and demonstrated in all external signs of humiliation and amendment.'

Although these were public chastisements they were integrally linked to household domination. In some towns arrangements were made for employing the branks within the home, 'In the old-fashioned, half-timbered houses in the borough [Congleton], there were generally fixed on one side of the large open fire-place, a hook; so that, when a man's wife indulged her scolding propensities, the husband sent for the town jailer to bring the bridle, and had her bridled and chained to the hook until she promised to behave herself.'[13] According to this observer, men often used the threat of the branks to attempt to silence their wives, 'If you don't rest with your tongue, I'll send for the bridle and hook you up.' In this example, we see how patriarchal domination and state domination were intricately intertwined.

The ducking and branking of women were not infrequent occurrences in British communities, where the family was a significant locus of economic, social and moral activity. Women who were seen as transgressing the patriarchal and religious order were viewed as serious offenders whose crimes/sins must be punished. These punishments were intended to discourage the offender through the application of pain and humiliation while the accompanying ceremonies and processions were meant to serve as moral lessons and deter those who watched. They also had deeper, more symbolic meanings. Most importantly, the spectacle of processions and public punishments symbolised the power to punish.

The common feature of these physical and symbolic punishments was that the body was the 'point for the manifestation of power.' In this way the guilty unwillingly colluded with the powerful, with their bodies serving as heralds of their transgression. The body provided the immediate signs of wrongdoing, and, if branded or mutilated, the disfigurement provided a lasting sign demonstrating the power to punish. Thus, through irregular, intermittent, sporadic punishments, the patriarchy, church and monarchy demonstrated their political power through their right and ability to punish.

Systematic Confinement in the Sixteenth and Seventeenth Centuries

These responses to crime and deviance were very different from the institutional forms of punishment and correction that emerged in the late sixteenth century. Systematic confinement came into being in the context of the social, economic and ideological changes associ-

ated with the demise of feudalism, the rise of agricultural and mercantile capitalism, and a virulent Protestant ideology.[14] The breaking
up of the traditional feudal order and, in England, the dissolution of
the monasteries, created extraordinary social disruptions resulting in
the dislocation of the labouring poor. These dislocations were often
generated by widespread enclosures of the common land for the
purpose of intensified agricultural exploitation. The labouring poor
were forced from the land to accommodate the demands of primitive
capital accumulation.[15] Such economic measures often created an idle
poor, forced to wander the countryside in order to find employment
or to beg to survive.

These material developments were linked with a new religious
ideology and a changed conception of the poor. Protestantism, and
especially Calvinism, stressed the importance of individual
responsibility and the demonstration of individual worth through
sustained labour.[16] All should work and those who did not, or could
not, should be punished for their slothfulness and mendacity. Ideals
of this nature, coupled with burgeoning numbers of the wandering
poor, meant that the poor were no longer seen as part of a religious
and social mosaic in which their presence benefited the souls of the
rich through pious almsgiving. Instead, they began to be seen as
sinful, lazy, unproductive and even dangerous, and, thus, in need of
suppression.[17] Conceptions such as these were mainly ideological
since most women and men who were forced to wander or beg were
neither dangerous nor lazy. They were usually displaced agricultural
labourers, servants, textile workers and pedlars who were merely
looking for employment.[18]

Despite this reality, these conceptions and fears generated
demands for new responses, and by the mid-seventeenth century,
the mercantilist state began to conceive of a solution in measures
aimed at the conservation of labour. The value embodied in the
labour power of the poor and criminal was not to be squandered and
idled away through the traditional methods of work, but efficiently
used and controlled in order to produce a surplus that could be
transformed into capital.

Although wandering and vagabondage were economically
necessary for the labouring poor, the propertied classes saw this
behaviour as detrimental to their own economic interests and created
harsh labour and penal laws intended to maintain a stable and
exploitable labour force. The state created new regulations aimed at
enforcing maximum wage limits, fixing periods of employment and
lengthening the working day. Harsher penal laws were enacted to

punish wandering and begging by flogging, mutilation and death for repeated offences. This 'bloody legislation' as Marx called it, was geared to linking labour to local demands and allowing for a more certain exploitation of the poor.

These negative sanctions were supplemented by the new positive mechanism of systematic confinement.[19] The new ideology of work as personal salvation and a means of attaining national superiority created ideas about confining the poor and criminal and forcing them to labour. By the end of the sixteenth century, and throughout the first half of the next, numerous suggestions for such schemes were produced, especially in England and the Low Countries. As early as 1516, Sir Thomas More had proposed in *Utopia* that the poor should be set to work as a means of relieving their suffering and reducing the burden and threat to the state.[20] One of the most prominent proponents of these ideas was the Dutchman Coornhert, who, in 1567, proposed that the poor and criminal of Holland were worth much more alive than dead. He argued that the potential labour power of the poor should not be wasted or incapacitated through mutilation and execution. His solution was to confine women and men and force them to work in order to support themselves and the state.[21]

In the seventeenth and eighteenth centuries temporary confinement in jails, castles and towers was relatively common throughout Europe, but long term confinement in convents, nunneries and monasteries was a much older practice. Women had been entering convents for centuries.[22] Voluntary entrants were almost entirely aristocratic and upper-class women, while the women forced into convents were usually political prisoners, illegitimate, disinherited by their families and/or physically deformed or mentally defective. Fathers and husbands used convents and nunneries to dispose of their unwanted daughters and wives. The enforced confinement, accompanied by strict rules of enclosure and silence, which forbade speaking or leaving the precincts of the cloister, made many of the monasteries very like prison.[23]

The difference between these early methods and more systematic forms of confinement was in intent and duration. Houses of correction were not intended to be mere temporary holding places prior to punishment, institutions devoted primarily to religious other-worldliness or locations for torture and punishment. Systematic, 'positive' confinement was directed at creating a new individual, one who had been corrected, trained and transformed into an ideal encompassing the qualities of docility, malleability and hard work. Such labourers would meet the needs of a nascent capitalism.

The first examples of these houses of correction were opened in the towns and cities of Protestant England, the Netherlands and Germany:[24] the first in London in late 1556 in the old, disused Bridewell Palace of Henry VIII.[25] This Bridewell, which gave its name to similar institutions in Britian, was intended for the confinement of idle, criminal and destitute women and men. By 1576, an Act specified that similar institutions, modelled on the London Bridewell, were to be established in all English counties, and by 1590 over twenty-one of them existed in England.[26]

The London Bridewell was created by prominent merchants, statesmen and soldiers who intended it to deal with the poverty and idleness of London's streets, 'not by statute but by labour'. Initially Bridewells were linked to extant punishments and traditional forms of power. For example, idle and 'lewd' women were often whipped or carted through the streets prior to their confinement, and the Bridewell itself became a location for physical punishments. In 1556, at the London Bridewell a woman was whipped on her bare back, dragged through a mob and pilloried with a paper on her head proclaiming: 'Whipped at Bridewell for having forsaken her child in the streets'.[27]

It was not just magistrates or the governors of these institutions who were empowered to send women and men to Bridewell; husbands, parents and masters could confine disobedient and wayward servants, apprentices, wives and children. The new positive mechanisms of systematic confinement did not supplant older forms of punishment and authority, but added them to the power of individual patriarchs and to the older public forms of punishment of the body.

Though the first houses of correction appeared in England, it was the Dutch who established the most sophisticated examples of confinement for men and women and the first distinct penal establishment for women. The first Dutch house of correction, 'Tuchthusien', was opened in Amsterdam in 1596.[28] It was an all-male establishment in which inmates were required to rasp hard African wood into small chips that were used by the Amsterdam textile guilds for the production of dyes – an occupation that gave the house its popular name, Rasphuis. A year later, the first unique penal institution for women was opened, significantly in St Ursule's Convent.[29] When this institution was destroyed by fire, a new establishment was opened in 1645, probably the first truly purpose-built penal institution for women. In the beginning, the Spinhuis, as it came to be called, housed mostly poor, wayward and 'disrespectful' women and girls, but within ten years it began to house women committed for prostitution, theft and other forms of crime. It was intended to be a paternalistic house of correction as the motto over the door attested, 'Fear not! I do not exact vengeance for evil, but compel you to be good. My hand is stern, but my heart is kind.'[30]

The regime of the Spinhuis incorporated features that were precursors of penal developments in the nineteenth century. It could accomodate 78 women who resided in dormitories containing ten partitioned stalls or cubicles. Eight of these stalls contained three women sleeping in the same bed, with the remaining two allocated to single accomodation for older women. Inmates worked in a communal setting and were initially engaged in spinning when Holland was in the forefront of textile production; later, they made nets and sewed linen goods. There was a specialized staff consisting of a seamstress, spinning master and warder and his wife who were called the 'house father and house mother.' Such staff and the conception of the institution as a household unit would become integral features of reformatories for juveniles and women created in the late nineteenth century.

By the seventeenth century, systems for classifying and segregating inmates were introduced. In 1663, a visitor described a rudimentary one, with cellular confinement for the correction of girls and women 'who cannot be kept to their duties by parents and husbands' and a separate congregate section divided into 'three sections [dormitories] of prisoners; one for drunks; one for the prostitutes from public brothels; and one for those whipped in public.'[31]

Amsterdam city officials were proud of their two penal establishments and the Spinhuis soon became 'the biggest sight of the city'. It was often visited by those interested in progressive penal schemes who praised its orderliness, discipline and sustained labour. Work was to be the most important feature of these early examples of systematic confinement; indeed, the initial title of the London Bridewell was House of Occupation.

The statesmen and merchants responsible for the creation of the first houses of correction in England and on the Continent were convinced that the idle and criminal could be transformed through the positive mechanism of incessant labour. Endless tedious labour would act as a punishment and deterrent. It would avoid the sins of idleness and instil the habits of mind and body associated with wage work. Those who created the Spinhuis desired an institution that would teach girls and women 'a suitable trade' and by the mid-seventeenth century the London Bridewell was turning out between one hundred and two hundred trained apprentices every year.[32]

The labour of inmates was also intended to fulfil two main material purposes for the institution, socially necessary labour and commodity production.[33] The labour power of women was especially important in maintaining and operating the institution itself by providing domestic work. From the beginning of systematic confinement women were required to cook, clean, launder, and provide general services for both male and female inmates. A central feature of the London Bridewell was the washing tub and hemp block. Inmate labour power was also used to produce commodities. For example, women in English Bridewells produced silk lace gloves and felt hose and the Amsterdam Spinhuis produced cloth and linen goods. Commodity production was organized in two ways. Commodities could be closely tied to the institution itself with the operators of the house selling the commodities in the market place, or it might be linked more directly to capitalist enterprises through contracts with outside entrepreneurs.

Two main systems were used to connect capital to houses of correction. The 'leasing out' system involved producers leasing either the labour power of the inmates alone or the entire institution. This was done in exchange for bearing the cost of maintaining the institution and supporting the prisoners, a system widely used in England. The second practice, more common on the Continent, was for the entrepreneur to provide the raw material for production, with the state/city managing the labour process and the upkeep of the institution. This was the system that prevailed in the Amsterdam Spinhuis and Rasphuis.

One of the most notorious English attempts at exploiting prison labour in order to make a profit occurred at the London Bridewell in 1602. The Governors of the Bridewell agreed to lease it and its inmate labour power to three gentlemen 'drapers and tanners' who were to 'set the idle people and ruffians to work'.[34] Ignoring the charter, the 'gentlemen' proceeded to operate the institution as a brothel. Women no longer wore the simple, austere 'blue livery' of the house, but reputedly 'flaunted in brave apparel . . . and supped very sumptuously . . . on crabs, lobsters and artichoke pies, washed down with gallons of wine.'[35] Some women were reported to have 'voluntarily' taken part while others were forced to participate through beatings and intimidation. The use of women's bodies as commodities was not endorsed by the Guardians of the Bridewell, and, in October of the same year, they divested the 'gentlemen' of their right to control the institution without punishment or detriment to them.

By the middle of the seventeenth century, examples of systematic confinement with labour had emerged in towns and cities in Sweden, Germany, Belgium, Holland and England. Similar institutions, such as the *hospitaux généraux* in Paris and the Galera de Mujeres in Madrid, were established in France, Italy and Spain.[36] However, these institutions were rather different from the houses of correction created in predominately Protestant countries. They were intended more for the relief of the poor and sick and as 'hospitals for the soul' than as institutions devoted to punishment and reform.[37] Clearly it was not just Protestant ideology or the materialist and social demands of capitalism that provided the impetus for the houses of correction. Rather, it was a combination of these material, social and ideological factors. Indeed, Scotland, a strongly Protestant country during this period, did not create houses of correction until the middle of the eighteenth century.[38] Although the ideological conditions and legislative apparatus were in place by the seventeenth century, the necessary administrative structure did not develop until later.

Houses of correction provided the models upon which the modern penitentiary would be fashioned in the nineteenth century. Institutions such as the Maison de Force in Ghent and the Amsterdam Spinhuis, with their systems of orderliness, rudimentary methods of classification and segregation, and programmes of systematic labour would provide the reference points for the late eighteenth-century English reformers whose efforts provided the impetus for the creation of the modern penitentiary. John Howard, one of the most important early penal reformers, gives explicit credit to the Amsterdam institutions as his model for the 1799 Penitentiary Act. He looked to the Continent for examples because by the late eighteenth century, English Bridewells had degenerated into institutions that were very different from those created in the two preceding centuries.

Eighteenth-century Crime and Punishment

The English enthusiasm for houses of correction began to wane by the late seventeenth century. The decline and neglect of these institutions must be assessed against a background of intensified capitalist exploitation, the undermining of traditional rights, and the resulting struggles between the propertied ruling classes and the people. The enclosure of land and the erosion of customary agricultural and manufacturing practices that began in the sixteenth century were intensified during the next two centuries. Social and economic activities of the common people, once considered legitimate by both the propertied classes and the people, became criminal offences, many punishable by death. Villagers and agricultural workers had customarily been entitled to the gleanings at harvest time, the trimmings associated with leather production, the underwood from forests and hedges, and had been allowed to trap and hunt a certain quantity of game from common lands.[39] These economic activities were crucial to the well being of the common people since wages played only a small part in the subsistence economy of the period. The ruling classes attacked these ancient, common rights and customs in order to take the fruit of the land for themselves. They enacted new laws, created and/or expanded networks of overseers, gamekeepers and constables to stamp out these rights and customs, and punished infractions with draconian penal measures.

The people, and not merely the poor, fought the attacks on their ancient rights with an extraordinary ferocity. Women played an important part in these efforts, especially in such economically important activities as gathering wood and gleaning. The new laws against 'stealing faggot wood' and 'breaking a hedge and cutting' were broken by women such as Audrey Grave who convinced her friends to tear down a fence of a landholder because, she argued, it was common land.[40] On the occasions when women were apprehended for these offences, they often fought back or argued that they had not committed a crime. In 1762, when Ann Osborne was apprehended for gathering wood, she pleaded that she 'did not know that there was any harm in it.'[41] Other women reacted more strongly to being caught. In one case, a Surrey constable who arrested two women for gathering wood was attacked by the mother of one, thus allowing them to escape apprehension.

Possibly the most important area of resistance for women was the popular protests associated with bread production and distribution.[42] Attempts to manipulate markets and prices were widespread during the eighteenth century. Both entrepreneurs and bakers attempted to hoard grain and raise prices to exorbitant levels. Such measures often provoked a strong reaction from members of the community who considered their objections to be morally just. E.P. Thompson has argued that such actions were part of the 'moral economy' of the period, and that 'it is most probable that the women most often precipitated the spontaneous action' of the community.[43] Sometimes the protests were indirect and symbolic, involving ritualized forms of collective demonstrations and noise-making, but more often they were direct and physical, aimed at the millers, bakers and transporters of grain and bread. For example, in Horsham (Sussex) in 1800

> A number of women . . . proceeded to Gosden wind-mill, where, abusing the miller for having served them brown flour, they seized on the cloth with which he was then dressing meal . . . , and cut it into a thousand pieces; threatening at the same time to serve all similar utensils he might in future attempt to use in the same manner. The Amazonian leader of this petticoated cavalcade afterwards regaled her associates with a guinea's worth of liquor at the Crab Tree public-house.[44]

At the end of the eighteenth century and well into the nineteenth, Scottish women played a significant role in community efforts to resist the clearance of people from the Highlands in order to allow the land to be used for farming and the grazing of sheep instead of the traditional crofting.[45] They were usually at the front of groups, sometimes the entire community, confronting bailiffs and sheriffs sent to serve eviction notices or to remove them from their cottages. On occasion, they were extremely bold and direct, berating, even attacking, officials and humiliating them by stripping them of their clothing. Both Scottish and English women felt morally justified in their attempts to protect their traditional rights through protest and resistance.

Political offences directed at new laws or new economic measures were, of course, not the only reasons women found themselves in court during this period. Beattie, who has carried out the most comprehensive analysis of the crimes of women in the eighteenth century, has detected both a change and an increase in women's offences during that time.[46] As today, Beattie's analysis of crimes in Sussex, Surrey and London, reveals that women committed few acts of violence against others. Thefts by women such as housebreaking, theft from dwellings, shoplifting and pick-pocketing, were primarily an urban phenomenon, with over 82 per cent of these charges being brought in towns and cities.[47] The majority of women appearing before the courts were charged with theft and larceny, accounting for approximately 28 per cent of all urban property offences and 13 per cent of the rural rate. When women did use violence, it was usually against members of their own household such as children and servants. Such women were primarily charged with assaults on children and servants as well as infanticide, a charge only brought against women.

Beattie and others have argued that the urban setting was a great deal more liberating for women than for men. Life in cities meant that women had wider opportunity for employment and a greater range of leisure and entertainment options than life in rural districts offered. Migration to towns and cities resulted in greater independence because of the severing or weakening of the local ties of family and village authority. But towns and cities also had obvious drawbacks. Many women experienced periods of prolonged unemployment and most suffered chronic underemployment and low wages. Throughout the century, women's wages were not more than 50 per cent of those of men. Although the family ties of the country could be stifling for young women, they might provide support when economic conditions were poor, something not usually available to young women living in towns and cities. Women who migrated to towns and cities had considerable freedom, but they sometimes suffered greater hardship and the pressure of need. These conditions, coupled with improved opportunity to participate in a wider range of social and leisure pursuits, constituted the context for the commission of more crimes.

The apparent rise in crimes of theft and the continuous struggle between the possessing classes and the people brought about an extraordinary response from the powerful. Members of the propertied classes were not interested in confinement at this time; they preferred to rely on spectacle and terror to crush disorder and to demonstrate the paramount importance of property. By the end of the eighteenth century over 200 offences were punishable by death, the overwhelming majority for some form of theft. For example, in 1713, theft from a dwelling house, a law mainly directed at domestic servants who were mostly women, became a capital offence. Importantly, although the number of capital convictions increased during this century, the rate of execution was not as high as it had been in the seventeenth century. Only about half of those who were sentenced to death were actually executed. The survivors were usually transported, pardoned, or sometimes sent to prison. Yet, both the threat and reality of the gallows played a significant role in the class struggle of the time.

As well as increasing the number of capital offences, the state expanded the network of 'justice' by developing a more elaborate system of local magistrates.[48] Magistrates, who were usually members of the landed gentry, were given greater powers of summary justice (trial without jury) over an expanding range of offences during the first half of the eighteenth century.

While the magistrates often held proceedings in their own homes, the occasion for judicial spectacle took place in the bi-annual visits of the red-robed, elaborately wigged justices of the Assizes. The Assizes sessions were usually reserved for serious offences, especially those punishable by death. Spectacle was imbedded in the proceedings of the high court justices; indeed, it even preceded them:

> They [the judges] enter the town with bells ringing and trumpets playing, preceded by the sheriff's men, to the number of twelve or twenty, in full dress, armed with javelins. The trumpeters and the javelin-men remain in attendance . . . during . . . their stay, and escort them every day to the assize halls and back again to their apartments.[49]

The importance of awe-inspiring spectacle was explicitly recognized by the judiciary. As Blackstone put it, 'the novelty and parade of appearance have no small influence upon the multitude.'[50]

Spectacle was fused with pedagogical intentions at two crucial junctures in the judicial proceedings. The first occurred when the charge was communicated to the grand jury. Judges took this opportunity to articulate the proper order of things – the propertied to rule and the poor to obey and labour. In some ways, these were statements of government policy; opportunities to translate policy directly to the multitudes. A second occasion for spectacle and pedagogy was when the judges donned their black caps to pronounce sentences of death. The judges' performance was to be perfectly timed, progressing from the least to most serious punishment, ending with the most brutal. Oratory and theatre preceded the actual pronouncement, with judges pointing out the errors of criminal ways and taking the opportunity to instruct the audience:

> A wise judge will never neglect so favourable an occasion of inculcating the enormity of vice, and the fatal consequences to which it leads. He will point out to his hearers the several causes . . . which have conducted step by step the wretched object before them through the several shades of guilt to a transgression unpardonable on earth. He will dwell with peculiar force on such

of those causes as appear to him the most likely, either from the general principles of human nature, or from local circumstances, to exert their contagious influence on the persons whom he addresses.[51]

Pronouncement of the sentence was not always the culmination of the spectacle and the lesson. In the case of a death sentence, the climax of the process was the execution itself. Solemn terror was to be punctuated by the rituals and brutality embodied in the violence of the state. The processions that accompanied public executions in France and England were to be solemn affairs in which the condemned would proceed along the busiest thoroughfares, such as Tyburn Road in London, traversing the most populous districts and important junctions, often stopping at these junctions for the condemned to be exposed as a lesson to all. At the site of the execution, the behaviour of the condemned provided a focus for this theatre of terror. She should die well and bravely, preferably confessing her guilt and beseeching the spectators to mend their evil ways. The dying speeches of two colonial American women aptly represent the ideal confession.

> I believe, the chief thing that hath brought me into my present condition, is my disobedience to my parents: I disputed all their Godly consels and reproofs; and I was always a haughty and stubborn spirit.

> Here I am to die a shameful death, and I justly deserve it. Young people take warning . . . Be obedient to your parents and masters . . . Oh run not abroad with wicked company, or on Sabbath day nights. . .[52]

The hangman's role was also crucial. He should perform his legitimate violence in a stylized, ritualistic, solemn and efficient manner, otherwise the lesson would be tainted. The power to punish should be executed in an efficient and merciful fashion bringing immediate death.

A new dimension of humiliation was added to the gallows early in the century when the barber surgeons and physicians began to snatch or otherwise obtain the corpses for dissection and experimentation.[53] Although it is certain that the progress of anatomy and empirical medicine was advanced by these actions, the poor feared and hated them. They perceived this scientific use of their bodies as unjustly aggravating the punishment, and the denial of a Christian burial threatened their souls. On the day of her execution, Sarah

Wilmshurst's main concern was 'how her body was to be disposed of.' The aggravation of the surgeons was, however, a footnote in the overall pageantry of the gallows because the main intent was to impart a moral lesson, not to aid science or antagonize the crowd. If all went well and everyone played their allotted role with alacrity, the execution confirmed justice and 'had the effectiveness of a long public confession'.[54]

The confessional and pedagogical elements of the execution were expanded beyond the immediate event through the publication of broadsheets and books conveying the accounts of condemned women and men. These Accounts, the most famous of which appeared in the *Malefactors' Register* and *The Annals of Newgate*, both published in 1776, included details of the condemned's life, her employment history, religion, reputation as a criminal, details of the specific offence for which she was executed, an account of the trial and always a confession and apology.[55] The vast majority of Accounts were recorded by the ministers, or ordinaries of prisons, especially at Newgate, London. The selling of accounts brought in a tidy annual income for the ordinaries because they were widely distributed and constituted a significant feature of the popular literature. These Accounts were for public consumption; mechanisms for circulating the lessons of the gallows. By the nineteenth century, these life histories and confessions of inmates would be used by proselytizing clergy, in a less public manner as a means of invoking guilt and exposing the fallen's path to sin and crime as a necessary prelude to reclamation. Later, psychiatrists and psychologists would begin to expropriate the case history and confessions as the means of revealing the mental and psychic clues to the criminal mind.

Terror and pedogogy were intended to deter potential or actual criminals. Solemn, sober ceremony, dying speechs and the Accounts of the condemned were to be fused into a fable of morality. Yet these intentions were often thwarted. Solemnity and sobriety appear to have been sparsely represented among the spectators at Tyburn hanging tree. A hanging was usually the scene of raucous behaviour, riot and general disorder; workshops closed, pubs and taverns were full and the pickpockets apparently had a field day in the drunken throngs. Far from deterring crime and disorder, executions often created a setting for it.

Very often the ceremony was ruined. Sometimes, the condemned refused to repent, remained mute or protested her innocence, damning her accusers and the judges, thus generally failing to confirm the legitimacy of justice. Women might refuse to give accounts, reject the ordinaries and behave in a 'blasphemous, irreverent manner'. Ordinaries responded by denying the sacraments and threatening eternal damnation. Even in the face of death without sacraments, defiance often prevailed. This did not stop the ordinaries and others from creating their own 'authenticated' accounts, such as the one reputedly revealing the deeds and confessions of the famous Brittany bandit, Marion Le Godd. She reportedly exclaimed from the scaffold,

> Fathers and mothers hear me now, watch over your children and teach them well; in my childhood I was a liar and good-for-nothing; I began by stealing a small knife . . . then I robbed pedlars and cattle dealers; finally, I led a robber band and that was why I am here. Tell all this to your children and let it be an example.[56]

Accounts such as these often reproduced the language and values of the pious prelate rather than those of poor women and men. The poor may have seen through these efforts, thus lessening their impact as deterring lessons.

Many avoided the finality of the scaffold by having their sentences commuted to transportation. Beginning in 1717, transportation was employed either as a direct punishment or as an alternative sanction when a sentence of death was commuted. The British transported over 30,000 women and men to North America prior to the outbreak of the War of Independence in 1775. After that avenue was closed, transportation began to Australia in 1787 and ended in 1852. Nearly 150,000 convicts were sent to Australia, and 24,960 of them were women.[57] These young women, most in their teens or early twenties, were usually transported for petty thefts, often their first or second offence. Once in Australia they were allocated to two forms of punishment: under the assignment system they were used as domestic or farm labourers, or beginning in 1821, they were imprisoned in 'female factories'/prisons.

The conditions for female transportees were much worse than those for men. Assignment to households and farms was usually nothing less than forced prostitution and the factories were overcrowded, repressive establishments often operated as open brothels or forced marriage markets. In 1812, the Committee on Transportation observed that women were '. . . indiscriminately given to such of the inhabitants as demanded them, and were in general received rather as prostitutes than as servants. . .'.[58] The British Government transported women for the purpose of preventing unrest among the free and convict male population by providing convict women as sexual commodities.

The ending of transportation to America was something of a watershed in British penal history. The crisis created by the temporary cessation of transportation was overcome by the creation of the hulks, disused ships moored in British rivers from which inmates were required to work in dockyards and dredge rivers and harbours. Creation of the hulks and the temporary halt to transportation were important features in the growing interest in prisons as an alternative to capital punishment and the inept and corrupt administration of local gaols.

By the end of the eighteenth century the local gaols and Bridewells had deteriorated to disease-ridden holding places allowing for all manner of what reformers saw as contaminating influences. Newgate, London, was often singled out for special condemnation but other prisons and Bridewells were adjudged as equally bad. Two observers of the time described Coldbath Fields prison in the following manner:

> Men and women, boys and girls, were indiscriminately herded together, in this chief county prison, without employment or wholesome control; while smoking, gaming, singing, and every species of brutalizing conversation and demeanour tended to the unlimited advancement of crime and pollution.

> . . . a sink of abomination and pollution; and so close was the combination amongst its corrupt functionairies, that it was difficult to acquire any definite notion of the wide-spread defilement that polluted every hole and corner . . . the whole machinery tended to promote shameless gains by the furtherance of all that was lawless and execrable.[59]

Reformers of the late eighteenth and early nineteenth centuries began to reject capital punishment, localized justice of magistrates, and corrupt and contaminated gaols as inefficient, inhumane and ineffective. Their preferred remedy was systematic imprisonment.

3

Penitentiaries for Women

The period from 1760 to 1840 was one of intense debate regarding the appropriate response to crime, disorder and poverty. This was a tumultuous era, characterized by numerous disorders, a rising incidence of crime and a growing distrust and fear of the labouring classes. The Gordon Riots, the machine breaking of the Luddites, the Peterloo massacre and numerous other disturbances and demonstrations punctuated life in British towns and cities.[1] Disorders and popular protests, once relatively tolerated in rural areas, began to be seen as more threatening, even revolutionary, within an increasingly urbanized Britain. The creation of the modern penitentiary in the 1840s was rooted in these upheavals and the new demands for control that emerged during this period.

The intermittent spectacles of the pre-industrial era and the disorganized and inefficient responses to crime that characterized the eighteenth century were eventually replaced by more systematic and continuous forms of regulation. By the mid-nineteenth century the British had created new institutions to survey, punish and reform the labouring classes, including the police, an organized judiciary, prisons and poorhouses.[2] Prisons were at the apex of this system, serving as a model of the new disciplines and forms of regulation meant to bring a social and moral transformation of labouring women and men.

We will analyse the ideological background to the creation of the modern penitentiary by considering the proposals for penal regimes, giving special consideration to the ideals of Elizabeth Fry and members of the Ladies' Society for Promoting the Reformation of Female Prisoners, who were especially important in shaping institutional regimes for female criminals. We will also consider the way these ideas were initially implemented within the prison context and how the practice of confinement diverged from the reformers' proposals. Finally, we will outline the development of forms of imprisonment from 1842 through to the creation of penal servitude in the 1860s. In contrast to some historical research emphasizing the reformative, even benevolent elements of these ideals and regimes, we will consider how the reformers were interested in creating institutions based on humiliation, punishment and rigid discipline.

Penal Reformers and Early Model Prisons

Sytematic imprisonment had not been fully accepted as the best form of 'secondary punishment' by the end of the eighteenth century. Many observers and jurists continued to argue for the use of capital and corporal punishment or argued for the continuation of transportation. However, the temporary cessation of transportation in 1776 because of the American Revolution, continuing disorder and a perceived rise in the rate of crime led the public and jurists to contemplate other reactions to crime. The outstanding contender was confinement.

By the first quarter of the nineteenth century there were three main proposals for the reform of prisons. One group, the reactionaries, argued that prisons should be places of punishment and irksome toil. A second, the Benthamites, followed Jeremy Bentham's proposals and sought to create institutions based on continuous surveillance and labour. The third group, the Evangelicals and Quakers, sought to transform criminals by religion and useful toil. All three shared the common goal of wanting to create a more certain and exacting form of response to crime and disorder. The debate concerned the exact method for doing so.

Irksome Labour and Continuous Surveillance

The ideas and efforts of the early nineteenth-century reformers were preceded by the work of two eighteenth-century penal reformers, John Howard and Jonas Hanway.[3] Howard, motivated by an evangelical asceticism, rejected the appalling physical conditions in British and European prisons and proposed penal regimes based on cleanliness, orderliness, useful labour and solitary seclusion. Although Howard was neither solely nor explicitly concerned with the plight of women in Bridewells and jails, he nevertheless objected to their indiscriminate mingling with men and the more demeaning conditions under which they were at times imprisoned.

Hanway's work preceded that of Howard by a number of years. Unlike Howard, he was a wide-ranging philanthropist who sought to improve the general physical and economic conditions of the poor. In 1758, Hanway and Robert Dingley established a Magdalen House for the voluntary confinement of penitent prostitutes where women were kept to a sparse diet, subjected to religious instruction and required to labour in solitude.[4] During the first year of its existence the house received 2,415 women. As a result of his operation of this institution, Hanway published in 1759 *Thoughts on a Plan for a Magdalen House* in which he provided details of his approved plan of confinement. The plan included continuous seclusion through the provision of separate cells for each inmate, enclosed cubicle chapels, and useful labour. Hanway and Howard both thought that prisons should be places of religious meditation, orderliness, silent solitude, and useful employment.

It was however, Howard's plans, supported by his indefatigable efforts, that brought about the first tentative step on the road to the creation of the modern penitentiary, the passage of the Penitentiary Act of 1799, which he helped to draft. The Act specified that jails should be built for the solitary confinement of each inmate and operated on the basis of silent contemplation and continuous labour. Despite this interest in penal reform, very few changes actually occurred in the operation of most penal institutions. A few model prisons were established, such as the Gloucestershire, Glasgow and Edinburgh Bridewells considered in more detail below. These sought to follow many of the precepts of the Evangelical reformers such as Howard. Yet most of the activity during the first quarter of the century was rhetorical, involving the proposals, claims and counter-claims of various reformers.

Reactionary reformers such as C. C. Western and the Reverend Sydney Smith were, in many respects, responding to the model regimes that had been created in a small number of institutions in Britain. They saw these regimes as over-indulgent, with too much food, education, religion and interesting work. Writing in 1821, C. C. Western argued that prisons should be places that humiliate and degrade. For him punishment should be

> . . . commensurate with the crime, deprive it of all incentive to stimulate courage, or excite a hope of fame or celebrity, give the culprit time for all his passions to subside, and the better feelings of his nature to resume their influence, exhaust the animal spirits which supply him with fortitude.[5]

In order to achieve this end, imprisonment should not involve 'cheerful industry'. What was needed were institutions with 'a judicious system of correctional discipline, hard labour, hard fare, hard lodging, seclusion from society, accompanied by proper moral and religious instructions. . .'.[6]

In contrast to the proposals of Howard and Hanway stressing useful labour, Western wanted prisons devoted to grinding toil: '. . . In every prison, there must be the machinery for hard labour, such as capstan, lever, or tread-wheel. Light employments are quite out of my consideration.'[7] Western was especially keen on the tread-wheel since it occupied numerous inmates and 'both sexes may be employed upon it'. Women should be subjected to the same grinding toil as men – the only specific interest in their 'treatment' was a concern for segregating them from men.

Sydney Smith endorsed Westerns' proposals for penal regimes but wanted to improve the legal and judicial methods of responding to crime in order to guarantee the rights of the accused. His concern for the 'rule of law' was accompanied by an equally strong commitment to punitive penal institutions.[8] Smith sought to protect the rights of the accused through a system of legal regularity and even mercy, but felt that once convicted, the guilty should be subjected to punitive confinement in order to deter them from the commission of future crimes; '. . . a gaol should be a place of punishment, for which men recoil with horror – a place of real suffering, painful to the memory, terrible to the imagination. . .'.[9] An important part of this punishment would be a deprivation of diet. Thieves, he argued, are 'gluttonous and sensual', therefore there is nothing they feel 'more bitterly in confinement than a long course of water-gruel and flour puddings.'[10]

Hard work and deprivation of food and accommodation, not seclusion were his answer to the problem of crime, and this was prescribed for men, women and children. 'There should be no tea and sugar, no assemblage of felons round the washing-tub, nothing but beating hemp, and pulling oakum, and pounding bricks, – no work but what was tedious, unusual, and unfeminine.'[11] The ideals of the reactionary reformers are neatly summarized by Smith: 'There must be a great deal of solitude; coarse food; a dress of shame; hard incessant, irksome eternal labour; a planned and regulated and unrelenting exclusion of happiness and comfort.'[12]

Jeremy Bentham, the eccentric, utilitarian and rationalist reformer, proposed more positive methods of responding to crime, disorder and poverty. Bentham sought to reform the law and the existing methods of dealing with offenders in order to create a more certain and encompassing system that would penetrate deep into the minds and habits of the labouring classes. Physical punishments, 'chains and shackles', would be suppressed within prisons because they were not capable of changing habits or orientations. What was needed were methods that would reconstruct individuals as thrifty, diligent and respectful workers. Unlike many reformers, Bentham was exceedingly clear about his motivations and the purposes of his proposed reforms. His work was not philanthropic; it was a rational, calculated effort to impose power. This goal was most explicitly articulated in his plans (first proposed in 1787) for the construction of a panopticon building allowing for the continuous surveillance of prisoners.[13] Bentham proposed this because he thought that criminals, especially young ones, were incapable of acting rationally. Their weakness, he wrote

> . . . consists in yielding to the seductions of the passing moment. Their minds are weak and disordered, and though their disease is neither so clearly marked nor so incurable as that of idiots and lunatics, like these they require to be kept under restraints, and they cannot, without danger, be left to themselves.[14]

The only certain means of protecting the public from crime and bringing about a reformation in the habits of delinquents was 'perpetual superintendence' and 'unremitted inspection'. In order to achieve this object, Bentham proposed that inmates should be confined in 'circular or polygonal' buildings in which they would be subjected to positive solitude within separate cells open to continuous inspection by warders stationed in a multi-storey, circular tower located in the middle of the building.[15] Through the use of inverted venetian blinds, warders would be able to see the inmates without being seen. Since prisoners would not know they were observed, this was a method that controlled by anticipation.

Prisoners would also be required to engage in continuous useful labour and subjected to 'instruction' by chaplains, teachers and work masters. Labour was a central feature of the panopticon. It would enable inmates to learn a trade and to experience 'new faculties and enjoyment' as a result of sharing in the profits of their labour. Bentham wrote that this labour would eventually defray the entire cost of the institution: 'after a short time it [panopticon] would cost the government nothing.' The entire scheme was oriented to encouragement, not punishment. Bentham even proposed that unmarried prisoners might be 'allowed to marry' since this privilege would 'operate as a powerful spur to those aimed at attaining this reward.'[16]

Such an institution would also provide a moral lesson to those who witnessed its external features and internal operation. Panopticons would be constructed in the most populous areas of the cities where 'those who required to be reminded, by penal exhibitions, of the consequence of crime' would be most likely to see them. Their very facade and appearance would awe and subdue. 'The appearance of the building, the singularity of its shape, the walls and ditches by which it would be surrounded, would all excite ideas of restraint and punishment.'[17] Panopticons would be open to continuous inspection by magistrates and members of the public as a means of providing additional surveillance and preventing administrative abuse. Public inspection would also have a moral effect on those who witnessed it, providing an extraordinary lesson:

> And what would they see? – a set of persons deprived of liberty which they had misused – compelled to engage in labour, which was formerly their aversion – and restrained from riot and intemperance, in which they formerly delighted. . . . What scene could be more instructive to the great proportion of spectators? What a source of conversation, of allusion, of domestic instruction![18]

Through a 'simple idea of architecture', the panopticon would achieve 'Safe Custody, Reformation and Economy' and provide a moral lesson for the wider community through its very presence and through the observation of its inmates.

Bentham was a great propagandist for his panopticon, which he considered appropriate not just for prisons but also for nurseries, schools, factories and workhouses. His mechanical, impersonal methods, emphasizing 'Glass and Iron' as moral weapons, could be used throughout society to create an extraordinary individualization of punishment and correction. This individualization would break up the dangerous masses associated with the streets of London and reproduced in gaols such as Newgate. In this abstract, impersonal world no special provisions would be made for women. They would be placed under the same continuous surveillance and subjected to the same perpetual labour as men. Ideally, this surveillance would bring about an internalized commitment to lawful behaviour. The fear and anticipation of detection and punishment of errant behaviour would produce a moral conscience to check criminal motivations once women were released into the community. Bentham apparently delighted in the prospect of creating a technology which, he argued, would be 'a way of obtaining power, power of mind over mind, hitherto without example.'

Elizabeth Fry and the Reform of Women's Prisons

Elizabeth Fry was the first penal reformer to devote her attention solely to the plight of imprisoned women. Her ideals for penal reform were based on the precepts of the Society of Friends (Quakers).[19] Where Bentham sought impersonal, mechanistic techniques, Quakers emphasised personal, paternalistic means of correction, and their main instrument of reform was religion. Quakers had a long association with prisons, not only as reformers but also as prisoners. The founder of the Society of Friends, George Fox, and the 'Mother of Quakerism', Margaret Fox, had been imprisoned in the seventeenth century for their dissenting beliefs and practices.[20] Both were shocked at the conditions they witnessed in the Derby Bridewell and at Lancaster Castle, especially the promiscuous 'herding of inmates'. Prison reform was not just a matter of middle-class concern for Quakers, it was partly the result of a history of a sense of shared oppression.

Penal reform was only one of a variety of philanthropic and political activities of early nineteenth-century Quakers. Others included peace movements, the anti-slavery agitations, the creation of schools for the religious and secular education of the poor, and Soup Societies to feed the unemployed.[21] Quaker women and men were involved in these various reform movements, although women had a rather restricted and 'special' role. Fry, like many of her women brethren, was involved in benevolent 'visiting'. Most of these women were educated and keenly interested in the social life of the time, but were usually prevented from participating fully in the wider social and economic world in which they lived. Quaker precepts did, however, point to the possibility of helping others through benevolent visiting as a means of bringing the message of salvation to the poor. Visiting involved the women in entering hospitals, asylums, poorhouses and the homes of the poor. Prison visiting was merely one aspect of this wider benevolent effort to rescue the poor. However, visits to prisons brought the most public attention, primarily through the work of one Quaker, Elizabeth Fry.[22]

Born into the prosperous and influential Gurney family of Norwich, she benefited from and participated in the rich social life of her generation of the Society of Friends. From a struggling seventeenth-century sect, the Quakers had by the late eighteenth century become an established, though still dissenting, religion with a number of families attaining considerable levels of prosperity through business activities. Prosperity led some families to abandon the Quaker principles of austere dress and personal asceticism. The Gurneys, for example, were known as 'gay Quakers'. Some Quakers began to have doubts about the moral effects of this wealth and social status, and by the time Elizabeth Fry was a young woman she rejected the family trappings of material success and adopted the strict principles of the Society of Friends. She wrote in her journal that she abandoned 'her flirtatious and worldly ways' and adopted the plain dress and bonnet of the early Quakers.

After marrying the London businessman, Joseph Fry, she became one of the most prominent members of strict Quaker groups in London. Her religious and philanthropic work in this group was an important foundation for the penal reform that eventually led to her worldwide reputation. Although Quaker doctrine and practice did not allow women a complete role in religious activities, the doctrine of 'direct inspiration' made it possible for women to become ministers. Long before her work in prisons, she had become a minister of considerable renown, noted for her 'peculiar gift of exhortation'.[23] She also practised the Quaker tradition of philanthropic work, and in 1797 wrote, 'I love to feel for the sorrows of others.'[24] Her own public preaching and philanthropic work, as well as the prison work of other Quakers such as Samuel Hoare and Fowell Buxton, constituted the significant background for her work in prison. Even so, Elizabeth Fry's role was a very unusual one, and her public commitments in the field of prison reform sometimes brought condemnation for being a neglectful mother.

The apparent catalyst for the start of her penal efforts was the visit in February 1813 of a group of American Quakers. When they visited Newgate they were 'shocked and sickened . . . by the blaspheming, fighting, dram-drinking, half-naked women.'[25] Their report and the persistent encouragement of Samuel Hoare were important in Fry's decision to visit Newgate in December 1813.

Newgate held both women and men who were awaiting trial, sentence, execution or transportation. The section for women was known at the time as 'hell above ground' with the women described as savages and wretches. The conditions for women prisoners were much worse than those for men. They suffered greater overcrowding since half of their allocated space of 190 square yards for 300 women and children had been appropriated by prison authorities for the confinement of upper-class prisoners of the Crown.[26] Women were also likely to be more impoverished than their male counterparts. This meant that they would have been unable to pay for the necessities and luxuries of prison life, such as food, ale and heating.

One of the most vivid and common public images of the women of Newgate was of them begging through the bars and grates of the prison. One of the 'ladies' who accompanied Fry on her initial visit described the scene in this manner, 'The railing was crowded with half naked women, struggling together for the front situations with the most boisterous violence, and begging with utmost vociferation.'[27] Fry was shocked by such scenes and she told Buxton,

> All I tell thee is a faint picture of reality; the filth, the closeness of the rooms, the furious manner and expressions of the women towards each other, and the abandoned wickedness, which everything bespoke, are quite indescribable.[28]

Despite the strong impression of this initial visit, she did not begin her famous work until late in 1816. This was against the objections of the Newgate authorities and the advice of the ordinary (minister), who warned that 'this, like many other useful and benevolent designs for the improvement of Newgate, would inevitably fail.'[29] She proposed to the women prisoners that they establish, with the guidance of herself and other visiting ladies, a school for the instruction of their children. The women were to consider this proposal, and, if agreed, to choose a 'schoolmistress' from their own ranks. When Fry and her associates returned the following day the women announced that they had embraced her proposal and selected a former schoolmistress to teach the children.

It is significant that the initial concerns of Fry and her colleagues centred on the children and not the women prisoners. The women, it seems, were considered to be almost beyond redemption. As one of the early visitors put it,

> the reformation of these women, lost as they were in every species of depravity, was scarcely an object of consideration, much less expectation . . . the utmost we could hope for, was to prevent these miserable creatures from becoming worse and worse. . . .[30]

The reformers, like Newgate officials and the public, initially considered women prisoners to be despicable savages. The same visitor described them as:

> . . . of the lowest and worst description, the very scum both of the city and country, filthy in their persons, disgusting in their habits, obscene in their conversations, and ignorant, to the greatest

degree, not only of religious truth, but of the most familiar duty and business of common life.[31]

Fry apparently shared this outlook, though possibly not so strongly. She tended to concentrate on the behaviour of women rather than their moral corruptness. For example, she noted in one of her early observations,

> It was in our visits to the school, where some of us attended almost every day, that we were witnesses to the dreadful proceedings that went forward on the female side of the prison; the begging, swearing, gaming, fighting, singing, dancing, dressing up in men's clothing; scenes too bad to be described. . . .[32]

Whatever Fry's initial conceptions of the women, she soon began to see them in a very different light, and to go beyond the first stereotypical impressions. By April 1817, she noted that 'Already, from being like wild beasts, they appear harmless and kind.'[33]

From an initial focus on 'convict children', Fry and her associates quickly expanded their horizons to improve the physical conditions for the women and develop and introduce plans for their reformation. One of the first steps was the formation of the Association for the Improvement of the Females at Newgate. The Association was composed of Fry, a clergyman's wife and eleven members of the Society of Friends.[34] The general aims of the Association were to

> . . . provide for the clothing, the instructions and the employment of these females, to introduce them to a knowledge of the holy scriptures, and to form in them as much as lies in our power, those habits of order, sobriety, and industry, which may render them docile and peaceable whilst in prison, and respectable when they leave it.[35]

These goals were to be achieved through a regime of work, orderliness, scripture reading and education. Fry considered systematic work of paramount importance,

> I found that nothing could be done, or was worth attempting for the reformation of the women, without constant employment; as it was, those who were idle were confirmed in idleness, and those who were disposed to the industrious, lost their good habits.[36]

The daily routine of the women was regulated by a system of rules that 'strictly prohibited' begging, the use of 'bad words', swearing, card playing, reading of 'plays, novels and other pernicious books' and the singing of 'immoral songs'.[37] Immoral habits were to be replaced by persistent labour, attentive listening to the holy scriptures, nominal education, cleanliness in all respects, and constant respect and deference. The entire system would be overseen by the ladies who were to be assisted by inmates elevated to positions of authority. Thirteen monitors were appointed, each to oversee twelve women in order to report on their work and to render an account of their efforts. A ward woman was also chosen to attend to the cleanliness of the ward and a yard woman appointed to nurse and assist in the sick room. At the apex of this inmate hierarchy would be the matron and submatron chosen from the most 'orderly and respectable'.

Fry and her colleagues also specified the most appropriate techniques for dealing with inmates. Members of the Association always attempted to adopt a personal, direct approach and stressed the importance of gaining the cooperation of inmates. Fry recommended that it was always important when embarking on the reform of women to call them together in order to 'express sympathy' with their position and to 'soothe them with words of gentleness and kindness as a means of gaining their trust and cooperation'.[38] Another member of the Committee pointed out that '. . . it has been our constant endeavour to associate them [prisoners] with ourselves in the object . . . all rules are first submitted to them and receive their voluntary consent.'[39] The practice of attempting to gain the direct assent and cooperation and the stress on a personal approach characterized by 'kind superintendence' were the distinguishing characteristics of the Ladies' Association's method. They, more than any other reformers, stressed the importance of obtaining the cooperation of inmates as a means of producing the 'willing subjects' who would voluntarily participate in their own transformation. This was the essential step in creating a profound and lasting reformation.

Newgate was transformed through the changes introduced by the Association. The most important change was an alteration in the living conditions. Women were provided with regular and sufficient food, proper bedding and decent clothing. Members of the Association also boasted that there had been radical changes in the 'manners and habits' of the women, '. . . from drunkenness to sobriety, from riot to order, from clamour to quietness, from obscenity to decency.'[40] The women had also apparently been transformed into diligent workers 'employed in patchwork, coarse needlework, spinning and knitting.'[41] It was not merely the 'visiting ladies' who observed and praised these changes, so did many of the frequent and prominent visitors. Only a short time after the transformation of Newgate the Association was honoured by a visit from the lord mayor and aldermen of the City of London. The lord mayor was astounded at the changes in Newgate.

> On my approach, no loud or dissonant sounds or angry voices indicated that I was about to enter a place which, I was credibly assured, had long had for one of its titles that of 'Hell above ground'. The court-yard into which I was admitted, instead of being peopled with beings scarcely human, blaspheming, fighting, tearing each other's hair, or gaming with a filthy pack of cards for the very clothes they wore, which often did not suffice even for decency, presented a scene where stillness and propriety reigned. I was conducted by a decently-dressed person, the newly-appointed yards-woman, to the door of a ward, where, at the head of a long table, sat a lady belonging to the Society of Friends. She was reading aloud to about sixteen women prisoners, who were engaged in needlework around it. Each wore a clean-looking blue apron and bib, with a ticket having a number on it suspended from her neck by a red tape. They all rose on my entrance, curtsied respectfully, and then at a signal given resumed their seats and employments. Instead of a scowl, leer, or ill-suppressed laugh, I observed upon their countenances an air of self-respect and gravity, a sort of consciousness of their improved character, and the altered position in which they were placed.[42]

These remarkable transformations were to be kept out of the public eye during the early stages of the Newgate 'experiment'. Publicity was something Fry and her associates sought to avoid. Throughout her life, following Quaker precepts, she attempted to dissociate herself from worldly success and acclaim. In her writings she often proclaimed that, as she was merely an instrument of the will of God, it was not right that she, a mere humble Quaker, should achieve such fame. Yet, at the same time she appears to have obtained considerable pleasure from the public homage and contact with society's elites that came from her prison work.

Whatever Fry's own sentiments regarding her work and the publicity it received, the Newgate experiment was immediately thrust into the public arena. Right from the beginning of their efforts the Ladies' Committee needed the cooperation and support of the authorities and in order to obtain it they had to demonstrate their successes. The lord mayor's visit was a perfect example of the sort of notables who came to view the 'experiment'. Not that these visits were always successful in gaining support. The lord mayor, for example, expressed praise for the extraordinary achievements of the Association but was unwilling to expend any additional resources on the institution. Official reluctance to finance and operate penal institutions was a continual issue throughout most of the nineteenth century. As a consequence, the Association's work was usually supported through private donations from the Society of Friends.

Despite the Association's attempts to keep its work out of the wider public arena, reports of its successes and Fry's public preaching at Newgate brought an extraordinary number of visitors, a flood of enquiring letters and often prominent press attention. One of the most important examples of this notoriety was the publication in April 1817 of a letter from Robert Owen in many London newspapers. Owen was well known as a reforming, even radical, industrialist through his operation of the industrial village at New Lanark, Scotland. Owen praised Fry's work, citing her success as 'proof of the effects of kindness and regular habits.'[43] There were numerous examples of such praise, and what was probably the most important was published in 1818 in Fowell Buxton's book, *An Inquiry Into Whether Crime and Misery are Produced or Prevented by Our Present System of Prison Disciplines*. In all of these works, Fry's gentle, persistent and religious efforts are juxtaposed against the savage, barbaric nature of the criminal women at Newgate. On the one side we have the pious middle-class woman acting as a saviour entering the bowels of hell to confront the depraved unwomanly creatures who were to be transformed through personal religious ministrations. This extraordinary transformation was mysterious, remarkable and beyond comprehension to those who considered women prisoners beyond redemption. Such views were not those of Fry, who always stressed that all were sinners and all could be elevated to a state of grace.

With the early successes at Newgate behind her, Fry set out in 1818 with her brother Joseph Gurney to tour northern England and Scotland in order to inspect the much neglected jails and to attempt to establish more Ladies' Associations. During their travels they inspected scores of small gaols, lock-ups and Bridewells and found most of them to be characterized by a lack of segregation which meant that the old and young as well as men and women were often housed in the same ward or room, a dearth of steady employment, insanitary and insecure accommodation and, unique to Scotland, confinement of the mad within prisons and the use of a rigorous system of *Squalor Carceris* for debtors.[44]

The existing conditions of women prisoners throughout Britain are aptly illustrated in the accounts of the Aberdeen County Jail and the Edinburgh City Gaol. At Aberdeen they found:

a small room, about fifteen feet long by eight in breadth, set apart for female criminals. There were four women in it, a man (husband of one of them), and a child. The room was most offensively close and very dirty . . . the impropriety of the man's being thus confined in company with women needs no remark.[45]

At an Edinburgh gaol she found that the women were segregated from the men, but such nominal arrangements were inadequate since

Neither was there any classifications attempted with the women, who were all together day and night; for in consequence of their night cells being so placed as to afford the opportunity of conversation with the men, they were under the necessity of sleeping in their day-rooms. This was an evil of no small magnitude. . . .[46]

Such accounts are typical, and Fry and Gurney judged almost all of these places of confinement wholly inadequate, with the exception of three Scottish Bridewells in Aberdeen, Edinburgh and Glasgow all of which held women and men in separate accommodation. The Aberdeen Bridewell was admired for its nursery for children and the full employment of women in weaving, spinning and oakum picking. Edinburgh Bridewell was praised for its unique architectural design. It housed primarily women and was the closest approximation to Bentham's panopticon ever constructed in Britain. As such, it employed a sophisticated form of continual surveillance.[47] The institution was a four-storey building built in a semi-circular or D-shaped fashion with the cells on the curved outer perimeter. Each inmate had a separate working and sleeping cell in which they were subjected to continuous solitary confinement. Gurney and Fry's description conveys the nature of this 'celebrated plan':

. . . In each of these four storeys there are thirteen working cells, open in front, and looking inwards towards the tower. In that tower there is, on the second storey, a semi-circular apartment fitted up with several long and very narrow windows, from which the inspector, without being discerned himself has a complete view of what is passing in all the working-cells . . . on the outside of the watch tower, in the court . . . is the pulpit, from which the minister may be distinctly seen and heard by the prisoners whilst they continue in their respective cells; thus the whole forms an excellent and commodious chapel.[48]

While the inmates laboured in seclusion, 'weaving linen, cotton and woollen stuffs' they were under continuous surveillance to ensure that they did not shirk their appointed tasks. Fry and Gurney were pleased to witness these forms of continuous labour and attempts at ceaseless solitary confinement, but they reserved their highest praise for the Glasgow Bridewell.

This institution operated what was called the silent congregate system with inmates working in silent groups during the day and sleeping in solitary cells at night. The Bridewell was primarily used for female offenders – of its 210 inmates, 160 were women. It was chiefly a 'house of labour' with the majority of women employed in textile production. In order to ensure industry, prisoners were required to labour on a task work basis and 'If these tasks are not completed, the prisoners are punished by the loss of a meal, which is found to have a powerful effect.'[49] The living conditions were judged to be superior to most prisons; inmates were reportedly well-fed and clothed and had decent bedding.

Fry praised these conditions and the useful labour which defrayed almost the total cost of confinement. She also appreciated the good work of the Committee of Ladies, which sought to 'instruct the ignorant, to provide the unemployed with work, to promote a daily reading of the Scriptures, and to watch over these criminals individually, not only when in prison, but, as far as possible after they leave it.'[50] Despite the achievements of these two Scottish institutions, Fry and Gurney were not satisfied with their regimes. They objected to an extreme emphasis on profitable labour and to the overcrowding that made the provisions for solitary confinement impossible. They proposed more religion and improved forms of classification in order to prevent the contamination caused by overcrowding.

The Perfect Prison for Women

Fry's most explicit and detailed statement of her preferred penal regime did not appear until 1825 in her short, but influential book, *Observations on the Siting, Superintendence and Government of Female Prisoners*. This work is one of the most detailed documents written by penal reformers of this era. Reading the works of Howard, Buxton, Western, Hoare and other male reformers who had certainly visited innumerable prisons, described their abuses and argued for legislative and administrative reforms, leaves one without many firm proposals. Fry, however, provided the concrete, explicit details for operating penal regimes missing from the works of most other reformers. Her direct and continual dealings with civic authorities, prison administrators, and prisoners provided a firmer and more convincing foundation for writing about the entire process of penal reform. Not only did she minutely describe her preferred form of penal discipline, she also gave solid recommendations as to how to operate a social movement directed at the amelioration of penal conditions.

Fry proposed that women should form themselves into local Visiting Committees. Her experience had convinced her of the futility of the efforts of lone reformers. A committee of several women arrives at 'sounder and wiser conclusions' because 'the Ladies may mutually assist each other's judgement.'[51] An organized committee was also likely to be more efficient and successful than a lone refomer, because 'when one labourer fails, the work will not cease, and others will be ready to supply her place.'[52] Specialization was also important for ensuring the efficiency of the committees, perhaps with one member oriented to classification, one to religious instruction and another to employment. Measures such as these would 'increase order, regularity and method' and greater numbers would lend more weight to the Committee's deliberations and deputations.

Once formed into a committee, the ladies should proceed with considerable caution when seeking to enter their local prisons. Visiting ladies, Fry advised, should never confront or interfere with those in authority. Visitors must be 'at once *wise as serpents and harmless as doves*. . .' – interesting advice from a woman who did not shrink from confronting established convention and municipal and penal authorities. Deference and delicacy were not needed when dealing with inmates. When visiting ladies first approached the inmates they were to adopt a position of authority, albeit one that sought to gain the cooperation of those subjected to it. Fry, following her own precepts, recommended a direct and personal approach, beginning with a meeting with the inmates at which members of the Committee might

> . . . express their sympathy with them under their afflicting circumstances and endeavour to hold up in strong colours, the danger and misery of vice, the beauty of holiness, and the innumerable advantages which attach to a life of sobriety, industry, honesty and virtue.[53]

Fry argued that if 'tenderly treated' in this manner women would willingly submit to the authority and discipline imposed by the Association.

After visitors had made their entry into the prison and gained the cooperation of inmates they should embark upon the implement-

ation of a strict regime of discipline. The rather loose and generalized system of scripture reading accompanied by silent needle-
work begun at Newgate was no longer seen as an adequate basis for
reformation. Fry certainly retained her emphasis on the importance
of a personal approach, continual employment, self-reflection,
classification and religious instruction, but she was now proposing
new forms of discipline and technologies of correction.

In contrast to her earlier conceptions, inmates were no longer seen
as primarily subjects who could be involved in their own transformation. It was now considered dangerous to leave them to their own
self-reflection. Presumably their deeds and attitudes had rendered
them unworthy participants in their own reformation; they were
now conceptualized as objects to be processed through an 'engine of
reform'. Perhaps because of her experience within prison and the
unwillingness of some inmates to accept 'kind superintendence',
Fry no longer trusted them to participate in their own reformation.
Where she once argued for a benevolent and loose system of
supervision over inmates, she now proposed 'Vigilant and
Unremitting Inspection.' Similar to Bentham she suggests the
creation of prisons where the arrangement of cells, day-rooms and
airing grounds would allow matrons to be 'able to see all the
prisoners while at work, and in their hours of recreation, and to
overhear them during the night.'[54] Continuous surveillance was one of
the *'most essential points* in a correct system of discipline.' The
panopticon principle was to be an important mechanism for assuring
that the new disciplines would be systematially applied and received.

The new regimes would also employ continuous degradations,
unremitted routines of labour, and religious and secular instruction.
Continuous, useful labour was to be an integral feature of prisons
because it had moral and material benefits, 'No prison can be
considered complete, which does not afford the means of *hard*
labour, which properly pertains to a reforming *discipline*, and forms
an important part of the system of *punishment.*[55] This statement
illustrates the usual twofold purpose of penal labour; as a means of
discipline leading to good order within prison and reformation of
habits and punishment intended to deter women from the
commission of crime.

At this stage in her career of penal reform, Fry appears to have
altered her ideas regarding work. In her early penal efforts she
stressed the benefits of regularity and orderliness arising from
labour, whereas her later proposals also emphasised its punitive
nature. Although Fry appears not to have been especially keen on

the use of purely punitive forms of labour for women, she did not rule them out. In 1835, when she testified before the Parliamentary committee established to investigate 'The State of Gaols and Houses of Correction in England and Wales' she objected to the systematic use of treadwheel labour for women. The Association of Lady Visitors thought treadwheel labour 'reduces health and reduces moral standards.'[56] Members of the Association and Fry did not, however, totally reject the use of purely punitive labour. As Fry indicated 'There is a wheel called a Crank-Wheel, which I consider better suited for women.'[57] There were numerous types of the crank-wheels; one of the most common was described as:

> . . . a narrow iron drum, placed on legs, with a long handle on one side, which, on being turned, causes a series of cups or scoops in the interior to revolve. At the lowest part of the machine is a thick layer of sand, which the cups, as they come round, scoop up, and carry to the top of the wheel, where they throw it out and empty themselves, after the principle of a dredging machine.[58]

This form of punitive labour was not to be applied to all women, only those described as 'recalcitrant'.

Fry and the Association continually stressed the importance of useful labour, 'better work is needle work and the best work is . . . giving a poor woman a knowledge how to cut out and make up articles of clothing.'[59] With such skills 'she goes out better able to perform her domestic duties . . . teaching her to wash properly, and to iron and mend; all these things help her after she quits the gaol.'[60] The vision of the perfect institution for women included continuous labour that created orderly habits, regulation within prisons and training for employment in domestic settings and clothing production.

The other instruments of reform to be used in Fry's ideal institution were religious instruction and teaching in the rudiments of reading and writing.[61] Women were to be taught to 'read and cipher as well as to make a ready and profitable use of the needle.' Intellectual development was only a secondary aspect of teaching, a more important outcome would be the elevation of the 'moral habits' and 'tastes' of female prisoners. Secular education would play only a minor role in prisons for women. Fry argued that 'everything sectarian must be rigidly avoided'. The major thrust of instruction should be religious.

Religious instruction would involve a regular, ideally daily, reading of the Holy Scriptures and attendance at chapel where women should be 'separated from the sight of men'. During scripture reading and religious services 'Nothing should be allowed to divert their attention, or to interrupt the solemnity of the occasion.' Religious instruction and scripture reading should be carried out by visiting ladies, and a chaplain of 'established character' appointed to conduct services. Chaplains were necessary, but Fry apparently did not trust males to preach to women in private. In 1835 she argued before the Parliamentary Committee that '. . . I would not have private instruction given by Gentlemen to Female Prisoners; and I am quite convinced that Instruction would be best received from their own Sex. . . .'[62] Fry preferred the personal and direct approach as the main instrument of religious reform; through this method visiting ladies should 'endeavour by private persuasion and instruction, to lead them into the path of virtue, religion and peace.'[63] Like most Evangelicals and Quakers, she had great faith in the ability of religious ministrations to bring about profound 'amendments in life'. She suggested, for instance, that the simple 'declaration of the Gospel has a powerful *tendency* to produce' repentance and reformation.

Fry's new, more elaborate schemes went far beyond instruction and employment. The additional elements of her proposal were intended to make reforming technologies and accompanying punishments more certain and specific. In order to decrease the deleterious effects of contamination and to ensure the application of punishments and rewards to specific inmates, a complex system of classification, progressive stages and marks was proposed. Classification would be based on two general categories: women who were awaiting trial and convicted women. Convicted women would experience four stages of confinement through which they would progress depending on 'their general character and degree of criminality'. The first class would be composed of women nearing the end of their sentence whose crimes were considered to be indicative of 'no deep moral dye'. Women in this stage/class would enjoy considerable advantages denied other inmates; for example, better clothing and less irksome labour for which they would be given a small pecuniary reward to be obtained upon release. Members of classes two and three would be in a privileged position but given fewer privileges than first-class women. Class four would be composed of those who must 'undergo *peculiar privations and hardships.*' Members of this class would be women who had served more than one sentence, 'the most hardened and desperate'. Still, there was some hope for these women who might 'with great care and deliberation . . . be raised step by step into the higher classes.'[64]

Classification and segregated living arrangements would distribute women in a hierarchy of relative guilt and worth and prompt them to behave in a diligent and industrious manner as a means of achieving greater rewards and privileges. To ensure the regimentation and performance associated with the duties of each class, an explicit method of accounting was required. A system of badges had been introduced at the beginning of the work at Newgate, but Fry developed a more exacting scheme by 1825. She proposed that each woman wear a 'ticket inscribed with a number by which she would be distinguished, and shall agree with a corresponding number in the class list.'[65] The wearing of numbered badges would allow a more precise and continuous differentiation of individuals, guaranteeing the systematic application of rewards and punishments. Inmate numbers would be recorded on a 'class list' that would operate as a conduct register. In this way the daily 'approbations and disapprobations' of each inmate could be registered. Orderliness and certainty would be enhanced since each inmate and members of staff would know her exact location relative to others. Classification and a system of badges would be a great benefit 'in promoting that strictness of discipline which is essential to the order and regularity of the *whole machine*.'[66]

A continuous system of moral accounting was to be aided by the wearing of a uniform for different classes. A distinct uniform for each class would provide a continuous sign of an individual's location within the overall 'machine' and embody a permanent and continuous form of degradation. A uniform dress should be 'perfectly plain and simple', clearly distinguishable from the women's usual apparel. Women were to be denied any expression of individuality or 'vanity' in their dress and deportment, 'Ear-rings, curled hair, and all sorts of finery and superfluity of dress . . . must be absolutely forbidden; and the caps worn by them must be close, plain, and not of transparent material.'[67] The humiliation associated with personal appearance started at the beginning of confinement with the ritual of cutting the woman's hair. Felons' hair, Fry argued must be short cropped and remain short throughout their sentence. Short hair would have a double impact, operating as a 'certain, yet harmless punishment' and promoting 'that humiliation of spirit, which, for persons so circumstanced, is an indispensable step to improvement and reformation.'[68]

The implementation and operation of this new regime required a full-time female staff aided by visiting ladies. Fry proposed to ban all males from the daily supervision of female inmates, only allowing chaplains access on a regular basis. Since female felons were of 'light and abandoned character' it was impossible and unreasonable to 'place them under the care of *men*. . .' because it 'seldom fails to be injurious to both parties.' Accordingly, she considered it 'Absolutely essential to the proper order and regulation of every prison, that the female prisoners should be placed under the superintendence of officers of their own sex.'[69] Matrons and female officers should be of a 'decidedly religious' character, possessed of 'respectable, orderly and active habits' and 'plain in dress, gentle, yet firm in . . . demeanour.' They should be a 'consistent example of feminine propriety and virtue' and practice 'vigilance and impartiality' in dealing with prisoners. Through the implementation of this plan, prisoners would no longer have important positions of authority as they did at Newgate; a professional staff would now be responsible for carrying out the rules of the institution, though the ultimate authority would reside with the lady visitors.

Importantly, Fry's system, like many of those that followed, combined elements of the symbolic signification associated with pre-industrial forms of punishment with the new, emergent forms of human accounting and correction. In contrast to the method of distributing signs associated with the scaffold and community shamings, the new technology of confinement provided a more continuous and certain form of symbolizing the guilt and humiliation associated with crime. They also departed from the traditional forms of humiliation in that the signifiers of guilt were no longer public. Humiliation and degradation were to be significant elements of the new penal regimes, but were to be used in more meaningful and useful ways.

Fry's ideas and her work within prisons were significant elements in the fierce, intermittent debates that took place over penal policy during the first forty years of the nineteenth century. The British Ladies' Society for Promoting the Reformation of Female Prisoners, established by Fry in 1821, and the, mainly Quaker, Prison Discipline Society, played key roles in these debates. The Ladies' Society, and its supporters claimed important and lasting effects for their new penal methods. Not only did they report changes in the 'manner and habits' of female prisoners at Newgate and elsewhere, they also claimed extraordinary successes in preventing relapses into crime after release. After the first two years of operating the women's side at Newgate, the Society reported that '*only four* have returned to us convicted of fresh offences. . . '.[70] In 1835, Fry claimed before a Select Committee of the House of Lords, that:

> I think before I leave speaking of Newgate I may say, as to the system of instruction and employment and classification such as we have been enabled to adopt, after trying it for eighteen years, we are increasingly confirmed in the utility of the plans, and we never felt more satisfied than we have of late years, for we have had more instances of women turning out well. . .[71]

Antagonistic observers were not as confident of the success. They argued, for example, that 'kind superintendence', useful labour and reasonable living conditions did not reform or deter women; rather, it made them see imprisonment as something to seek out, an enjoyable respite from the hardships of the street and crime. Reactionaries, such as Western and Smith, argued that prison conditions should be worse than the living conditions women and men experienced outside of prison. Opponents also attempted to refute the claim of permanent reformation. For example, in October 1833 a letter to the *Times* rejected the Society's claims for lasting improvement in female criminals, citing the reports of outrageous conduct of female transportees once they left Newgate.[72] Additionally, many of the regimes and improved living conditions implemented by the visiting ladies had apparently not been maintained in prisons. Regardless of the material results of the Society's efforts, their ideas, and especially the work of Fry, would have a profound effect on the creation of the modern penitentiary.

The Creation of National Penitentiaries

The first halting movement towards the creation of a system of national penitentiaries occurred in 1816 with the opening of the massive Millbank prison.[73] Millbank was to be a model prison, providing an example for all local and county officials. Religion, constant inspection and regular employment were to be the cornerstones of the discipline but its initial operation failed to live up to expectations. Religion did play a significant role in the prison, exemplified by the appointment of religious ministers, such as Wentworth Russell, to the position of governor. These governor/ministers attempted to enforce strict religious observances and practices on prisoners and staff. Preaching and exhortation did not, however, have the desired effect. Inmates resisted efforts to impose religious doctrines and often rebelled in chapel (see Chapter Four).

Overcrowding usually prevented the implementation of labour schemes and the attempts to isolate inmates in individual cells also failed. These problems, when coupled with outbreaks of disease and illness, brought continuous criticism from the press and public. Millbank, rather than providing an answer to crime, actually generated greater demands for improvements in prison discipline.

As indicated above, there were two major and competing forms of penal discipline during this period, the congregate silent system as practiced at the Glasgow Bridewell and continuous solitary confinement such as that enforced at the Edinburgh and Gloucestershire Bridewells.[74] Both systems were primarily aimed at preventing the contamination caused by direct contact of prisoners. Basically, the congregate silent system was one in which prisoners worked in groups in absolute silence. Continuous solitary confinement meant housing prisoners in separate cells without any form of contact. Supporters of the congregate system argued that it prevented contamination by prohibiting conversation and contact amongst prisoners, provided the best form of industrial training for inmates which helped to defray the costs of confinement, and avoided the 'unnatural' features and adverse results of prolonged solitary confinement. Those who supported prolonged solitary confinement urged its adoption as the only sure means of preventing contamination. According to the opponents of solitary confinement, it led to physical and mental breakdown and the necessity of a separate cell for each inmate was deemed prohibitively expensive.

The debate was not settled until 1839 with the passage of the National Penitentiary Acts for England and Scotland. These Acts came about through the vigorous efforts of two well-known penal reformers, William Crawford and Wentworth Russell. Their campaign began in 1834 when Crawford was sent to the United States to inspect and report on the penal experiments being conducted there.[75] Crawford inspected a number of institutions but his attention focussed on four prisons in New York and Pennsylvania: the Walnut Street Gaol and the Eastern Penitentiary in Philadelphia and the Auburn and Sing Sing prisons in New York. The New York institutions relied on the congregate silent method and classification to prevent communications and contamination. The two Pennsylvania institutions were based on a rigorous system of continuous solitary confinement and cellular labour.

In his report on these institutions, Crawford enthusiastically endorsed the general principles of the solitary system and rejected the congregate method. He thought the latter failed to prevent communication and led to attempts to circumvent the silent rule which often resulted in severe punishments such as whipping. Crawford praised the silence, order and regularity of the solitary system and pointed out that such techniques were first employed in Britain in the Glasgow and Gloucestershire Bridewells. He did not, however, fully endorse the solitary systems as they were operated in the United States. He judged them inadequate in the provision of religious instruction and made it clear that the evils of this system had primarily come about because of lengthy confinement without labour.

Crawford's report did not immediately usher the solitary system into British prisons. It was, however, an important step towards the creation of the modern penitentiary with solitary confinement at its core. Crawford's campaign was helped enormously when, in 1835, he and Russell were appointed to the newly created positions of prison inspectors. The creation of a prison inspectorate, long proposed by the Discipline Society, resulted in the institutionalization of penal reform and offered a privileged position to those who performed these duties.[76] From this position Crawford and the zealous Russell pressed for the adoption of solitary confinement as the approved method of penal correction. In numerous official reports and private representations they began to discredit the congregate system and urge the adoption of what they began to call the Separate System.

The Separate System was eloquently and precisely detailed in the third *Report* of the Prison Inspectorate. The use of the term 'separate' was intended to distinguish their proposed regime from total solitary confinement while stressing the importance of holding each prisoner in separate cells. Separate did not mean total unrelenting solitude. Solitude was to be used as a means of enducing compliance and acquiescence but it would be interrupted by visits from warders, taskmasters, educators, prison matrons, prison governors, and most importantly for Russell, prison chaplains. Separation meant being cut off from friends and associates, not from reforming influences of the new professional penal staff. Through this system prisoners would be educated, exhorted, improved and required to pay close attention to the Bible and their allocated labour. Useful labour was to be an integral feature of the new separate system, a reward providing relief from solitude, though it was rarely used in this way. The majority of women and men sent to prison after the implementation of the separate system, in fact, were required to labour right from the start of their confinement.

Crawford and Russell proposed no special arrangements for women prisoners other than the provision for confinement separate from men, usually within wings of the same institution. They did, however, invoke the supposed inadequacy of matrons and female officers as an additional reason for imposing the separate system. According to them, 'it had been found utterly impossible to enforce the discipline of the congregate system with women prisoners.'[77] Female officers were deemed to lack judgement and firmness to enforce the congregate system in an efficient way, thus requiring continual attention from the governor. The weakness of women officers and the continual intervention of the governor supposedly had an adverse effect on women prisoners. It led to '. . . a feeling of contempt for authority, a banishment of all serious reflection, an absence of subordination, demoralizing intercourse, and a release from the salutary discomfort and restraint which it ought to be the aim of every penal system to produce.'[78] Accordingly, the introduction of the separate system was meant to overcome the individual idiosyncrasies of women officers and guarantee an exacting and uniform system.

The relentless pressure of Crawford and Russell finally led to the passage of the 1839 Penal Act which specified the separate system as the approved method of confinement. The English Act and its Scottish equivalent, enacted in the same year, provided a mandate for the building of two model penitentiaries, Pentonville in London and Perth in North Central Scotland.[79] When these institutions were opened in 1842, they operated rigorous systems of separate confinement involving 23 hours of daily solitary confinement and twelve hours of continuous labour, relieved only by an hour of exercise and periodic visits from chaplains, taskmasters, warders and educators. Inmates were confined in these conditions for an eighteen-month period prior to being transported.[80]

The 1840s were characterized by efforts to introduce the separate system into all British prisons. In 1852 the Surveyor General of Prisons, Joshua Jebb, reported that fifty prisons had been erected or improved for the operation of the separate system, with accommodation for 12,000 prisoners in England and Wales and 1,000 in Scotland and Ireland.[81] It is clear, however, that the inspectorate misrepresented the degree of implementation and operation of the system. Many local city and county jails continued to operate the congregate silent system after 1839, or practised no form of systematic confinement.[82] Even those institutions built or redesigned to enforce the separate system rarely achieved the goal of total separation. Overcrowding, lack of sufficient accommodation and demands for labour meant that separation was only applied to a small proportion of inmates.

Despite the nominal implementation of a vigorous separate system in most British prisons, its operation attracted a great deal of immediate public attention and concern. From the beginning especially at Pentonville, penal officials and press reports expressed considerable concern about the mental and physical impact of prolonged solitary confinement. The first efforts to alter the system were directed at reducing the length of confinement, first to 12 months and then to nine. Vigorous attacks on the separate system and transportation throughout the 1840s resulted in new developments in British prisons.

The disillusionment with transportation and its virtual cessation in 1852 meant that the British penal system was required to absorb a growing number of convicts who would have been punished by transportation rather than imprisonment. The Penal Servitude Acts of 1853 and 1857 were intended to create a system to absorb these convicted criminals and develop new harsher institutions to punish and rehabilitate them through hard, congregate labour.[83] Penal servitude was linked to the separate system through a progressive stage system that provided solitary confinement during the early months of imprisonment followed by hard, congregate labour outside the prison.

Under the Penal Servitude Acts male convicts were to be placed in solitary confinement for the first four months of their prison sentence and then transferred to a hard labour prison like Portsmouth, Chatham and Dartmoor, where they were forced to engage in hard labour, such as dredging marshes, quarrying stone or building harbours. After the expiration of two-thirds of their sentence they would be released on licence through the ticket-of-leave system, a forerunner of parole. Women sentenced to penal servitude were initially sent to Millbank prison for the first stages of their confinement, where they also underwent four months of solitary confinement. They would then be transferred to Brixton to complete their sentence in partial separation, primarily engaged in silent congregate labour inside the prison. Unlike male convicts, women did not engage in outdoor labour beyond the prison walls, and they were not automatically released on licence after serving two-thirds of their sentence. Rather, they were required to continue to labour within the prison and were sometimes sent to a third institution, a Refuge, after the expiration of their sentence. The

Penal Servitude Acts marked the beginning of distinct official differences in the treatment of women offenders who were not allowed to go out to labour and were subjected to a tighter regime than their male counterparts. Women were more closely confined in this new regime created specifically for them.

By mid-century, the British had created unique and austere institutions that usually provided secure, sanitary conditions for prisoners. Following the dictates of most reformers, they had separated women from men and appointed women warders, matrons and, later, lady superintendents to oversee the women's side. The corrupt and insanitary conditions that predominated in the late eighteenth and early nineteenth centuries had generally been replaced by new forbidding fortresses of discipline and punishment. In contrast to the United States where women were held in cramped, insanitary gaols and often subjected to sexual assaults by warders, it seems that women in British prisons had been granted a fair degree of security and protection by this time.[84]

The new and improved prisons of this period combined degradation and humiliation with the positive elements of reform and discipline. In some ways the regimes were similar for men and women. Yet it is clear that patriarchal and paternalist conceptions played a crucial role in the responses to women right from the beginning of the modern prison. The work provided for women was always predicated on assumptions about their natural skills and limitations, and the surveillance and regulation was always closer and more onmipresent than that usually directed at men. The personal and direct approach initially played an important role in some institutions. However, the impersonal and more abstract approaches increasingly gained acceptance along with an emphasis on humiliation, degradation, human accounting, hard useful labour and religious exhortation.

4

Penal Regimes

The period from 1840 to 1870 ushered in the age of the 'great confinement' with thousands of men and women sent to English, Welsh and Scottish prisons, jails, asylums and workhouses. In 1849, for example, 157,273 women and men passed through English and Welsh prisons. In the same year 24,335 prisoners were received into Scottish prisons.[1] Women constituted a considerable proportion of these commitals. From 1842 to 1853 they comprised nearly a quarter of all commitals in England and Wales.[2] In Scotland, the ratio of women to the total prison population was even higher; in 1844 they constituted 37 per cent of the total intake of 19,319; 36 per cent in 1850 (total 23,736) and 40.7 per cent (total 19,018) in 1855.[3] Some English and Welsh areas, such as Cumberland, Lancaster, South Wales and Northumberland approached this high proportion, though they were never as high as the Scottish level. At the beginning of the age of the 'great confinement' both women and men usually served rather short sentences, often three to six months and sometimes even less than a week. Short sentences predominated during the nineteenth century, but after the enactment of the Penal Servitude Acts some prisoners began to serve much longer sentences of five and seven years in convict prisons such as Brixton and Dartmoor. Our purpose in this chapter is to analyse the nature of the regimes experienced by women in the new and reconstituted prisons of Britain, and consider women's reactions to this confinement.

The Operation of Penal Regimes for Women

Most prisons in the nineteenth century held a mixed population with distinct wings allocated to males and females. For example, Millbank in London and Perth prison in Scotland held both men and women under the separate system. Millbank was the transportation depot for England, Wales and Scotland where women and men were confined under the separate system before being transported to the penal colonies. After the cessation of transportation, Millbank became the main English prison for the reception of women sentenced to penal servitude, with a daily average of around 500. Other prisons, although mandated by the 1839 Act to operate a rigorous regime of separate confinement, usually enforced the congregate silent method of work and discipline. Most local and county jails and houses of correction, such as Tothill Fields prison in London and the Glasgow Bridewell held women and men in separate wings under the discipline of the congregate system. Solitary confinement was often used, however, as the first stage of imprisonment in the rudimentary stage systems that existed in many prisons. These types of prisons usually held convicted prisoners. Women and men awaiting trial were increasingly being segregated in distinct institutions such as Newgate or in separate wings of mixed prisons.

In 1853 the first purpose-built prison for women was opened in Brixton, London. It was rebuilt after the Penal Servitude Acts to accommodate 700–800 women. The reconstructed Brixton and Millbank were initially used in combination to house penal servitude women who were subjected to a progressive stage system involving four stages.[4] At the beginning of a five- to seven-year sentence, women would be sent to Millbank to go through the first two stages of imprisonment, probation and the third class. During the first four months of probation prisoners were confined in nearly total isolation with their 'cell-doors bolted', picking coir matting or heckling old ropes in 'perfect silence'. They were not allowed visitors during this probationary period and could only advance out of the probationary class by 'their industry and good conduct'. If after two months they proved to be well-behaved, they were allowed to engage in needle-work within their bolted cell. Continued improvement would result in promotion to the third class. Women in this class were allowed a visit after two months and were sometimes given lighter work, such as needlework. Women remained in this class until they were transferred to Brixton to complete their sentence.[5] The lengths of time served in Millbank probably varied a great deal depending on a woman's conduct and, more importantly, the availability of accommodation at Brixton.

Once transferred to Brixton, women had to pass through two additional stages. They continued in the third class for a period of six months until they had demonstrated diligent conduct and exemplary behaviour. Promotion to the second class brought additional privileges. A woman in the second class wore a badge with the number '2' on it, a mark of honour, and she was allowed to labour in silent association. She earned 'a small gratuity of from sixpence to eightpence a week for her labour' that she received upon release. Continued good conduct for another six-month period resulted in promotion to the first class.[6] First-class women were allowed to wear a badge marked '1' and entitled to a gratuity of eightpence to a shilling a week. They were also given additional privileges, such as greater silent associated labour and, most importantly, the possibility to talk with their fellow inmates for two periods during the day, about an hour and a half. The progressive stage system also worked in descending direction; women who were judged to be recalcitrant or troublesome might be demoted in rank and sent back to Millbank where they lost all of their privileges. This system of rewards and punishments was adjudged very useful by penal authorities, one of whom considered it 'most beneficial in promoting continued good behaviour.'[7]

Not all British prisons for women operated such an elaborate system of classification and progressive stages, yet most had some variant of this progressive method. What all the prisons did have in common was a commitment to penal regimes that were more rigorous and exacting than those existing before the 1839 Act; regimes that combined punishment, degradation, correction, reformation, education, and labour.

The initial stages of a woman's sentence, as Fry and others had proposed, were characterized by degradation, isolation and 'penal coercion'. Penal coercion involved sparse, even punitive diets, enforced silence, rigid rules and harsh punishments for infractions. Degradations and humiliations took two general forms, those designed to isolate women from the supports provided by the wider social and inmate world and those oriented to reducing women's self-esteem. Solitary confinement and the severe restriction of visits would eliminate material and symbolic support, and the shaving of women's heads and wearing of uniforms would reduce, even eliminate, individuality and vanity. According to contemporary reports, women found the cutting of their hair a severe degradation and often attempted to resist this ritual. As the matron of Millbank prison put it, 'they'd sooner lose their lives than their hair.'[8] The cutting of hair was followed by the issuing of a 'plain and simple' uniform distinct from normal apparel. The women at Brixton wore a 'loose, dark, claret-brown robe or gown, with a blue check apron and neckerchief, while the cap they wore was a small, close, white muslin . . . with brass figures on their arms, numbers 1 and 2.'[9] In the Female House of Correction at Holloway, London women wore

> . . .three wincy petticoats in winter, and two in summer; a blue gown, a checked apron, a blue checked neckerchief, a small printed pocket handkerchief, and a white linen cap. A pair of blue worsted stockings, and a thick substantial shawl, both knitted by the female prisoners.[10]

The daily routines of discipline at many women's prisons, such as Perth, Millbank and Brixton, were remarkably similar.[11] Importantly, the new regimes and the regulations relating to their operation were oriented to bringing about exacting behaviour from both *staff* and *inmates*. The daily routine for matrons, warders and inmates was regulated by an explicit timetable, often marked by the ringing of bells. At Millbank the first bell at 5:30 was the signal for matrons and warders to rise and prepare for duty. A second bell at 5:45 was the signal for the warders to assemble and for prisoners to rise. By 6:00 every prisoner was expected to have put out her 'night vessel', arranged and swept her cell, washed, and be 'standing in her cell, ready to show herself to the matrons on the ward.' After inspection, women worked until 7:30 when a breakfast of cocoa and a four-ounce loaf of bread was served. After a short break for breakfast (some prisons allowed ten minutes) women resumed their labours.

Under the rigorous separate system and in the initial period of the stage system, women worked in silence within their cell. Yet many imprisoned women, even during the most vigorous period of the separate system, worked in communal silence. Individual and/or associated labour continued until 12:39 p.m. when water was served with dinner at 1:00. After a short interval for dinner, work resumed and continued unabated until 4:30 or 5:00 p.m. when women returned to their cells and prepared for supper. Once supper was finished, needlework continued, usually within the cells or in associated silence until 7:30 or 8:00 p.m. depending on the particular prison. At this point the order was given to 'sling hammocks'. Inmates were allowed to read approved texts until 8:30 and the final bell was rung at 9:00 p.m. as the signal to close the prison. Routines such as this were intended to instil the ideals and patterns of behaviour associated with sobriety, orderliness and punctuality.

This exacting routine of silent labour was interrupted only by periods of teaching, preaching and exercising. At the beginnning of these regimes, women were only allowed to exercise individually. For example, at Perth prison exercise was taken alone in enclosed, covered courtyards intended to prevent any contaminating influences through social contact. Authorities went to extraordinary lengths to prevent communication under the separate system. In the chapels at Perth and Pentonville inmates were enclosed in separate cubicles during service and at a number of prisons were required to wear a veil or mask to prevent recognition by and communication from other inmates when moving to and from exercise yards. With the relaxation of the separate system, they were allowed into the 'airing yards' to exercise together, first in a group but separated from each other, walking in single file in a circle; later in pairs, engaged in quiet conversation.

Secular instruction was given by teachers hired specifically for that purpose, but its aim was primarily disciplinary and limited to imparting rudimentary skills. As the superintendent of the women's prison in Mountjoy, Ireland (under British administration) put it, education should 'awaken the minds of the prisoners, and improve their natural comprehensions, to make them more docile, more easily brought to see the value of cleanliness and order, and to inspire them with a considerable self-respect. . . .'[12] Secular education, as Fry had proposed, was limited and its main purpose was moral and social.

These purposes were, of course, even clearer in the work of the chaplains who were significant features of prison regimes during this period, with many of them acting as both governor and chaplain. Prison chaplains used exhortation and scripture reading in their efforts to bring about atonement and redemption. They were the first penal professionals and their reports, pamphlets and books were given considerable prominence in official reports and public debates.

From the beginning of the era of the modern penitentiary, chaplains wholeheartedly adopted their role as instruments of penal reform. They saw themselves as engaged in benevolent, philanthropic labour. Many of them rejected other mechanisms of punishment and correction such as the separate system and argued that only religion reformed. As the chaplain of Pentonville Prison, Rev Joseph Kingsmill, put it:

> We are led by our own observations to value it [separation] but little as an *active agency* for reforming criminals, but to allow it a high place as auxiliary, in general, to that which is reformatory in the highest degree. *Christian instruction in the hands of Christian men.*[23]

Solitary confinement and the rigours of the timetable of discipline were mere auxiliaries or adjuncts to the reforming mechanism of religion. Some chaplains did recognize solitude as the bedrock of reformation. The Rev Clay of Liverpool prison saw it as his responsibility to 'endeavour as much as possible to make the prisoner welcome religion as an alleviation of this punishment.'[14]

The process of 'alleviation' usually took on a similar form in most institutions. Using a variant of the modern casework method, chaplains sought to coax prisoners to reveal their life history, to admit guilt, to repent and to vow that they would apply themselves in a diligent manner to the rigours of the penal system. Exhortation and scripture reading were the chaplains' tools. The chaplain of Edinburgh prison indicated that:

> the scriptures, with all their warnings, counsels, instructions, admonitions, precepts, promises, and threatenings, are firmly and permanently lodged in their minds, and may be present to restrain them in some future day of temptation, or to tell them where to look for pardon in the hour of death.[15]

Similar techniques were employed by visiting ladies who, it is said, were extremely distressed if they were unable to invoke guilt in their subjects.[16] Although some inmates often resisted these efforts (see below), it is likely that chaplains and lady visitors were reasonably successful in extracting confessions from those subjected to isolation and humiliation, though much less successful in bringing about the 'profound submission' and lasting reformation they sought.

The major technology of discipline and reform was sustained labour. The use of purely punitive labour, such as the treadwheel and the crank, had been relaxed by mid-century, though some institutions, such as Coldbath Fields, continued to employ them. Most penal reformers and administrators had no doubt that continuous useful labour should constitute the most significant feature of penal establishements. Frederick Hill, the first prison inspector for Scotland, was a lifelong, ardent supporter of useful penal labour. Hill argued that a system of paid piece-work would lead to moral redemption, benefit prison management, and defray the costs of confinement. It instilled self-respect, diligence and ambition. His annual reports are filled with accounts from governors, matrons, and chaplains suggesting the beneficial, reforming effects of useful labour. As the matron of Edinburgh prison reported,

> I got on with my prisoners remarkably well last winter, because we had a very busy winter of various kinds of work, most of which was

well paid. My prisoners were tasked daily, and their diligence and spirit were delightful. . . . There was no idleness in getting up in the morning; each was more anxious than another to get to their work.[17]

Hill zealously extended useful labour to all Scottish prisons. Useful, 'productive' work, he argued, was '. . . the most efficacious means of improvement, and ought not therefore to be represented in deterring ardours, or mingled with the ideas of punishment.'[18] English authorities, such as the Reverend Clay and the reformer, Mary Carpenter, echoed these views, and female prisoners of English prisons were usually employed in useful work.

In 1861 the matron of Brixton reported that her '. . . prisoners are always very anxious for employment . . . and as a body . . . are very industrious.'[19] She endorsed useful labour and concluded, 'My experience satisfies me that female convicts, as a body, cannot bear to be idle.'[20] Mary Carpenter concurred, 'Hard work is a most important element of training, and a great aid to subduing bad passions.'[21] As we have seen, penal reformers had continually suggested useful employment as a means of reformation and good order, and with few exceptions most British prisons during this period, especially Scottish ones, employed women and men in useful and productive labour.

The upkeep of prisons involved cooking, baking, cleaning and, most importantly, laundering. The laundry was often the hub of a woman's prison, with a large proportion of inmates employed in washing, drying, ironing and folding clothes and linen for both women's and men's prisons and some outside contractors. A few penal authorities rightly equated laundry work with the hard labour of male convicts working in the dockyards and quarries.

Brixton laundry was probably the largest within the penal system, supplying clean clothes and linen for Brixton, Pentonville and Millbank. In one year the laundry provided over half a million pieces of clean linen and clothing for the 1800 prisoners in these prisons.[22] Workrooms and laundries were of great interest to penal authorities, and Henry Mayhew described the operation of the Brixton laundry in the following manner:

> Here the majority of women . . . habited in their light-blue checked over-dresses, are found, standing on wooden gratings, washing away at the wooden troughs ranged round the spacious washhouse which forms the lower part of the building. Here some, with their bare red arms, are working the soddened flannels against a wooden grooved board that is used to save the rubbing of the

clothes, while the tops of the troughs are white and iridescent with the clouds of suds within them. . . .

From the wash-house we ascended to the drying-rooms over-head, and here one of the doors of what seemed to be a huge press was thrown open and an immense clothes-horse drawn out, with rows of unbleached towels and blankets across its rails, while the blast of hot air that rushed forth was even more unpleasant than the dampness of the atmosphere below. Hence we passed into the iron-room, and as we approached the place, we knew by the smell of burnt flannel the nature of the occupation carried on within. Here were gas-stoves for heating the irons, the ordinary grates being found too hot for the sumer, and there was a large blanketed dresser, at which a crowd of clean-looking women were at work, in very white aprons, while the place resounded with the continued click of the irons returned every now and then to their metal stands. On the floor stood baskets of newly-ironed clothes, and plaited, and looking positively like so much mounded snow; whilst over-head might be heard the rumbling of the mangles at work on the upper floor.[23]

Prisoners not employed in the laundry or bake house or in cleaning the prison were engaged in producing commodities. For example, in Brixton, Millbank and Perth, women were primarily involved in the production of textile goods, such as prison uniforms, shirts, blouses, sheets, towels and numerous other articles of clothing and linen. Most of this work was carried out under the silent congregate system and in some prisons authorities had gone to great lengths to design workrooms that would prevent con-taminating communication. One of the best examples of such efforts was the knitting room at the Female House of Correction at Tothill Fields which was designed like a chapel with 'high wooden partitions' at the back of each row of prisoners.

This place is about the size of a village school-room and contained 35 women, all ranged on the slant, . . . in long narrow pews, stretching diagonally across the room. Just peeping over the tops of the partitions, the white caps of the prisoners could be seen, while ranged along the wall upon the raised gallery, stood a couple of warders looking down into the sloping troughs, as it were, and crying occasionally, 'I can hear some one talking there.'[24]

Associated silent labour did not always take place in workrooms. For example, the women convicts at Brixton, who were usually engaged in labour within their cells, were allowed to work in silent association outside their cell doors for one hour a day.

From eleven to twelve, the women located in the wings pursue their needlework in silence, and seated at their doors; and then it is a most peculiar sight to see the two hundred female convicts ranged along the sides of the arcade, and in each of the three long balconies that run one above the other round the entire building, so that you behold nothing but long lines of convict women . . . stitching away in the most startling silence, as if they were so many automata.[25]

This was the ideal form of labour envisaged by Fry and other reformers, continuous application with total concentration on the task, no diversions of conversations or other 'extraneous' social activities.

Commodity production by women prisoners was very important in penal institutions. It defrayed the costs of confinement and was often prodigious. In 1854 the women in Brixton produced '20,000 shirts, . . . 10,000 flannel drawers and waistcoats, 1,200 shifts, 3,500 petticoats, 5,700 sheets, 2,000 caps, 3,700 pocket-handkerchiefs, 2,800 aprons, 2,300 neckerchiefs, 1,200 jackets, and just upon 3,400 towels. . .'[26] All of this from a daily average population of only 700 women. The bulk of these articles were for prison consumption, such as shirts for Portland, Pentonville and Millbank prisons. However, a considerable proportion was for London firms. In one year, 1860, the female prisoners of Millbank (about 500) produced 50,822 shirts and mended and completed 96,541 bags for city firms.[27] Prison authorities often contracted with manufacturers or merchants for the production of goods. The usual method was for the prison to provide the raw materials for production, although on a few occasions the manufacturer would provide the necessary materials. Only rarely did the manufacturer also supervise the labour process, a common practice in the United States.[28] Useful and productive labour was highly valued by penal authorities who were keen to defray the cost of these new public institutions. Perth prison even operated its own retail shop for the disposal of goods that were not produced for the prison service or for outside merchants.

Penal labour was linked to capital in other, less direct ways. Manufacturing was not dominated by the factory at this time; cottage industry and the 'putting out' system were still common, especially in textile industries. Manufacturers using the putting-out system, giving workers the raw materials for production at home, sometimes appear to have preferred prison labour to 'free' labour. They even used penal work as a yardstick to assess free labour. For example, in 1842, the Inspector of Scottish Prisons reported that:

It is a curious fact, and one bespeaking a great change in prisons, that finds needle-work [by women] is now sometimes sent to be done in prisons, on account of the great cleanliness of the place as compared with ordinary cottages; and, what is yet more striking, work is sometimes sent in consequence of the absolute security against *dishonesty*! It has happened several times at Glasgow, that when a manufacturer has had reason to suspect that part of his material has been stolen, he has sent a given quantity of it to the prison to be worked up that he might see how much cloth it would really produce.[29]

Thus, prison labour, which was clearly forced and unrelenting, was sometimes used as a measure for 'free' labour performed by women in the home, both in terms of the quality and quantity of the final product.

Penal labour was also linked to capital in a social and moral cause. Industrial capitalism required workers with at least rudimentary skills, and the inculcation of labour skills and diligent work habits was an integral feature of confinement. The prison reports often recounted the number of prisoners taught new skillls. In an eighteen-month period, 700 Scottish women were taught to knit in Kirkcaldy prison and the matron of Edinburgh prison reported teaching '700 prisoners to knit stockings, well and without assistance, while 100 more had learnt imperfectly.'[30] The storekeeper of the Wandsworth house of correction in London indicated:

> The great mass of prisoners of various ages are inferior nee-
> dlewomen. Many come here who cannot sew, but who become
> tolerably proficient before they leave the prison. At first . . . we
> give them towels and handkerchiefs to hem. As they progress, they
> get better work, such as shirts and day-caps. . . . Some are very
> awkward, and others are tolerably good sewers. I teach them to
> sew, and find them very grateful for my instruction.[31]

Labour was also intended to be more than a 'mere' material enterprise or training exercise; according to many reformers and penal authorities, its main purpose was moral. In the Third Report of the Inspectors of English Prisons for 1837–8, they argued that labour should be oriented to instilling permanent '*habits of industry*' that would last far beyond prison sentences, 'it is the habits and feelings with which he [she] returns to the world, which determine whether his [her] training and treatment have been judicious or otherwise.'[32] Again, the intention was to produce the willing subject. How successful these efforts of permanent reform were is hard to say. It is safe to conclude that the new penal experts and technicians did succeed in teaching women new skills and in producing vast quantities of commodities.

In many respects the major features of penal arrangements for women were similar to those operated for men. What was different was the way the two systems functioned, with greater control and surveillance often evident in prisons for women. Another important distinction was the provision for children.

Not all prisons had nurseries, but those that did, such as Brixton and Tothill Fields, had special dormitory accommodation for women and their children. The nurseries at these two institutions could hold up to 30 children and their mothers at any one time. Most children were under the age of two, although children of four were sometimes retained in prison. The children, like their mothers, wore a prison uniform 'a spotted blue frock . . .'.[33]

Women in these circumstances were not allowed to escape prison discipline. At Tothill they were required to pick a pound and a half of oakum every day and at Brixton 'convict mothers' sewed in the dormitory. Some Victorian observers believed that under the silent congregate system mothers were not allowed to speak to their children, but this was not the case. Apparently they were only prohibited from speaking to other women, not their own children. The operation of these nurseries epitomizes the paternalistic approach to women. Penal paternalism allowed some latitude for women, in this case mothers, but always in the context of discipline and relative to the dictates of those who held power over them.

Widening the Carceral Net

Once a woman had completed her sentence in a convict prison she might not be allowed to escape the institutional nexus. Reformers had created unique institutions for the reception of female convicts, and the young of both sexes, after their release from prison. Instead of the outright release or release under licence given to men, some women were required to enter refuges where they experienced an indeterminate period of confinement. Other institutions emerged during the first half of the nineteenth century that were intended to confine and train women and girls as a means of preventing an irreversible slide into sin and crime. Such institutions were usually of a 'voluntary' nature, but it is certain that women and girls were sometimes pressured into them by zealous reformers, the police and judiciary. These refuges, asylums, reformatories and shelters were not necessarily penal, but what they established was a wide, interlocking carceral network, based on the assumption that females needed a firm paternalistic hand to guide their development.

One of the earliest forms of such 'voluntary' confinement for women dating back several centuries was the Magdalen House or Asylum for prostitutes, and it was resurrected in the nineteenth century under the influence of purity leagues.[34] The purpose of these institutions, sometimes called asylums, shelters, refuges or penitentiaries, was identical to that of the prisons: to alter the habits, behaviour and orientations of female prostitutes and to restore and create, through religion and labour, a new reformed woman. The two largest, the Magdalen Hospital and the London Female Penitentiary, each housed around 100 inmates. Similar, though usually smaller, institutions were established in a number of British cities, such as Liverpool, Birmingham, Bristol, Leeds, Newcastle, Manchester, Edinburgh and Glasgow.[35]

Religion was to have an even more central place in these asylums or refuges than it occupied in the prison. Asylum reformers, like prison chaplains, stressed religion as the only sure route to reform. One of them argued, for example, that a fallen woman needed 'A religious house, a spiritual hospital . . .' where she should be given 'her retirement, quiet; opportunity of devotion, help to reflection, spiritual ministrations, especially directed to her condition. . . .'[36] As in prisons, the chapel was to be the most 'prominent object' within the overall scheme and the most important member of staff was the resident chaplain, who, with the visiting ladies, encouraged women 'to confess doubts and struggles, to make free communications for the relief of their souls.'[37]

As well as having the principles of religion strictly inculcated, 'idle, neglectful women should also be subjected to education and instruction in ordinary household duties' and 'trained to industry and activity.'[38] As the governors of the London Female Penitentiary for prostitutes put it, the regime of the institutions was intended '. . . to destroy the habits of idleness and vice and to substitute those of honest and profitable industry, thus benefiting society whilst the individual is restored.'[39] Most of those who ran these 'industrial institutions' relegated religion to a secondary position.[40] In the London penitentiary for prostitutes: 'Each female is regularly engaged in some useful and profitable employment. Thus habits of application and diligence are forming, the dangers of idleness repelled, and the means of virtuous and honest subsistence put into the hands of many. . . .'[41] The nature of labour was also similar to that performed in prisons. Women were engaged in 'plain needlework, washing, ironing and mangling family linens' as a means of preparing them for domestic service.

Women served indeterminate periods of time in these institutions; once admitted it appears that it was rather difficult to obtain voluntary release. Institutional experts argued that the length of confinement should be variable, long enough to '. . . wean them from those habits that were both immoral and offensive, and to train them to new ones. . . .'[42] In order to ensure that women stayed a 'responsible' period of time, some of the asylums shaved heads and required absolute seclusion during the early stages of confinement. For example, at the London Female Penitentiary 'every female on admission, *has her head shaved*' and is confined 'in a room apart from the other females for two months after admission.'[43] After this initial degradation and period of solitary confinement, women were segregated according to their 'moral condition' and usually allowed to work in silent association.

It is not clear how long women were kept in these institutions. According to reformers, eventual release should ideally be contingent upon previous experience, the amount of instruction absorbed, behaviour within the institution and the possibility of finding employment in 'pious and respectable families.' Admission as servants into a 'pious family' was considered by some observers to be the 'only safeguard for future good behaviour.'[44] The ideal pattern for assuring the reclamation of the 'fallen woman' involved a period of indeterminate training and religious instruction within an institution followed by employment in a respectable household. Thus creating a complete, encompassing system of surveillance and tutelage that should allow no deviation and reversion to old habits.

Other institutions were aimed at rescuing young women and girls who had not yet fallen into a persistent life of crime and/or prostitution. Scores of reformatories and refuges were created during the nineteenth century for the purpose of saving and reforming girls and young women. In contrast to the manufacturing work preferred and often practised in the prisons and asylums for prostitutes, inmates in these refuges were primarily engaged in household labour. This was not so much to train them to be efficient housewives as to provide them with the background to fulfil the enormous demand for household servants.[45] Two of the earliest of these institutions were created in Scotland in the early 1840s, the Shelter for adult women and Dean Bank refuge for young girls below the age of 16 who had committed petty thefts. The girls were trained 'with a view to their becoming servants, and were taught sewing, household work, washing, and ironing.'[46] Much of this work was productive, including washing and ironing for local families.

According to the officials of Dean Bank, the proceeds from work nearly defrayed the entire cost of the institution. Since they were destined to work in middle-class households, the girls were also subject to moral and religious instruction to create 'docility and decorum'. The institutional order was oriented to 'preparing them for honest service.'[47]

These two Scottish institutions, and similar ones thoughout Britain, were based on assumptions about the limited capabilities and potentials of working-class women and girls. They were explicitly oriented to the demands and needs of the 'benevolent ladies' who established them. They constituted some of the first institutions aimed at the systematic training of women, and helped overcome the perceived problem of procuring 'good servants'. Many of the graduates of these institutions appear to have been highly sought after. For example, the Matron of Dean Bank reported 'that she found no difficulty in getting situations in respectable families for such of the girls as she could recommend, the training which they receive being considered a great advantage, and, as to render the girls superior to the ordinary run of young servants. . . .'[48]

A third type of institution created explicitly for the reception of women was what we would now term an intermediate prison, an institution established for the reception of women released from convict prisons. The two major ones were Fulham Refuge in England and the Golden Bridge Reformatory in Dublin. Both were established around 1856 and were intended to receive women released from Brixton or Mountjoy. Men who completed their sentences in a convict prison were usually released on licence into the community but many women were required to enter one of these intermediate prisons. In 1863, the superintendent of Golden Bridge, Sister Kirwan, offered a number of reasons for this different treatment. She argued that women must be detained for a longer period of time than men because: (1) it was generally admitted that women are more difficult to reform than men, (2) upon their release, men would be engaged in outdoor work whereas 'women are generally engaged in household duties, often with valuable property under their charge, therefore they require more time for training and testing', (3) women must be 'untaught and then retaught since females of the criminal class are essentially idle and ignorant to helplessness.'[49] Women were punished not only for their past but also because of their gender and their hypothetical futures.

Golden Bridge and the Fulham Refuge had similar regimes. Like Scottish shelters and Magdalen Asylums, they operated a system of labour and moral reform, though unlike pre-prison institutions their regimes were backed up by the ability to return women to prison. Fulham held about 170 inmates, most of whom were 'first class women with few reports' from Brixton. The Refuge was described as placing women in the *intermediate condition* between the prison and 'the world wherein lurk all the old temptations to which offenders formerly succumbed. . . .'[50] The object of the institution, according to the governor, was to 'raise the women up in the social scale, as respects personal character and aspiration . . . and [help them] forward in future endeavours to lead an honest and steady life.'[51] The major method of achieving these goals was labour. According to the Prison Inspector Joshua Jebb, the women were '. . . engaged in every kind of industrial employment, such as washing and needle-work, but especially washing. . . .'[52]

Golden Bridge offered similar forms of labour with a strong emphasis on domestic work. Uniquely, the reformatory also employed women in 'outdoor gardening, potato cultivation, and the care of pigs and poultry.'[53] After a visit to the institution in 1862 Mary Carpenter observed, 'the care of animals is generally ben-eficial, and intercourse with nature always is so.'[54] This agrarian theme and outdoor work for women was quite unique for this period. The philosophy upon which it was based would become a persistent theme in the late nineteenth-century justifications for the siting and operation of American reformatories for women and juveniles.[55]

Intermediate institutions, Magdalen Asylums and pre-prison refuges constituted significant developments in the extension of a carceral net of supervision and correction for women. Under this network girls and women could be confined prior to the commission of crime or upon apprehension, often apparently without formal proceedings. If convicted and sentenced to hard labour in a convict prison, a woman might have her sentence extended on an indefinite basis. The extension of her sentence would not be based on the passage of time as decreed by judicial mechanism; rather, it was based on her assessed character which determined her release and/or return to prison. As the superintendent of Golden Bridge put it,

> She is removed to the refuge at the appointed time, where she is taught all the duties of a domestic and farm servant, and when she acquires habits of industry, self-control, and self-respect, she is [released and] provided with suitable employment and perseveres in a good life for the future.[56]

Resistance and Adaptation; 'Bold and Strategic' Women

An expanding network of institutions for females was created by the 1860s, ranging from reformatories and shelters for girls through local prisons for adolescents and adults to the top of the hierarchy with convict prisons and their appended refuges for receiving women after their release from Millbank, Brixton and Mountjoy. Reformers and penal administrators worried a great deal about the success of their model regimes. The measure of success then, as often today, was the recidivism rate. The evidence of reconvictions indicated that prisons were not successful; between one-third and half of all offenders re-offended after being sent to prison.[57] The reformers sought perfection and these results indicated the contrary. Another way of assessing the success of regimes was to attempt to chart the impact of prisons on prisoners. Did prison subdue and humiliate, correct and reform? There are some good and surprising sources of information about women's responses to prison, such as official prison reports and, very occasionally, accounts written by women themselves.[58] These tell us less about the successes or failures of regimes and more about the techniques of resistance and struggle or individual and collective attempts to adapt to oppressive and humiliating circumstances.

Penal authorities often included accounts of inmate behaviour in their official reports. Some of the early reports of the inspectorate indicated that many women responded to these new penal regimes in a bemused, resigned and even accepting fashion. Scottish women were reported to be easy to deal with and accepting of the 'benevolence' of their warders. The Scottish inspector, Frederick Hill, reported that women worked diligently, obeyed the rules and generally conducted themselves in an exemplary fashion, and stated that the general feeling among the women under the rigorous separate system at Perth was that of 'penitence and gratitude.'[59] An important indicator of these feelings was the apparently good relationship between prison staff and women prisoners. As one of the women at Glasgow reported, 'Miss Cameron [prison officer] is a mild nice girl over us, she has a soft word on her tongue to us, and shuts the door and opens it cannily; she does not bang it through your head till you are all in a tremble.'[60] These observations were reinforced by accounts of minimal infractions of the rules and few punishments.

Hill's early reports reveal that few women resisted or overtly struggled against regimes. It is likely that Hill over-emphasized the

degree of acquiescence and especially acceptance, yet it may very
well be that there was considerable outward compliance with early
penal regimes. There are a number of possible explanations for this
apparent acceptance. It could be that many women actually did
accept their sentences, their guilt and the regimes under which they
were held. It is also likely that some of these early prisons were
operated in an essentially paternalistic fashion with female staff
being concerned and interested in their charges. Hill often remarked
on the affectionate and concerned response of the female staff. For
instance he commented on the favourable orientation of female staff
at Glasgow, and cited the sympathetic remarks of the chaplain at
Edinburgh prison in two of his early reports.

> Glasgow – The tone of the warders, no less than that of the matron
> and teachers, in speaking of the prisoners is uniformly that of a
> desire to benefit them, and of their strong conviction that it is by
> mildness and kindness that they are most successful in managing
> prisoners.[61]

> Edinburgh – I find the prisoners, almost without exception,
> attentive and even affectionate, and I think if they could be
> screened from the temptations which beset them when they leave
> prison, very many of them would do well.[62]

More straightforwardly, many women received short sentences
which meant that the deprivations and rigours of confinement had to
be endured for a brief period and might be more readily tolerated.
Furthermore, many of the women and men sent to prison in the
early nineteenth century came from rural backgrounds and would
have found the prison experience extremely frightening and
bewildering. The rigours of the separate and congregate systems
would have subdued those unaccustomed to continual isolation,
silence and indoor labour. Finally, some women were committed to
prisons and Bridewells as a means of relieving extreme poverty and
deprivation, especially in Scotland, and they would probably not
wish to jeopardize this 'accommodation', for which there was no
alternative, by breaking the rules.

Despite this general outward compliance, there were also
persistent resistances to penal regimes, strong reactions and adoption of a variety of methods for coping. Protests, challenges and
resistances were usually individually based, although women occasionally demonstrated collectively. The most notable collective
responses occurred at Millbank. From its inception, Millbank was
the scene of protest and rebellion of both women and men. The early

attempts to enforce silence, harsh diets, continuous inspection, and a steady round of religious exhortation met with strong protests from women. One of the main areas of protest was the quantity and quality of food. Only a year after the creation of Millbank, a number of women refused to eat or work, protesting that they were 'half starving' and demanding an 'increase of half a pound of bread'. In the same year the women presented a petition to the governor expressing their objections to the overzealous punishment of two prisoners. The culmination of this year of protest occurred in the spring when a 'mutiny' broke out.

The focus of this 'mutiny' was again food, inferior bread. At breakfast on the day of the 'outrage', both women and men refused to eat, and the women especially complained of the 'coarseness' of the bread. The following day the prisoners accepted their loaves not because they had given up their hunger strike but because they had devised another form of collective protest. This protest occurred in the chapel during daily services when the men hammered their kneeling benches to the floor and the women started chanting 'Give us our daily bread.' This was accompanied by the throwing of bread and further chanting of 'better bread, better bread'. The men continued their protest for only a short length of time, but the women persisted until they were forcibly removed from the chapel.[63] The 'riot' was quelled the following day when the Bow Street Runners (forerunners of the modern police) were brought in to handcuff the most 'refractory' prisoners. The 'ringleaders' of this uprising were punished, but it did not stop the general protest and resistances of the women. In 1823 another general disturbance broke out, accompanied by attacks on wardswomen and the matron. According to the governor's report, this uprising included a plan to murder the matron, one female officer and the chaplain.[64]

The most notorious outbreaks of violent, collective protests in nineteenth-century British prisons occurred at Millbank and Brixton prisons between 1853 and 1859, when transportation was replaced by sentences of penal servitude. The end of transportation meant that women and men who would have spent one to two years at Millbank or Brixton prior to being transported for five to seven years were now facing the same sentence to be served entirely in prison under rigid penal regimes. These protests of women were described in 1862 by the reformer Mayhew in the following manner:

> . . . when they became aware that they were to be eventually discharged in this country after a protracted penal detention, disappointment rendered them thoroughly reckless; hope died

with them; they actually courted punishment. . . . They constantly destroyed their clothes, tore up their bedding, and smashed their windows. They frequently threatened the officers with violence, though . . . they seldom proceeded to put their threats into force; and when they did so, some among them . . . took the officers' part to protect them from personal injury.[65]

Direct collective protests and demonstrations constituted an intermittent and persistent aspect of penal institutions for men and women throughout the nineteenth and into the twentieth century, though this is much less true of institutions for women. The focus of these collective, sometimes violent, protests was often physical conditions, such as the quality and quantity of food. Collective protests were relatively infrequent occurrences; indirect forms of protest and resistance were much more likely.

Women and men reacted to penal regimes and penal authorities in a variety of overt and covert ways. The vigorous preaching and exhortation that characterized prisons such as the early Millbank and Liverpool prisons were often rejected by inmates. Wentworth Russell, an especially ardent supporter of religious indoctrination, experienced considerable resistance to his efforts at Millbank. Prisoners responded to his preaching by speaking in mock biblical cant, rejecting his sermons and generally resisting rigid religious doctrines. On one occasion the protest was direct and physical, 'just as the sermon began, a loud scram or huzza was heard among the females . . . the next moment a half-a-dozen Prayer Books were flung at the chaplain's head in the pulpit.'[66]

Women responded to other elements of penal regimes by trying to circumvent restrictions, especially enforced silence. Women, like their male counterparts, developed diverse forms of silent communication, or *prisoner freemasonry* as it was dubbed by penal observers. They attempted to talk to each other on their way to exercise or at chapel by mouthing words, whispering or making signs. One of the major means of communication involved passing written messages. At Brixton, women used gas lighting paper to write messages called 'stiffs' that were slipped under a neighbour's door or passed along during chapel. One of the most ingenious techniques of overcoming rules of silence involved the use of a system of knocks. Prisoners worked out elaborate systems of serial knocking – a 'knocking alphabet' – which allowed them to communicate quite long and complex messages by knocking on the walls of their cells.[67]

Women also worked hard to overcome the humiliations associated with attempts to standardize their personal appearance. Prison authorities considered the vanity of women a sin that led to crime. This 'universal weakness' was to be stamped out through shaving women's heads and banishing any adornments or refinements in dress and make-up. They were to be indistinguishable in their plain, drab uniforms. Some women considered personal appearance essential to maintaining self-respect, a fact even recognized by a few penal authorities. Mayhew noted, 'In civilized communities dress enters so fully into our notions of individuals, that a particular kind of garment has as much human character about it as even the definite form of countenance.'[68] Yet, Mayhew, like most penal authorities, went on to praise the spartan uniforms and close-fitting caps of women prisoners. The women did not, however, accept such uniforms with deferential respect. Young women were especially keen to resist the degradations of dress and a few were notoriously adept at this enterprise. The prison matron of Millbank described some of the more ingenious methods of overcoming dull attire.

> One woman, I give you my word, took the ropes off her hammock and put them round the bottom of her dress so as to make the skirt seem fuller. Another we had filled her gown with coal round the bottom for the same object; and others, again, have taken the wire from the dinner cans and used it as stiffeners to their stays. One actually took the tin foil from under the buttons, and made it into a ring. You would hardly believe it, perhaps, but I have known women scrape the walls of their cells and use the powder of the whitewash to whiten their complexion. Indeed, there is hardly any trick they would not be at if we did not keep a sharp eye upon them.[69]

Behaviour such as this confirmed the prevailing conceptions of criminal women among penal authorities who believed that '. . . the majority are inordinately vain and incorrigibly mischievous.' Through such means women displayed a rejection of their 'degraded' dress and countenance.

As we have indicated, penal regimes were intended to strip inmates of their disrespectful behaviour and to create deferential, obedient workers. Some penal observers, primarily men, were disturbed when women failed to exhibit outward signs of shame and subservience to authority. Mayhew made numerous references to the outward appearances of women who had clearly not been subdued by their prison experience. On some occasions women did demonstrate deference as when Mayhew and the Brixton chaplain inspected them sewing quietly outside their cells. As they passed, 'each woman rose from her little stool, and curtseyed.' This was not the usual sight that greeted Mayhew on his extensive visits to London prisons. In most of the prison workshops he observed women who 'stared' boldly into his face with 'all the brazen look of the streets'. Many of the women in the workshops at Westminster Female Prison and Tothill Fields House of Correction were clearly not subdued or beaten down by their confinement.

> *Westminster.* As we glanced along the three rows of white caps, there was not one abashed face or averted eye to be seen, whilst many grinned impudently on meeting our gaze. *Tothill Fields* . . . the callous brazen smile on every lip, and startling shamelessness in every glance.[79]

A few women chose more direct forms of demonstrating their disaffection with the regime and its enforcers. One supposedly notorious prisoner of Millbank was reported to have 'refused to take her dinner, tearing up her Prayer-book, singing loudly all the fore part of the evening, and refusing her breakfast, grazing her nose. . . .'[71] Singing loudly, shouting and making noise were a common form of protest and self-expression, which is not surprising given the silence rule. Women often protested by drumming on their cell doors with their feet. Sometimes this would 'spread' to the entire prison. In Millbank one episode of drumming by the whole population went on for weeks, creating a terrible noise because, according to the governor, the 'badly hung doors rattled like mad'.[72]

The most common form of protest and self-expression involved individual outbreaks of aggression. Rather than aim their personal demonstration at prison personnel or other inmates, as men generally did, women tended to direct their aggression at their cell and its contents. The superintendent of Brixton prison reported that women 'Rarely injured themselves or those around them' but they could be 'terribly violent indeed.'

> . . . they tear up and break everything they can lay their hands on. The other day one of the prisoners not only broke all the windows in her cell, but tore all her bed-clothes into ribbons, and pulled open her bed and tossed all the coir in a heap on the floor; and then she wrenched off the gas-jet, and managed to pull down the triangular iron shelf that is fixed into the wall at one corner of the cell.[73]

Mary Carpenter described such actions as 'revolting scenes' and they came to be known as 'fits' or 'breaking out'. Penal authorities and reformers like Carpenter usually saw these 'fits' as expressions of irrational female personalities. A few observers were more careful, even sympathetic in their attempts to explain these actions. The medical officer of Brixton reported that such outbreaks were more common among women, especially young women, than men and that he 'knew of no bodily or organic reason to account for them. . . .'[74] He added that 'female prisoners, *as a body*, do not bear imprisonment so well as the male prisoners; they are anxious and restless, more irritable in temper, and more easily excited, and they look forward to the future with much less hope of regaining their former position in life.'[75] He did not, however, point to 'unique' female characteristics to explain this behaviour. For him the greater likelihood of 'fits' among women could be explained by their different treatment within prison.

He pointed out that the circumstances of male convicts made it easier for them to reconcile themselves to their confinement. A male convict always experienced a change of prison at least once, but most importantly, according to the medical officer, '. . . he looks forward to the time when he will be employed *in the open air* on public works.'[76] Women convicts experienced very different, more restricting, forms of imprisonment. A woman would be subjected to longer periods of close confinement, sedentary forms of labour, and an uncertainty about the 'duration of that portion of her sentence which is to be passed in prison'. The Brixton medical officer concluded that 'all [of these factors] tend to make a sentence more severe to the woman, than a sentence of the same duration to the man.'[77]

For a few women, prolonged solitary confinement and/or the relentless pressure of the prison regime proved intolerable and they attempted to escape or protest by self-mutilation, 'wanton destruction of health', and, on rare occasions, suicide. Penal authorities sometimes demonstrated considerable insensitivity to this behaviour, describing such women as 'troublesome prisoners' who were merely attempting to gain entry into the infirmary where they might converse with other women and receive an improved diet. One woman who covered her body with her own excreta for six months was described by the Brixton medical officer as engaging in 'deceitful behaviour'. He was referring to what he judged as her attempts to feign madness, and it seems not to have occurred to him that her persistent behaviour could have anything to do with the nature of her confinement.

In retrospect, we might see such incredulity and insensitivity as a reflection of a failure to understand the outward manifestations of prolonged confinement under an extremely tight regime; a failure to comprehend the now well-established link between human behaviour and environment. However, by this time, 1863, much had already been written about the effects of the rigours of solitary confinement and penal regimes in general. At this juncture some penal professionals were beginning to adapt the more abstract, distant and detached view of their charges that would come to dominate the future operation of the prison machine; empathy was not an integral feature of this machine.

Punishments

Penal authorities were equipped with a wide range of punitive reactions for these outrages and offences against prison discipline. Coercive penalty is the underlying foundation of all discipline. The demands for obedience, regularity, punctuality and attentiveness evident in schools, armies, prisons and factories are all backed up by penalties to ensure the compliance of many, and may be invoked to subdue the refractions of those who do resist. Prison warders and governors punished women by reducing diets, withdrawing privileges, confining them to special cells, and by applying various instruments, such as straight waistcoats, handcuffs and ankle straps, to restrain their movements.

Confinement in 'refractory' or 'darkened' cells was a commonly used technique of punishment. One of the punishment cells on the women's side at Millbank was described as:

> . . . intensely dark, with a kind of grating in the walls for ventilation, but no light-hole; and there was a small raised wooden bed in the corner. The cell was shut in first by a grated gate, then a wooden door, lined with iron, with another door outside that; and then a kind of mattress, or large straw-pad, arranged on a slide before the outer door, to deaden the sound from within.[78]

These cells were dubbed 'the darks' by prisoners since very little, if any, light came through the iron gratings. Women were usually sentenced to between one and three days' confinement, either on full rations or, just as likely, on bread and water. For those women adjudged especially troublesome, or continuously refractory, even more secure cells were created. We are not quite certain when these special cells were built but they were certainly in existence by the 1860s and were designed to prevent communication and stifle women's verbal protests. The 'hoppered cell' involved two doors between which was affixed an adjoining slanting hopper, a wedge-shaped device apparently similar to the trough used in corn mills to channel corn into the mill-stone. The hopper could be used to communicate with the prisoner and pass in food or other articles without opening the door of the cell. The most efficient means of taming these prison viragos was through the use of the 'dumb cell', literally a double cell fitted with a type of mattress on all the walls and affixed outside the door. Arthur Griffiths, governor of Millbank for many years, described the impact of these cells on refractory women:

> From the latter [dumb cell] no sound can possibly proceed: however loud and boisterous the outcry within, outside not a whisper is heard. When women feel that they are shouting and wasting their breath all to no purpose, they throw up the sponge.[79]

Solitary confinement, either in dark cells or in more restrictive and technological advanced cells was a widely used punishment. For example, in 1860 there were 1,077 punishments administered to 550 adult women at Millbank; 305, or 30 per cent, involved confinement in darkened cells.[80]

Another common punishment was the application of physical restraint, such as handcuffs or a straight waistcoat, for the duration of at least one day. In Millbank, this happened 126 times in 1860. Two forms of body restraint were used at Millbank, the 'canvas dress' and the 'straight-waistcoat'.

> The canvas dress we found to be like a coarse sack, with sleeves, and straps at the waist – the latter made to fasten, as we have said before, with small screws. With it we were shown the prison straight-waistcoat, which consisted of a canvas jacket, with black leather sleeves, like boots closed at the end, and with straps up the arm.[81]

Other physical punishments involved the application of a bread and water diet and the deprivation of a meal or part of a meal.

Women also received moral punishments such as reprimands. Most probably these were used for first offenders prior to the application of more severe reactions. Punishments in Scottish prisons were very similar, usually involving the loss of a meal, reduction in diet, confinement to a darkened cell and more frequent use of physical restraints, especially handcuffs and leather muffs. Frederick Hill observed that such punishments '. . . *arise from the strong and natural desire of the prisoners to communicate with one another, and most of them*, as might be expected by young prisoners.'[82]

There were distinct differences in the punishments administered to women and men that brought strong objections from penal reformers such as Mary Carpenter. Male prisoners, unlike females, could be subjected to severe physical chastisements such as whipping with the birch or cat-of-nine tails, although this was apparently a rather infrequent occurrence. In 1861, for example, only nine adult males and three juveniles were whipped with a cat or birch at Millbank. By contrast, no men were punished with the straight-jacket, whereas it was employed 287 times on adult women and 116 on adolescent girls. A few reformers such as Carpenter objected both to the use of physical and corporal punishment and to the differential application of physical restraints on women and girls. She argued that such 'severe and degrading' punishments as flogging and the strait-jacket had 'no place in Reformatories'. Her strongest objections focused on

> This remarkable disparity in the punishments inflicted on the two sexes, and the peculiarly severe character of the punishments of the women, leads to the conclusion that such punishments are in themselves quite inefficacious, and that some different system ought to be adopted.[83]

An additional distinction between women and men was the number of punishments. Female adult and juvenile prisoners of Millbank (daily average 489) were punished 1,716 times, while 515 males experienced only 891 punishments. Thus, on average, male prisoners experienced less than two punishments per year whereas female prisoners experienced about three and one-half per year. Importantly, over half of the punishments of males involved admonishments, while this accounted for only a third of those for females. Although Carpenter objected to the differential application of physical punishments, she, like the majority of prison officials, accepted that women were greater offenders than men because they were more emotional, wicked and morally degraded. She would have agreed with the chaplain of Brixton prison, who reported that 'Violence of temper is one great evil with female prisoners: they are so easily excited, and so subject to sudden impulses, that it is very painful to consider what misery they bring upon themselves, owing to the influence of bad temper.'[84]

We can, however, offer several other interpretations for the seemingly greater infractions of the rules and more frequent punishments of women. It is very likely that penal regimes for women were being enforced in a more rigorous manner than those established for men. Minor infractions by women would be less likely to be tolerated than those of males. Female prison staff may have had less tolerance for the 'offences' of their charges than male warders, especially since their task was constituted as more of a moral endeavour. As such, 'foul language' and 'brutish behaviour' might be subject to censor; behaviour that, if exhibited in males, would be less likely to result in a sanction.

Prison officials proposed numerous techniques for dealing with continuously refractory women, and one of the most radical was offered by the chaplain of Brixton Prison.

> Great difficulty is experienced in dealing with refractory women in an associated prison. . . . If I may venture to repeat what I have more than once expressed, it does seem most important that women of this class should be treated in a *special manner* and in a *special place*, and that they should be placed under medical treatment, as their presence among other prisoners operates most injuriously upon those around them, and constitutes one of the chief difficulties in carrying out the discipline of this prison. . . . And few can conceive the lengths to which they will go, and the strategies to which they will resort, in order to have their own way.[85]

Prescriptions such as these were most prophetic, anticipating the subsequent development of the fully elaborated treatment or medical ideology that emerged at the turn of the century.

Other experts and observers proposed more of the same, and some suggested even more reactionary measures. The governor of Coldbath Fields, George Chesterton, suggested, 'in the case of a set of abandoned young husseys, disgracing all feminine attributes, manual correction by a women, in the presence of women only, would infuse salutary intimidation, and tend to repress scenes too painful to contemplate.'[86] The Millbank surgeon suggested that penal authorities should be able to 'inflict upon them some sort of bodily punishment, it would be much more merciful. . . .'[87] Captain O'Brien, the superintendent of female convicts also recommended more traditional reactions. He reported to a Parliamentary Committee that existing punishments were ineffectual and '. . . lately it has occurred to me that the use of stocks might be a good addition to the present rules.'[88] When members of the Parliamentary Committee asked the Millbank surgeon for his view of the use of the stocks he said;

> If you put a woman into the stocks, so as to prevent her from following her *favourite amusement of lying on the floor and drumming* with her feet against the door, she still retains the use of her tongue, and will make a great disturbance. *Especially if she knows that the officers are sleeping near her. . . .*[89]

Penal technologies and punishments in prisons, refuges and other unique institutions for women were part of wide-ranging, innovative attempts to manage the poor and the criminal. Many of these innovations in institutions for women, such as the indeterminate sentence, specialized staff, rigid regimes, and the location and operation of 'reformatories', were unique to Britain and Europe until the last quarter of the century when they were introduced into the women's reformatories in the Northeast and Midwest of the United States. In the 1870s, the new American reformatories incorporated a number of features already prominent in the prisons and reformatories of Britain. The main difference was in the architecture. Whereas the British prison appeared as an impregnable fortress, the new American reformatories were based on a cottage style, generally with minimal security, perhaps because they held women adjudged less criminal and more salvageable than the working-class and black women who continued to be sent to America's county and city jails and state prisons.[90]

Penal developments in British prisons during the last quarter of the nineteenth century were primarily administrative and ideological. Two national penal systems were created in 1877, one for England and Wales and the other for Scotland. Under the directorship of Edmond DuCann penal authorities began to close scores of small local jails and standardize the operation of prisons in these two national systems. Much has been written about the deleterious effects of DuCann's reforms, and he is often held accountable for creating the extreme standardization evident in British prisons in the early twentieth century. What we have shown is that rigid, inflexible regimes existed long before DuCann became head of British prisons. He merely insured the enforcement of pre-existing penal discipline in a wider range of prisons.

The major developments in British penal affairs at the turn of the century were no longer in building prisons and developing new regimes. This had shifted to America. In Britain the emphasis moved to the development of theories of crime and delinquency, most directed at the explanation of the crimes of youth, and many concerned with those of women. A great deal has been written about a few Continental and American theorists' conceptions of the crimes of women, especially the Italian prison surgeon Cesare Lombroso and the American social psychologist, W. I. Thomas. Our task in the next chapter will be to explore the work of British theorists, especially those who were closely connected with the management of prisons, since it is they who would potentially affect the operation of the prisons.

5

Experts and the Female Criminal

Penal arrangements for women in British prisons changed very little during the final decades of the nineteenth century. The important developments involved consolidation of the position of the new penal professionals and promulgation of new theories about female criminality and imprisonment. Prisons and asylums were, as we have shown, locations for the operation of technologies of discipline and correction where new professionals experimented with behaviour as a means of creating more perfect human beings and from which perspectives emerged about female crime and deviance. Similar discourses also came from outside the penal system. Regardless of the location from which these observers spoke or wrote about women, their ideas were remarkably consonant, concentrating on the uniqueness of a criminal class populated by women and men who stood outside the bounds of acceptable morality and normality. Various accounts were offered, but most concentrated on outward physical features and biological functioning as explanations of criminality and behaviour within prison. First the physiognomist, then the physical anthropologist and evolutionist and, finally, the psy-professionals expounded theories about female criminality that are quite breathtaking in the ferocity with which they depict such women as depraved, desperate and degraded. Despite these conceptions about the crimes of women, the women themselves were for the most part involved in petty thefts and public order offences. But the rhetoric was harsh, damning first the biological make-up of the thief or prostitute and later her sentiments, psyche and sexuality. In this chapter we shall detail the nature of crimes resulting in imprisonment, examine the new methods of assessing and disciplining prisoners and consider the accounts of female criminality produced by the new penal experts.

Women's Crimes

Women sent to prison were overwhelmingly from working-class backgrounds, many experiencing extreme poverty because of the wildly fluctuating economic conditions. Frederick Hill, the first prison inspector for Scotland, felt that economic conditions led to the majority of crimes and his reports were filled with examples of the poverty experienced by Scottish women.[1]

> It was a sickly bairn, and when my husband deserted me I was fair distressed. I carried it about in my arms, and could do little but nurse it and try to hush its wailings for six months when it died. I took the fever with grief, and fatigue and poverty and went to the infirmary. When I came out I was sickly for some weeks after, but I got work. I wrought at the clipping of flowered muslin for curtains and ladies' dresses. I worked at home. I earned 3s 6d a week. If I rose at four in the morning and sat till past ten at night, I could make 5s a week. I paid 1s 3d for my lodging. Then no work was to be had and I was fair pressed . . . I did not apply to the kirk session for I thought shame to be refused, and they do not help the young and active.[2]

A consequence of these conditions was that women were placed in a predicament whereby their only recourse for survival was crime, especially theft. Throughout the century women and men were sent to prison primarily for crimes of theft, the bulk of which involved women stealing articles of clothing, food, and household provisions such as coal.[3] English and Welsh women from the poorest areas were convicted of stealing bread from pub counters, meat from stalls, and potatoes from garden plots.[4]

Many of those who worked in prisons recognised this pattern of crime, as the matron of Brixton observed in the early 1860s, 'the women are mostly in for common larcenies . . . and many of them have been servants; some have been gentlemen's servants and a good number have been farm servants. . . .'[5] Scottish authorities made similar observations and attested to the relationship between poverty and theft.

> Aberdeen Suprintendent of Police: . . . mostly thefts of very trifling value, . . . principally of small sums of money taken from the person, and articles of wearing apparel; and it may be mentioned, that in many of the cases, the offenders were wives who had been deserted by their husbands, boys and girls, deserted by their parents.[6].

Although the thefts resulting in the imprisonment of women were usually trivial, a few were more sophisticated in nature, involving careful planning and training. According to a number of contemporary accounts, women were especially adept at shoplifting and picking pockets. Mid-nineteenth-century literature is replete with accounts of women who dressed and behaved above their station in order to perpetrate crimes in shops and places reserved for the middle class. Reverend Clay, chaplain of Liverpool gaol, was especially fascinated by such women. In describing the mode of operation of female pickpockets he wrote, 'When the Omnibus leaves, they get into it, and being dressed like any gentlemen's girls, with one of these french baskets in their hands, they get close beside a lady, and contrive to place their shawl or mantle over the lady's dress pocket, which shades their hands.'[7] Under the cover of fine apparel and bourgeois pretences, women also entered shops in order to 'wire' articles of apparel or ladies' purses. The term 'wire' originally referred to the use of a wire to extract silk handkerchiefs from ladies' pockets and purses. Later, as in the following description it was used in a generic sense to describe pickpockets.

> Some of the female *wires* are dressed in the first style. There are three of them attending the shops where the most ladies go to: one woman acts as servant while the *wire* acts mistress. When they go into one of these shops, as any other lady might do, they are on the watch to see when purses are pulled out, and the 'mistress' gets close to a lady who has shown a purse, *wires* her of it, and then contrives to give it to the 'servant' who goes away, while the mistress remains in the shop, and if she is clever, gets another purse before leaving it.[8]

Commentators reported numerous forms of deception used by women to gain a livelihood. Two 'notorious' women practised sophisticated thefts of jewellery. They posed as a lady and her maid who requested jewellers to visit their impressive accommodation in order to show them their wares. Once in the house the jeweller would hand over the goods for inspection and the women would discreetly exit, leaving the shop assistant locked in the house.[9] Another example of such a ruse was the work of a Mrs Roberts, who frequented religious services as a means of relieving the faithful of their purses and wallets. 'She dressed with fashionable taste . . . and while others . . . were intent on prayer, she was busied rifling their pockets, or in disengaging from their sides their chains and watches.'[10]

While these exploits may be fascinating, we should not be misled by such sensationalized descriptions since their promulgation was more of an ideological enterprise than a statement of widespread practices. Women certainly did engage in well-organized and skillfully executed crimes, but most crimes of larceny involved minor sums of money or goods and were rarely carefully planned; rather they were opportunistic, related to immediate need.

Public order offences such as breach of the peace, public drunkenness and using obscene language were the other major types of crimes resulting in the imprisonment of women. One of the major tasks of the newly established police was the surveillance and regulation of cities, especially working-class districts.[11] A disciplined, punctual and sober workforce prepared to labour for twelve to fifteen hours a day, six days a week, was needed in the new factories and mills. Requirements such as these were not compatible with the recreational and leisure activities of the working classes. Women and men who spent their Sundays, evenings and numerous festive days enjoying themselves in public settings began to be subjected to increasing forms of surveillance and regulation. The police, often spurred on by the demands of purity and temperance associations, sought to enforce a moral order within the community that would constrict and even eliminate numerous traditional forms of leisure and celebration.

Ideals of 'Home and Hearth', disseminated by romantic idealists such as Ruskin, led to a view of the home as the centre of morality and social activity.[12] The numerous social purity and temperance groups in Britain and the United States stressed sexual chastity, chaste public entertainments and an idealized moral purity within the home. Public temptations on family and female morality, such as dance halls, gaming rooms, pubs and drink horrified reformers. They sought to eliminate or reduce these evils and thus protect and strengthen the family. Women were to be the moral centre of the well-ordered 'sacred place', the home.[13] In order to achieve this goal, the existing domestic arrangments of all classes would have to be transformed. Initially this meant that the middle-classes demanded domestic servants who were sober, honest and respectable. Much later such ideals were also directed at the transformation of working-class households, leading to considerable concern about the public morals of all women. Police attempts to curb the social and leisure pursuits of women occurred in the general context of attacks on working-class culture and specific efforts to regulate the public morality of women.

Each year thousands of women were given prison sentences, usually short ones, for public order offences, which in England and Wales reached their peak in the 1860s, with numbers dropping precipitously after 1870, whereas in Scotland the significant increases in prosecution for public order crimes occurred during the final decades of the nineteenth century and the first decade of the twentieth.

In the early 1870s, Scottish authorities, especially in Glasgow, Aberdeen and Edinburgh began to wage an intensive war on the public behaviour of working people. New Municipal and National Acts, such as the Police and Public House Acts of 1862, were enacted to cover a multitude of public behaviours. Prosperity brought more women and men onto the streets of cities where the enforcement of the Acts led to increasing numbers of commitals to prisons. From 1860 to 1901 the population increased only 25 per cent, while the annual number of commitals to prison rose threefold, from 19,102 to 66,769. The rate of imprisonment also increased from 80 per 100,000 per head of population in 1870 to 140 per 100,000 in 1901 and there were over 60,000 commitals each year beginning in 1900, a level maintained to the end of the first decade of the twentieth century and not exceeded since.[14]

The reason for this upsurge in recorded crime was the number of commitals for public order offences. Thousands of women went to prison for breach of the peace, drunkenness, using obscene language and causing a nuisance. In 1898, for example, 40,000 of the 56,000 commitals were for these offences. In 1901 the Glasgow police made 'strong efforts to check obscene language' in the streets and apprehended 12,000 persons. Scottish prison officials were concerned about this extraordinary rise, pointing to the passage of various acts that brought more women and men before the courts. While many were only fined, the inability to pay meant they ended up in prison. This pattern is clear in comparisons of prison statistics for England and Scotland. For example, in 1902, over half of those punished by a fine in Scottish courts were unable to pay, whereas only 16 per cent of those fined in England defaulted and were sent to prison. A higher rate of fines, about twice the English average, plus an inability rather than a reluctance to pay meant a much higher rate of imprisonment in Scotland.

Scotland also continued to have a much higher ratio of women to men in prison. English women apparently never constituted more than 25 per cent of the overall prison population and by the 1870s they represented a small proportion.[15] In Scotland from 1870 to the end of the first two decades of the twentieth century, women comprised 35 to 40 per cent of all commitals to prisons. At certain points Glasgow prisons were filled with women, in 1890 10,000 of the 12,000 prisoners were women.[16] This pattern arises partly because of the nature of criminal justice in Scotland and because of the economic and social circumstances of women. Scottish women, unlike their English sisters, were more likely to work in mills and factories and live more independent lives.[17] While young English women were also employed in industry, the major form of employment was in domestic service as maids, cooks, governesses and nursemaids. Domestic servants were often subjected to close scrutiny and regulation within the husehold and allowed little opportunity to engage in leisure activities.[18] These different employment patterns probably led to alternative risks of contact with the police. Once contacted and arrested women were probably just as likely to be fined for their offences as men, but there was considerable difference in their ability to pay since women's wages were often a fraction of men's. As such, Scots women were disproportionately represented in the prison population because of differences in economic and leisure patterns, opportunity to commit public order offences, inability to pay fines, and the zealous operation of the police. Much has been written about the cult of domesticity as an ideological force associated with driving women into the home and forcing them out of paid labour. These figures seem to show that the ideology was also reinforced by law and zealous police enforcement directed at regulating a large number of women and keeping them out of places of public entertainment and amusement.

Theft and public order offences were common to women and men, but there were a few crimes that were only relevant to women, prostitution being the most obvious. Though prostitution itself was not illegal, women were sent to prison for importuning, diplays of 'public indecency' and public order offences related to prostitution. Campaigns against prostitutes occurred intermittently throughout the nineteenth century just as they do today. The most notorious was the Contagious Diseases Acts aimed at protecting the soldiers and sailors of Her Majesty's forces from venereal diseases.[19] From 1866 until 1869 women suspected of being prostitutes in garrison and port towns in England were forced to register and submit to fortnightly examinations. Refusal could mean imprisonment. Initial police reaction was enthusiastic and the police succeeded in extending the Acts to London.

The London Metropolitan Police enforced the Acts in a most vigorous manner, extending their surveillance to shop assistants, needlewomen, domestic servants and milliners, in short to all working women. As one of the critics of the Acts wrote,

A register of the women examined was kept from which no woman could remove her name without formal permission, and any woman ordered to be examined, who refused to regularly submit herself to physical examination, might be imprisoned.[20]

The most iniquitous feature of the Acts was the power of police constables on mere suspicion to place a woman under arrest and have her name inscribed on the list of known prostitutes. These powers were praised by the police who employed them as a means of regulating all women in public places and there was a belief that the threat of detection and registration was 'very salutary' on the general class of women from which prostitutes were drawn. Indifferent to the effect upon women, a commissioner of the Metropolitan Police indicated that '. . . young women in the position of domestic servants, leave their male acquaintances directly the police appear in sight.'[21]

This surveillance and the discretionary powers of enforcement led to considerable public outrage from diverse groups. Josephine Butler, a vociferous and diligent critic, published numerous examples of harassment and inscription of respectable women in her magazine, *The Shield*.[22] Intense and continuous pressure on parliament first led to the elimination of the Metropolitan's special officer force, and in 1886, to the repeal of the Acts. The repeal of the Contagious Diseases Act did not mean the end of harassment and arrest of women for prostitution-related offences. Like today, certain cities or police districts waged aggressive campaigns on women working as prostitutes and on places of entertainment, and at least one other national campain emerged in the early 1900s as London police mounted an intensive campaign against prostitutes from 1901 to 1906.[23] We might speculate that the enforcement of the Contagious Diseases Act in England may have kept English women out of public places to such an extent that they were less likely than Scottish women to be arrested for all manner of public order offences and this may have also been important in the different rate of female incarceration in both countries.

Throughout the nineteenth century, Scotland and England imprisoned a small number of women for another unique offence, concealment of pregnancy, and this is still on the statute books in Scotland. The criminal justice system and the Kirk (Church) enforced this law to prevent women 'putting away' their newborn infants in order to avoid the shame of illegitimacy and/or the extraordinary burdens of single parenthood. The 1842 Scottish prison report contains a poignant example of a women of twenty who had been orphaned at an early age and placed in service where she was raped by one of the farm hands.

> I should have been glad to have told him [doctor] the truth, had he asked me any questions, . . . but I had not heart to tell what had happened. I gaed ill, and came away from my place. Then I wrought at the harvest, and then I went to another place, and I knew not one person there who had ever cared for me. . . . I knew not which way to turn or where to look to. I think whiles if I could have read I should never have been here, for I had heard heaps of girls talk of concealment of pregnancy, and I knew not the sin that was before me. When my mistress found I was ill she was really kind; she sent me to bed, and wrought my work. [She could not tell them she was in labour because of her shame] . . . and so they gaed to their beds, and I was left to my misery. I thought mayhap my mistress might come in the night, but she did not come back to ask me how I was; and I was very ill, and I put away the life of my wean, and I grat [cried] all night as it lay by my side. When morning came, I was in such a state that I scarcely knew what I had done.[24]

The prison inspectorate presented this case with sympathy and it appears that the courts dealt with the charges of concealment and infanticide in a relatively lenient manner.[25] This woman received a twelve-month sentence, whereas a charge of murder or causing a death could have resulted in execution or transportation. Despite the sympathy and relative leniency in this case, it would not have occurred to most church leaders and penal authorities that the woman's plight was a result of the church's stance on fornication and illegitimacy. Women concealed rape and pregnancy and 'put away' infants out of fear of the guilt and shame that would befall them. This problem barely affected the men involved.

Another unique route to prison for Scottish women, particularly during the first half of the nineteenth century, was through voluntary committals. These women had not committed criminal acts, though occasionally they would commit crime in order to be sent to prison. They committed themselves because of poverty and starvation created by economic depression often accompanied by the desertion or ill-usage of husbands.

> I was ill, and stupid, and doltish, my husband ill-used me and beat me; and he left me and the child day after day to starve.[26]

In 1842, forty women sought voluntary committal to the Glasgow Bridwell 'in order to obtain food and shelter'. Some remained as long as two years and all were subjected to the rigours of the separate system.

The depressed economic situation meant that many women could not find employment and, unlike their English and Welsh sisters, they could not obtain relief from the poorhouse. The Scottish reluctance to institute systematic forms of relief meant that women and their children were often forced into prison in order to survive. Frederick Hill, a vigorous supporter of systematic relief and an ardent critic of the Scottish failure to introduce an effective Poor Law, ends his eleventh report with a clear statement on this issue.

> . . . to provide for destitution and crime . . . a country neeeds two institutions, and only two, a workhouse for all who are willing to enter such an institution, there to labour, to live on plain food, and to submit to the other rules of a well-ordered establishment of the kind; and a prison for those who will not consent to enter a workhouse, or to live honestly and peaceably by their own exertion.[27]

Voluntary committals were stopped by 1850 because of over-crowding and judicial decisions clarifying the penal nature of such institutions.

Women also went to prison for a variety of other offences, such as, assault and assault and robbery. However, women did not usually commit violent offences and when they did it tended to be against a family member and often involved circumstances such as infanticide after rape, or killing a husband after years of physical brutality. It is important to reiterate that most criminal acts of women throughout the century, as today, were minor, involving petty thefts or frauds and public order offences. Given this, it is perhaps surprising that the new penal experts considered women who committed crime to be a distinct, degraded and biologically deficient group.

Assessing and Evaluating Prisoners

Prison experts emerged both from within the prison system and from a wider base of philanthropic interest in the working classes. Professionals within the prison were concerned with obtaining detailed knowledge about prisoners' behaviour inside the institution. One of their early tasks was the creation, operation, and assessment of the new techniques of discipline and punishment. They attempted to determine the effect of the separate system, dietary restrictions and physical punishments. As part of this enterprise they developed various techniques for assessing individual potential and conduct as well as biological, moral and, eventually, psychological differences. Prisoners were differentiated in a hier-archical manner as good or bad subjects who did or did not conform to the norm of appropriate behaviour determined by the prison regime or wider social ideals.

At the time, the ideal for women was becoming more narrowly circumscribed within the family and increasingly set apart from the public arena. The home was increasingly glorified as the sole setting for her skills. The Victorian ideal exalted the cult of domesticity and characterized normal, proper or good women as mothers, dependent wives, sexually passive and morally perfect.[28] By contrast, criminal women were by definition flawed, frequenters of the public world, unchaste, sexually deviant, morally aberrant, unmotherly and the like. At best, they were simply not proper women. At worst, they were monstrous, perhaps not even human. This ideal of the private, perfect woman served as the backdrop for evaluating all women and helps explain the ferocity of those who set about the task of constructing a view of women who found their way into prison.

The means of assessing women in prison, of deciding who was redeemable and who was not, was the examination. Through it moral corruptness, as revealed in physical attributes and psychological aberrations, could be assessed, measured and objectified.[29] It may be too much to say that the modern behavioural sciences are rooted in this evaluative and disciplinary net of the prison, but it is no exaggeration to say that prisons and asylums were the first locations to provide a laboratory able to hold and manipulate human subjects for long periods of time and with few restrictions on experimentation. Examinations create the objectified case. Women and men are no longer individuals, or only in the sense that they are reproduced in documents, files, tests and various forms of written assessment. Such information is seen as scientific, a truth above patriarchal and class assumptions, but, as we shall see, nearly all of these assessments were permeated with preconceptions about the inherent nature of women *per se* and especially of deviant women who were the mirror opposite of the ideal middle-class Victorian woman.

An early concern of the new professionals, especially prison inspectors, was the operation of the separate system. Frederick Hill, the first inspector of Scottish prisons, was simultaneously an outspoken critic and a supporter of the separate system. He defended the separate system by arguing that it 'can be applied with perfect safety, and (for moderate periods of time) with great moral benefit, provided the prisoner be placed under humane officers, and supplied with useful labour.'[30] He advised moderation and special consideration for age and mental condition. After only one year at Perth prison, he concluded, 'I am more and more convinced that to subject boys and girls for long periods of time to the solitary of the separate cell is to war with nature, and to run a danger of injuring their minds and bodies.'[31]

The greatest concern of Hill and others was the 'ill effects of the separate system on boys' judged to produce listlessness and 'stiffness of limbs'. To combat this, lads were allowed out of their cells to 'have a run once or twice a day in the corridor'. Females 'should be required at a word of command to go through a few simple exercises in their separate cells.'[32] Exercise would relieve the 'evils' of the separate system and serve as an adjunct to discipline. Hill noted, 'one advantage of the military exercises is the habit of prompt obedience which they tend to produce.'[33]

In 1842, Scottish doctors began to assess the physical conditions of prisoners undergoing separate confinement at Perth prison, measuring weight, muscular fitness, pliancy of limbs and general health. For tests of pliancy, 'The prisoner is required to close his arm so as to touch his shoulder with his thumb, and the principle of the arm is then felt to see whether it is hard or soft and a corresponding entry made under muscular firmness. . . .'[34] The measurements were 'duly registered' at the beginning of imprisonment and repeated each month to assess 'deterioration' based on three scores for muscular firmness, 'f. for firm, m. for middling and s. for soft'. Such assessments requried a new technical, scientific vocabulary as well as the means of measuring and recording results.

Women and men in prisons were also evaluated on their educational, moral and social characteristics prior to and during imprisonment. For example, in education both initial potential and eventual achievement were assessed. This provided a wealth of information such as the fact that in 1845 only one in fifteen of the population of 15,000 in Scottish prisons was judged capable of both reading and writing, while 3,000 could not read and 8,000 could not write.[35]

One of the most general tests involved judgements of conduct while in prison. Before release, each Scottish prisoner was assessed as 'good' or 'bad'. For example, of those released from Scottish prisons in 1844, 17,000 were adjudged 'good' and 674 'bad'.[36] At some prisons, notably Aberdeen, such general assessments began to be used as a basis of prediction of future behaviour. Their annual reports included a 'Table Showing What Hopes May Be Entertained of the Future Conduct of Prisoners.'[37] In 1842, eleven women were judged 'Hopeful', sixteen 'Hopeless' and twenty 'Doubtful'. In 1876 the character of convict women in England was being determined on a seven-point scale including categories of: exemplary very good, good, fair, indifferent, bad and very bad.[38]

The methods of making such evaluations were multi-faceted but centred on two major techniques. Registers of behavioural conduct first proposed and used by Fry, usually focused on completion of work tasks and yielded external, measurable forms of judgement. Those who failed to adhere to the regime and/or complete their task were obviously of poor character. The most sophisticated registers were the badge and mark systems developed under the penal servitude system. Under the mark system prisoners were given a specified number of marks each day if they completed their allocated work task. The second technique of evaluation was less physical and more psychological and involved what would now be called the 'case history'. Annual prison reports always included case histories thought to assess character and provide a predictive basis for future conduct. Chaplains considered their collection both a right and a duty, and two Scottish chaplains outlined their methods as follows:

> The plan pursued by me . . . is to acquaint myself, as far as possible, with the past history, present attainments, and future prospects of the prisoners; by which method I am the better able to instruct and exhort them, according to their circumstances.[39]

> On my first visit after their commitment, I endeavour to obtain from them all the information I can of their previous life and habits, and the causes that led them to their commission of crime.[40]

This confessional, life history approach dates back at least to the Inquisitions and formed an important element in the public drama of the execution. With the rise of the casework method the information was used for private, professional consumption rather than public display, yet there is some similarity of purpose. The confession of guilt, though often resisted, allowed the application of stigma and the association of guilt with an act of crime. In prison, this association was intended to be a foundation for individual reformation, rather than a public signifier of guilt as it had previously been used in conjunction with the gallows. Through this process prisoners could be brought to participate in their own lasting correction, with admission of guilt and personal subjugation as the first step. If one forgot their history, the chaplain was there to remind them and to exhort better behaviour.

These methods seem crude and unsophisticated compared with the assessment techniques of modern medicine and psychology. However, they represent examples of early attempts to categorize individuals and create typologies enabling penal administrators and experts to differentiate individuals and assess the new types of punishment and reform. In many ways these two types of assessment continue today and might be seen as the forerunners of modern psychological approaches, such as behaviourism with its emphasis on external behaviour and 'objective' testing, and psychiatry with its focus on internal dynamics assessed by subjective methods such as the case work approach.

Early Discourses on Criminal Women

The new professionals did not restrict their energies to creating, refining and assessing technologies of control. They also developed new 'theories' about the causes of crime and the nature of criminals. Experts, like prisoners, were also distributed according to the worth of their observations. Those closest to the prison claimed that their privileged position within the institution and their intimate knowledge of prisoners gave them greater credibility, and they eventually became *the* experts on crime and penal reform. Prison inspectors, doctors, governors, chaplains and matrons, and other penal officials began to reject those outside of prison officialdom and to argue in favour of their own knowledge of crime and forms of amelioration. Lady visitors and Elizabeth Fry herself had earlier been described as meddling, injudicious and incompetent, and attempts were made to exclude such outsiders from prisons and to discount their observations and proposals.[41] Independent observers often criticized the practices of those who operated prisons and proposed alternative regimes. Some developed elaborate theories about the nature of criminal women, and the ideas of a few gained considerable prominence, particularly Mary Carpenter, Francis Robinson and Henry Mayhew. In the remainder of the chapter we shall consider the ideas that dominated during the third quarter of the nineteenth century and into the twentieth, focusing on those about environment, physiognomy, physiology, psychology and psychiatry.

Poverty and the Environment

At the beginning of the nineteenth century some penal experts focused on economic and environmental factors as explanations of crime. Early prison reports for Scotland provide numerous accounts of the economic predicament of women, usually presented in a sympathetic manner. Some Scottish police superintendents, prison chaplains and governors saw a direct link between poverty and crime, and felt there was a strong connection between economic conditions and theft and prostitution. Other commentators were less sympathetic and argued that poverty was self-imposed, whereby the feckless and indolent nature of working people leads both to poverty and to crime. The chaplain of Perth prison reported:

> Dissipation is, in an overwhelming number of instances the predisposing and immediate cause of crime; . . . especially if the history of young criminals were fully known. How many of these may have been led to follow a vicious life, in consequence of dissipation on the part of the parents, and the destitution by which such a habit is invariably followed amongst the working classes, whose sole hope of success depends upon a life of sobriety and steady perseverance.[42]

Such arguments were based on the already 'confirmed' belief that an important root of crime was the unwillingness to labour. The concept of dissipation extends this idea to encompass those who are willing to labour but fail to follow a life of 'sobriety and steady perseverance', and thus dissipate their efforts. Similar explanations were apparently strong in France.[43] In both countries, penal discourses were linked with 'philanthropic' efforts to instil appropriate habits of savings in the working classes in order to increase the independence of 'free labour', break the bonds of community and kin dependence and reduce the responsibilities of the state in periods of economic distress.

Frederick Hill rejected attempts to blame the poor for their poverty, but such challenges were rare. He argued that while 'ignorance, idleness, improvidence and . . . indulgence to excess in drinking and other sensual pleasures' contributed to the commission of crime, most crime was brought about by 'economic fluctuations' and 'scanty wages' that caused 'extreme poverty' leading to 'pressures of temptations'.[44] Women were seen as particulary vulnerable to these pressures and during the first half of the nineteenth century their predicament deteriorated because of new labour laws excluding them from certain forms of employment. Hill pointed out that women 'are at present practically excluded from nearly all the most lucrative employments – even from several for which they seem to be peculiarly fitted [e.g., printing] and hence the low payments for female labour.'[45] One example was the Scottish law forbidding women from working underground in coal mining. Hill outlined women's struggles against the implementation of these laws, involving deputations to local authorities and dressing up as men in order to work in the more highly paid underground jobs. While regretting that women were forced to work in mines, he sympathized with these struggles, observing 'even this is not so bad as starving . . .'[46] He often provided evidence and authoritative accounts of the relationship between economic hardship, seduction of women and their 'drift' into crime.

> One terrible evil, caused in part, . . . by the small payment now made for female labour, is exposure to seduction, leading often to an after life of public prostitution and crime . . . societies for its prevention should direct their energy at remedying this cause rather than by trying to get stringent laws passed for the suppression of houses of ill-fame.[47]

Such interpretations were not widely shared, especially after mid-century, when alternative views of crime and the working classes began to develop. An official and often quoted rejection of the link between crime and poverty was put in 1838 by the Royal Commission on the Constabulary Force.

> We have investigated the origin of the great mass of crime committed for the sake of property, and we find the whole ascribable to one common cause, namely the temptations of the profit of a career of depredations as compared with the profits of honest even well paid industry . . . The notion that any considerable proportion of the crimes against property are caused by blameless poverty of destitution we find disproved at every step.[48]

The poor and working classes began to be seen as dangerous, depraved and often distinctly different from the bourgeoisie.

Physiognomy and Evolution

In the 1860s, influential commentators, such as Carpenter, Robinson and Mayhew stressed contamination and individual pathology as the root causes of crime. Francis Robinson's two-volume work, *Female Life in Prison* (1862) appeared as an anonymous account of a prison matron. Although fictitious, it is an extraordinarily accurate portrayal of life in prison, certainly drawing on official literature and probably benefiting from an acquaintance with women who worked in prison. It was widely read, and went through three editions in two years. Mary Carpenter received even wider acclaim for work with wayward and delinquent children.[49] Her massive two-volume work, *Our Convicts* (1864), was meant to be a comprehensive analysis of the penal servitude system. She devoted considerable attention to women, whom she saw as especially degraded and sinful. Henry Mayhew, a well-known philanthropist, was most noted for his work on the London poor.[50] His book on crime and imprisonment, *The Criminal Prisons of London* (1862), is a report of his thorough investigations of all of the London prisons and draws on his first-hand knowledge of crime and the conditions of the poor.[51]

Carpenter and Robinson were firm supporters of physiognomy, believing in a rather straightforward relationship between the physical appearance of individuals and their criminal tendencies. Mayhew, on the other hand, was an evolutionist who believed that criminals were a separate class who had evolved from a different 'race' or people. His ideas were more systematic and predated some of the later positivistic approaches. Although all three commentators were sometimes critical of the operation of prison, we should not assume that they always sought more lenient or progressive penal regimes, or that they held enlightened views on the criminality of women. They were often responsible for extraordinarily negative conceptions of the 'criminal classes' and at times proposed stronger measures of punishment and discipline than the experts within the prison system.

Carpenter was also adamant about the existence of a distinct criminal class that transmitted criminal traits through contaminating influences. More than most commentators, she identified women as the chief agents of the spread of crime, commenting:

> If we follow this wretched woman to her home, and see around her the companions and accomplices of her crimes, we may form some small conception of the baneful influence she must shed around her, and shudder at the life to which her infant must be destined.[52]

Her most virulent descriptions of the physiognomy and contaminating influences of women were published in June 1862 in the popular magazine, *Once a Week*. In this lengthy report on the Irish penal system, she discusses her visit to the nursery at Mountjoy which provoked a memory of an earlier visit to a nursery in an English prison.

> The room was full and the spectacle awful! The faces of those mothers can never be forgotten, for they exhibited every species of hideous vice and degradation. And these were to give the first impressions to the young immortal beings who were unhappily their children, and who were imbibing from them the tainted

> streams of life . . . all around there were other wicked mothers,
> whose looks and voices would be bad and even fiendlike at times:
> the poor little child would catch its first notions of life from the
> worst specimen of humanity.[53]

Robinson attempted to capture both the physical and moral attributes of women in a series of vignettes called 'Prison Characters'. He thought the faces of women told a complete story and revealed their inner character, '. . . there is a general likeness among thieves, which a little observation does not fail to detect. Knavery stamps all its votaries with a common seal. . . .'[54] Women prisoners, he observed, behave in 'wicked' and 'deceitful' ways, traits that are evident in their outward appearances. '*A physiognomist might have* guessed much of her character from her countenance – it was so disproportionate and revolting. A white-faced ape would have been something like her and there was a look in her black eyes which made one shudder to encounter.'[55]

The physiognomy of convict women was a sign of their location within a 'pariah class' . . . 'found to differ in many respects from those belonging to a higher sphere.'[56] Members of this class were not merely physically depraved, but morally corrupted. The women Carpenter observed were thought to be given to 'Extreme excitability, violent and even frantic outbursts of passion, a duplicity and disregard of truth hardly conceivable in the better classes of society . . .'[57] According to her they were a contaminating danger to civilization, an 'outcast society . . . which exists in our state as something fearfully rotten and polluted, and which diffuses its upas poison [a poisonous tree] around, undermining the very foundations of society.'[58]

Carpenter and Robinson's account of physiognomy belonged to a pre-scientific conception of human behaviour. Such descriptions did not posit crime and other human acts as *caused* by facial features; rather depraved looks and countenances were seen as outward signs of moral corruption and weak character. The greater the depravity, the greater the ugliness. Conceptions about facial features were strongest in early accounts of crime, but attention began to shift to inherited biological make-up.

Cesare Lombroso became the most famous exponent of biological, evolutionary conceptions of the criminal, yet his ideas were not original and had been proposed by British and Continental thinkers for decades before he achieved fame in the late nineteenth century. One of the most important and earliest of these theorists was Henry Mayhew who developed a systematic theory of crime based on the use of statistical information. Though often neglected as a criminologist, his elaborate theories about crime and about female offenders were widely read and are very interesting if only because they are so disturbing.

Mayhew proposed a universal, evolutionary theory intended to explain crime '*all over the world*'.[59] He divided the human race into two groups, 'wanderers and settlers', who evolved different social and moral habits. Wanderers were in the 'habit of *seeking and taking* what they require'. Settlers evolved habits of '*producing* and *growing* what they want.'[60] Criminals were the wanderers coming from the Bedouin Arab 'tribes'. Mayhew's explanation of the development of these criminal classes combines biological and environmental forces, though it is ultimately strongly biological. Anticipating Lombroso's conceptions of criminals as atavistic throwbacks, he claimed that 'Our criminal tribes . . . may be regarded as that portion of our society who have not yet conformed to civilized habits.'[61] Within the midst of the supposed highest civilization in Europe were members of an 'outcast race' with distinct evolutionary features of habitual criminal temperament. These features of the 'criminal and mendicant *races*' are inherited; 'if Jews engender Jews with minds and characters almost as Hebraic as their noses . . .' then it is not surprising, he writes, that criminals 'should beget natures like their own – deficient in moral and physical energy, and therefore not only averse to the drudgery of regular labour, but incapable of that continued tension of the will which we call moral purpose or principle.'[62] The evolutionary process was, he believed, intensified in the middle ages when outcast tribes sought sanctuary in specific locations where they

> *interbred* with the lowest class of women . . . and so served to render every one of the old religious haunts positive nests of vice, misery and disease-hatching felons, lepers, and mendicants, like vipers in a muck-heap.[63]

This elaborate evolutionary theory was supplemented by an equally developed conception of criminal women who were seen as possessed of unique qualities and patterns of behaviour that led them into crime. The idea that women's crime arose from employment in the 'rudest and most unfeminine labours', such as mining, was rejected and statistical returns for criminality were used to claim that 'We are . . . inclined to connect female criminality with unchastity [prostitution], rather than 'rude' employment . . .'[64] Prostitution was seen as the root of all women's crimes which in turn arose from innate features of women within the criminal classes. Members of the 'criminal classes' are disposed to an 'easy mode of living'; for men this leads to theft, for women to street-walking.

> . . . females, among the poorer classes of society, who are born to labour for their bread, but who find work inordinately irksome to their natures, and pleasure inordinately agreeable to them, have no necessity to resort to the more daring career of theft to supply their want, but have only to trade upon their personal charms in order to secure the apparent luxury of an idle life.[65]

The reasons for prostitution was also located in the 'natural' characteristics of women. Mayhew saw women as naturally good, chaste, modest and born to motherhood. Blessed with an extreme sensitivity to praise or blame, they live in 'acute dread of being detected in the slightest impropriety of conduct'[66] and 'naturally find the greatest delight in approbation . . .'[67] All humans need praise, but criminal women are inordinately vain and immune to the natural shame that arises from impropriety. Shame as an 'educated sentiment' comes about through training in 'decency and virtue', and yet the educated characteristics of civilized women may 'continue utterly unawakened in the ruder forms of female nature', a failure deriving from the living conditions of the 'wretched girls',

> . . . living almost the same barbarious life as they would, had they been born in the interior of Africa . . . [they have] become so hardened to scorn and reproofs of their fellow creatures as to be utterly barbarized and left without the faintest twinges of moral sense to restrain their wild animal passions and impulses.[68]

Once detected in sin and crime, these women are without shame, made

> reckless as to how their acts are regarded by others, viewed by the rest of the world as creatures in whom the brightest feminine qualities have been effaced, and whose natures and passions are subject to none of the ordinary principles of restraint.[69]

The confirmation of this process was to be witnessed in the prisons of London, where 'The most striking peculiarity of women . . . is that of utter and imperturbable shamelessness.'

A lack of restraint within the family was in Mayhew's account an additional reason why more working-class women took up prostitution and crime. He maintained that working-class girls are not naturally more unchaste than their middle-class counterparts, but subject to fewer restraints. Since their mothers are working, either in paid employment or in their own homes, the girls have more responsibilities that take them outside of the protection of their mothers. A working-class girl must run errands 'from the tenderest age' and 'once her limbs are strong enough to work, she is put out in the world to toil for herself.'[70] Once abroad in the community working they are less likely to be protected. '*She* has no maids to accompany *her* when she walks abroad, and often her only playground is the common court in which her parents reside.'[71] These observations lead Mayhew to the conclusion that mothers are a significant source of all crime, not just prostitution. If women would remain in the home in their natural nurturing and caretaking role, children would be educated in the appropriate sentiments and regulated within the home. Thus, the state of industrial Britain with women in paid employment was an unnatural one.

> In a natural state of things, it has clearly been intended by the Great Architect of the universe that the labour of the man should be sufficient for the maintenance of the family – the frame of the woman in itself evidence that she was never meant to do the hard work of society, whilst the foundations of life that she carries in her bosom, as well as the kinder and more affectionate qualities of her nature, all show that her duty was designed to be that of a mother and a nurse to the children, rather than a fellow-labourer with the man.[72]

Mayhew's discourses on the evolutionary nature of the criminal, and his conception of the unique features of the lives and characters of working-class girls were some of the most sophisticated of the period. Equivalent conceptions were to become the cornerstones of many of the late nineteenth- and early twentieth-century theories about female criminality.

The Fall of Women

Apart from theories about the causes of crime, additional indications of the supposedly unique nature of criminal women were gleaned from observation of their behaviour once inside the prison. Carpenter, Robinson and Mayhew all reported such observations and comparable accounts appeared in official prison reports. The essence of most of these reports was that women were naturally morally superior to men but once they descended into crime they became worse than men and were nearly beyond redemption. Mayhew noted that women in prison were more hideous 'because they are usually regarded as the most graceful and gentle form of humanity.'[73] Carpenter pointed out that women must descend a greater distance than men to reach the depths of criminal depravity.

> The very susceptibility and tenderness of woman's nature render her more completely diseased in her whole nature when thus perverted to evil; and when a woman has thrown aside the virtuous restraints of society, and is enlisted on the side of evil, she is far more dangerous to society than the other sex.[74]

She cites Tennyson in support of her thesis, 'For men at most differ as Heaven and earth. But women, worst and best, as Heaven and hell' and argues that once fallen, criminal women are 'entirely lost to shame or reputation'.[75] Robinson thought some 'less easy to tame than creatures of the jungle'.[76]

Women were also seen as much more difficult to manage while in prison. Male prisoners, according to Robinson, 'are influenced by some amount of reason and forethought . . .' whereas female prisoners 'act more like mad women unable to think judiciously.'[77] Female prisoners, he observed, are 'As a class, desperately wicked, deceitful, crafty, malicious, lewd, and void of common feeling.'[78] Male prisoners are no match for women; they are tame by comparison. 'In the penal classes of the male prisons there is not one man to match the worst inmates of our female prisons.'[79]

Arguments and conceptions such as these led to proposals for the development of unique responses to women convicts, and Carpenter, Robinson and the English prison inspectors agreed on this. Carpenter began her book with such views and emphasized them throughout, '. . . the treatment of females is far more perplexing than that of males. It demands, indeed, peculiar consideration and comprehension of the special difficulties to be grappled with.'[80] The influential prison reformer and inspector, Joshua Jebb, also observed that

> because they are not so amenable to punishment, their [penal] offences are of a different character, and depend very much upon impulse. If they quarrel one with another, they will set to work and break the windows in their cells, and tear up their clothes, all without assignable reason, and they will sit down and burst out crying. They are difficult people to manage.[81]

Thus, it was thought that women should be reacted to on an individual basis. 'Male convicts must be treated in masses rather than according to their individual character. Individuality must be more regarded with female convicts.'[82]

Although penal experts inside and outside the carceral system agreed on the importance of individualizing the treatment of women, they did not agree on the efficacy of the existing operation of prisons. Carpenter believed that little reformation occurred within British prisons. On the contrary, '. . . a torrent of vice from this sink of impurity annually pours forth into the community, and irrigates the length and breadth of the community, not with fertilizing, but with polluting streams.'[83] This 'polluting stream' was created through lax and indulgent penal administration. The English convict system for women and men is operated, she argued, '. . . on such indulgences and such avowed consideration of the wishes of the criminal classes, it can neither be a deterrent to them nor truly reformatory. . . .'[84] The warders who are responsible for enforcing discipline were judged to be overly indulgent because they were fearful of reprisal or because '. . . a sort of tacit understanding grows up between the Convicts and the warders.'[85]

In order to rectify these shortcomings, Carpenter proposed more stringent application of existing regulations, a sparser diet and, ironically, a more individual approach. 'Man is not a machine to be worked on mechanical principles.'[86] The personal and direct approach was the only means of bringing about a profound transformation, and women would not be reformed if prisons operated relative to 'preconceived theories, or mechanical arrangments, or desire of economy.'[87] The transformation Carpenter sought must not be 'outside the individual'. She thought that the '. . . will of the individual should be brought into such a condition as to wish to reform . . .' with reformation coming from 'the inner spirit. . . .'[88] The first step in this process was severe suffering through the application of lengthy periods of solitary confinement and sparse diet. This humbling procedure would subdue and 'bring the individual into a state in which he may be more easily made sensible of his criminality towards God and man.'[89] The outcome of this would be a complete willingness to admit guilt and submit to humiliation, 'The state of antagonism to society must be destroyed; the hostility to divine and human law must be subdued.'[90] As signs of their absolute subjugation, prisoners must 'perform willingly the very lowest drudgery, – to accept the least inviting food as more than he deserves, – to yield a cheerful obedience to the strictest regulations.'[91]

It is useful to compare Carpenter's discourses to Fry's earlier conceptions of prison regimes. Although both sought to achieve the complete subjugation of women at the hands of authority, in other respects their views were quite different. Carpenter saw a distinct pariah class contaminated by sin, degradation and crime. While Fry certainly conceived of criminals as morally degraded, she did not argue that they were an innately inferior group.

Carpenter's idea of a more individual approach implied also one that was more distant and detached, separating and isolating women in a web of discipline and punishment, rendering them more susceptible to techniques of allocating blame and guilt in order to break down resistance and make them more willing subjects in their own transformation.

Science and Bio-psychological Approaches

Early nineteenth-century reformers were primarily religious ministers and/or concerned philanthropists such as Fry, Carpenter and Mayhew. Yet, from the very beginning of systematic confinement, the medical profession was prominent in the creation and assessment of technologies of correction and punishment within prisons. They played a significant role in implementing, legitimizing and sometimes mitigating the technologies of discipline and punishment. At mid century, doctors began to promulgate new 'scientific' discourses on crime and imprisonment. Before them, Mayhew had used statistical methods and direct observations of crime in the community in an attempt to explain crime. For the new medical bio-psychologists, physiques, cranial configurations and other physical features provided indicators of moral degeneracy and criminality.[92] The difference between these new scientific approaches and earlier physiognomist ones was a reliance on statistical measurements of bodily features, what came to be called anthropometry. Most of these new ideas were deeply implicated in the eugenics movements of the late nineteenth and early twentieth centuries.[93] Physical measurements and eventually psychological tests would enable eugenicists to differentiate inferior 'races' and to identify and classify degeneracy within national groups. The analysis of women was particularly important in these efforts since women in their role as mothers were seen as the biological and social source of degeneracy, and patriarchal assumptions about the true nature of women led to attempts to identify and classify those who deviated from this norm.

Doctors working in prisons and asylums began to monopolize the new scientific discourses on crime.[94] Their ascendancy was due to their privileged position within society and direct observations of prisoners, and they offered explanations of crime that were comforting because they were based on individualized explanations and accepted wisdom. British doctors, and later psychologists, were important in this new approach to crime and degeneracy, although the credit for the development of the scientific or positivistic explanation of crime goes to an Italian prison surgeon, Cesare Lombroso.

Physiology, Anthropometry and Moral Degeneracy

Much has been written about Lombroso's unique contribution to the explanation of female criminality and it is only necessary for us to outline his major ideas.[95] He gained worldwide recognition for articulating in a didactic, often breathless style, bio-psychological ideas already gaining widespread acceptance in Europe, Britain and the United States. Lombroso concentrated on the measurement of physical features and basically believed that criminals were 'atavistic throwbacks', members of a distinct class of women and men who failed to evolve into normal European types. Women criminals were seen as 'pathological anomalies' who failed to develop the 'natural' instincts of their sex. These ideas were not unique nor especially original, but Lombroso's entrepreneurial genius was to combine concepts from social Darwinism, racial superiority, and physical anthropology into what appeared to be a coherent theory of crime. The widespread acceptance of his ideas had more to do with the persuasiveness of his arguments and their correspondence with long-standing folk wisdom than with originality or scientific evidence.

Lombroso's works were widely disseminated during the late nineteenth century and accepted by many criminologists from the Continent and fewer from Britain and America.[96] For example, Tarnowsky sought to establish that Russian women prisoners were physically distinct. She reputedly found that the majority of women imprisoned for murder and infanticide were under normal weight and that most women convicts were below average height and weight.[97] Italian physical anthropologists went furthest in the assessment of unique physical characteristics of criminals. Fornasari, for example, found that 'The thighs of prostitutes are consequently bigger than normal women's in proportion to the calves. The foot in proportion is also shorter and narrower than in normals.'[98] Another Italian, Maro, attempted to measure the cranial capacities of 'prostitutes, peasant chaste women, educated chaste women and thieves.' He found little variation in these women, but concluded that prostitutes have 'small cranial capacities' compared to other women.

Unlike the Italian physical anthropologists who focused on bodily dimensions and crime, many British experts emphasized the relationship between moral degeneracy and malfunctioning of the brain. This strong materialistic conception of the direct relationship between the mind (morals and sentiments) and the brain (the neurological functioning) was first given prominence through the work of Henry Maudsley who believed that crime indicated 'a congenital fault of mental organisation.' Moral feeling, like hunger or thirst, '. . . is a function of organisation, and is essentially dependent on that part of the nervous system which ministers to its manifestations as in any part of mental functioning.'[99]

Maudsley's most important contribution was the early identification and classification of the congenital nature of mental subnormality among the population in general. But unlike some of his American contemporaries, he did not give prominence to a connection between mental subnormality, low intelligence or feeblemindedness, and crime.[100] Instead, he saw the cause as moral degeneracy which was in turn caused by a failure of the brain to function properly. For Maudsley, not all criminality is inherited but most of it is. He claimed that '. . . of the true thief as of the true poet it may be indeed said that he is born, not made.'[101] Physiognomy also played an important role in Maudsley's formulations, with inherited outward appearances serving as simple indicators of membership in a distinct criminal class, '. . . an experienced detective officer or prison official could pick them out from any promiscuous assembly at church or market.'[102] Like Lombroso and many other experts of the time, he believed in a separate criminal class with clearly distinguishable features.

Maudsley devoted considerable attention to the deviance and criminality of women, and saw female prisoners as 'ugly in features, and without grace of expression or movement.' When reviewing Robinson's *Female Life in Prison*, he wrote that decent people are surprised to learn

> to what a depth of degradation woman sometimes sinks . . . she
> completely loses all sense of shame, modesty, self-respect, and
> gentleness, all her womanliness, and becomes violent, cruel,
> outrageously blasphemous, and impudently immodest; in fact, a
> sort of fiend with all the vices of woman in an exaggerated form,
> and with none of her virtues.[103]

He appears to have been one of the first British doctors to identify the normal functionings of women's bodies as a cause of insanity and deviance, arguing that normal menstruation, pregnancy and lactation could form part of a pathological condition.[104] Taking this materialist view of behaviour to its limits, he concluded that sexual 'deviations' in women were attributable to the '. . . irritation of the ovaries or uterus – a disease by which the chaste and modest woman is transformed into a raging fury of lust.'[105]

Tredgold was another influential physician who proposed a strong materialist view of human action. Following Maudsley, he argued that it is possible to identify the morally insane and the 'morally deficient' through physical indicators, and individuals born with these limitations exhibit persistent 'vicious or criminal conduct'. Tredgold's proposals provided a bridge between the primarily biological analysis of Maudsley and the rise of bio-psychological perspectives emphasizing the importance of emotions. As well as stressing the importance of moral degeneracy and outward appearances, four 'senses' or 'sentiments that go to make up the average civilized man' were identified: the 'intellectual, the religious, the aesthetic and moral or social.'[106] They emerge from 'special hereditary tendencies' and the 'nature of . . . early environment', and the ability to develop them was innate but lacking in certain individuals, 'the [criminal] class that we are now considering are fundamentally incapable of acquiring a moral feeling.'[107]

Tredgold offered a typology of the morally defective: (1) the morally perverse or habitual type, (2) the facile type, and (3) the explosive type. The 'facile' type was primarily composed of women, judged 'lacking in will power' and 'unable to steer a right course'. Their path to crime did not generally begin until adolescence when parental restraint was reduced and they were 'speedily in trouble'. The trouble for girls was usually sexual deviance. Tredgold claimed that about half 'the girls admitted to Magdalen Homes . . . and a considerable proportion of prositutes . . . belonged to this class of morally defective.'[108]

As a medical practitioner, Tredgold, like Maudsley, was primarily interested in charting and categorizing mental retardation and only marginally interested in human 'sentiments', which were to become the primary province of the newly emerging disciplines of psychology and psychiatry. Like their medical counterparts, psychologists argued that they were primarily interested in the usual and normal aspects of sentiments, emotion and personality, but like their medical colleagues they focused a great deal of attention on the wayward and deviant as a means of defining the normal. Two prominent British examples of early psychological work on deviance and crime were Havelock Ellis and Cyril Burt.

At the turn of the century, Ellis wrote a popularized account of bio-psychology and in it expressed regret at the lack of enthusiasm for the anthropometric method in Britain and celebrated Lombroso as the Columbus of criminology, '. . . who led the way to a fresh scientific region.'[109] Ellis elaborated and endorsed the 'evidence' relating to the physical attributes of the criminal: unique cranial and cerebral configurations, facial features, anomalies of body hair, general criminal physiognomy of the body and viscera and lack of physical sensibility. He sums up his views on 'born criminals' with a statement from Lombroso. 'It is in short, a type resembling the Mongolian, or sometimes the Negroid.'[110]

Another major theme was the relationship between immorality, insensibility and crime, with research on physical sensitivity converging to 'show that the criminal is markedly deficient in physical sensibility. This physical insensibility is associated with that moral insensibility . . . which is . . . the criminal's most fundamental characteristic.'[111] Like Mayhew and Carpenter before him, Ellis believed that criminals were usually, 'morally insensible and perverse, imprudent, lacking in foresight . . . incapable of prolonged and sustained exertion.'[112] Criminals are not just physically dwarfed or peculiar; they are also morally underdeveloped, a state revealed in their aversion to work, 'This constitutional laziness is therefore one of the chief organic bases of crime.'[113]

Ellis devoted considerable attention to the deviance and crimes of women who, like male criminals, were seen as atavistic, but in special ways. Criminal women in prison were reputed to have more body and facial hair than 'normal' women. He cites an Italian criminologist who reported '. . . considerable distribution of hair between the pubes and umbilicus (as in men) in 10 of the forty women he examined . . . [and] abundant hair in seven out of forty around the anus, a part in normal women rarely supplied with hair.'[114] An excess of down on the face was 'found with special frequency in women guilty of infanticide', revealing an animal vigour and repressed sexual instincts. Ellis believed that many women apprehended for crime were male-like in appearance. Citing another Italian, Maro, he notes that natural selection has played an important role in criminality since women in prisons are generally, 'Masculine, unsexed, ugly, abnormal women . . . most strongly marked with the signs of degeneration . . .'[115]

Ellis also linked female criminality with women's biology and supposed sexual proclivities, reporting that there is little doubt, as evidenced in prisons, asylums, and medico-legal opinion that the 'menstrual period favours a . . . general tendency to emotional instability' and that 'the sexual organs in women criminals very frequently reveal pathological conditions . . . menstruation is nearly always irregular or suppressed in female prisoners.'[116] As well as having marred biological functions, women criminals were also oriented to deviant sexual practices. Homosexuality in prison and other habits considered deviant by Ellis were examples of attempts to create excitement and diversion in otherwise vacuous lives. An image reminiscent of witchcraft lore is evoked in his description of the supposed practices of criminal men and women.

> The craving for excitement, for intoxication, for uproar, finds its chief satisfaction in the love of orgy, which is now almost confined, at all events in its extreme forms to the criminal and his intimate ally the prostitute.[117]

The orgy was a 'sacred festival' of criminals, and women prisoners who engaged in breaking out were perhaps performing their own auto-erotic orgy. Breaking out might be considered an 'exaggerated or vicarious form of orgy . . .'[118] One cannot help but wonder what evidence was available for comparison with 'normal' non-criminal women and to question how much of this science was voyeurism or pornography.

Cyril Burt became famous for his 'research' on intelligence and innate inferiority of the working class and was given a knighthood for this work.[119] It has now been thoroughly discredited because many of the findings, and indeed one of his research assistants, were fictitious. He also had a keen interest in delinquency, and his lengthy book, *The Young Delinquent*, first published in 1919, was widely read and went through several printings.[120] Initially given as a series of lectures to London school teachers, it expounded a wealth of ideas presented as scientific discourse, identifying delinquency as a serious problem that could only be solved through scientific investigations by professional psychologists. He proposed an overall methodology involving the creation of an abstract case built from detailed examinations of the individual. Psychologists, he argued, should begin with elaborate case histories detailing the physical, social, environmental, moral and family background of the delinquent. Additional information could be obtained by using the new instruments of psychological measurement and assessment. Thus, objective tests and subjective assessments of character would reveal the inner springs of motivation and immorality.

Burt's conception of the causes of delinquency are very broad, including physiological, psychological, and environmental factors.

Although he argued that only a minority of delinquents were 'congenitally criminal', that is the offspring of criminals, his basic message was that delinquents are possessed of underdeveloped sentiments which are inherited. A clear indication of this position was expressed in a lengthy passage he emphasized near the end of *The Young Delinquent*.

> *The commoner delinquencies committed by the young consist essentially, in almost every case, either of the hereditary reactions which constitute the universal human instincts, or else of slightly modified reactions elaborated out of, but still evidently springing from, these aboriginal modes of response.*[121]

Burt's influential work was based on the case histories of 190 London girls and boys who had committed a variety of offences, mostly trivial. The majority had come to Burt's attention for theft (79 per cent of the boys and 43 per cent of the girls). Other offences included: 'willing' sexual relations with the opposite sex (37 per cent of girls and 11 per cent of boys); 'excessive masturbation' (3 per cent of girls and 4 per cent of boys); gross obscenity, including talk (2 per cent of the boys and 8 per cent of the girls); incorrigibility and 'excessive' bad temper (19 per cent of the girls and 9 per cent of the boys); with only the girls finding themselves in trouble for 'false and dangerous accusations' (4 per cent). It is important to note that girls were much more likely to be identified as delinquent for purely 'immoral' behaviour, such as bad temper and willing sexual relations.

Burt and Ellis represent important examples of the way the newly emerging child-regulating movement and professional psychology began to define and map sexual behaviour as a form of human conduct worthy of scrutiny, classification and censure. This was not a new focus, but early reformers sought to circumscribe and regulate sexuality while generally ignoring its actual operation. The new professionals sought to reveal the intricacies of sex and sexuality, expose it to scrutiny and make its study a scientific enterprise capable of entering a wider social, moral and political discourse. Identifying and naming sexual features of human behaviour made the exploration and specification of normality legitimate. For Burt, aberrant sexuality, meaning sexuality that departed from espoused Victorian middle-class morality, was a clear indicator of immorality, revealing an inherently weak character requiring correction.

The case histories he gathered all began with a description of the physical appearance of the youngster, most revealing an extraordinary prejudice against working-class children, especially girls. For example, he described two of his delinquents:

> She had a fixed and foolish leer; and her head and features showed several slight anomalies, which might have been fastened upon as stigmata of degeneracy. Her forehead was bossed; her nose pinched and undeveloped; her palate high; and her teeth misshapen and irregularly packed. . . . From early childhood to the present she had exhibited, with remarkable consistency of career, the ineradicable habits of a *hopeless moral reprobate*.[122] [our emphasis]

> A big, burly, fierce-looking maiden, with a puckered scowl on her forehead and a square, under-shot, resolute jaw, she shouldered into my room with a policeman's blood literally moist upon her knuckles.[123]

These descriptions are not atypical and reveal Burt's orientation to working-class girls as well as a commitment to sensational descriptions and language geared to arouse public and professional interest.

Although Burt argued for the use of various 'objective' psychological tests such as the Association Reaction Test, Downey's Handwriting Test, and of course the IQ test, he had great respect for the use of subjective assessments of outward physical features as indicators of inner character. He lamented, 'Physiognomy, as a branch of individual psychology has fallen into curious neglect and ill-repute.'[124] He thought that for the 'observer who knows what to look for, the child's face, physique, and general deportment are always rich in significance.'[125] Much more than mental and emotional tests, a child's facial expression indicates the 'dominating mood and chief susceptibilities', with the body, physique and face suggestive of fundamental 'constitutional conditions'.[126]

Burt paid particular attention to the deviance of girls. Following his general physiological and hereditary arguments, he observed that since sexual differences were evident from birth, they 'must spring in part from some deeper and more general quality of the feminine body or mind.'[127] He thought women were ruled by biology and, in contrast to men, it is 'physiology rather than . . . physique that generally give rise to trouble.'[128] Females' sentiments were also distinctly different from those of males, 'One inborn sex-difference alone is well marked and well established, and that is the difference in emotions and instincts.' In explaining the criminality of girls and women he invoked various ideas, some emphasizing masculine traits, others stressing the unique characteristics of female biology. He observed that, 'Many of my female cases bear records of having been over-grown romps and tomboys while at school, and burly hoydens and

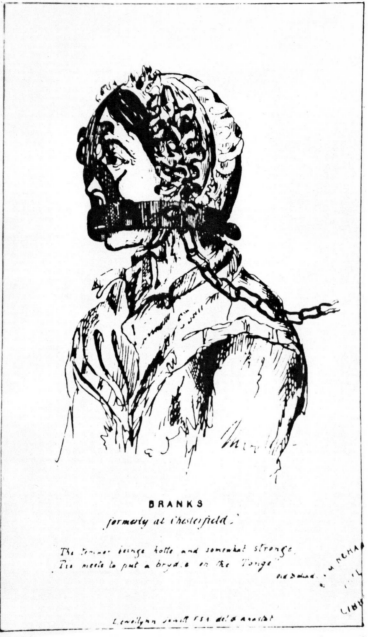

BRANKS
formerly at Chesterfield.

The *former things bothe and somewhat stronge.*
Tis neele to put a bryd.s on the Tonge

old School.

Llewellyn scull f s s deld arosbt

1 Woman chained to a branks, a not infrequent form of
punishment for 'shrewish' and 'nagging' women from the sixteenth
to the eighteenth centuries.

2 Women working in silence outside their cells on the sharply tiered galleries of Brixton Prison, c. 1860.

3   Brixton Chapel with staff sitting at the front and prisoners at the back, c. 1860.

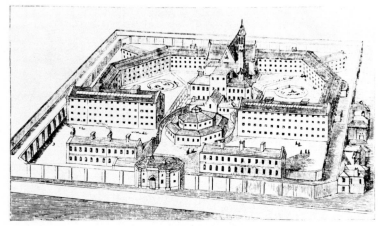

4 Women's Convict Prison, Brixton, established around 1817, expanded and adapted in 1853 for women sentenced to penal servitude.

5 Holloway House of Correction for women and men opened in 1852; it later became the main women's prison for England.

6 Prisoner wearing a veil intended to prevent the contaminating influences associated with seeing and talking to other prisoners. Surrey House of Correction, Wandsworth, c. 1860.

7 Mothers and their children exercising at Tothill Fields Prison, c. 1860.

8 Girls' School, Tothill Fields Prison, c. 1860.

9 Silent congregate labour at the House of Correction, Tothill Fields, c. 1860.

10 The laundry at Brixton, c. 1860.

11 Prisoner picking oakum, a task which involved untwisting lengths of tarred rope – a tedious and dirty task. Oakum picking was commonly performed by prisoners subjected to labour in their cells throughout the nineteenth and well into the twentieth century.

12 The laundry at Wormwood Scrubs in the 1890s.

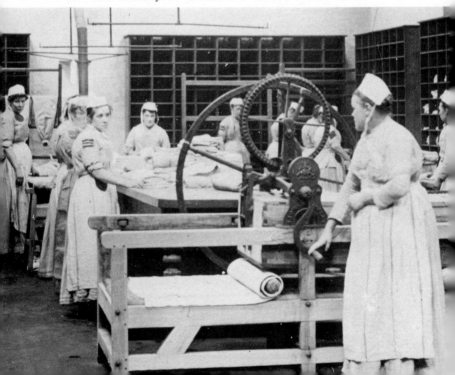

viragos in their later years.'[129] Like Lombroso he thought that many women murderers had 'masculine appearance and proportions.'[130]

One of the root causes of delinquency in girls was the onset of puberty and periodicity, 'specifically marked by the appearance of a monthly crisis' that results in 'mild but far-reaching disturbances of the mind.'[131] According to Burt, theft was a common result of the 'disturbances' of these periods, 'many young women of a neurotic and unstable disposition take to shop-lifting.' However, the most usual delinquency associated with periodicity involved sexual activities. Girls and women become sexually excited at this time, 'In both the pre-menstrual and post-menstrual phase, the commonest delinquencies are downright or manifestly substituted for, this particular impulse such as wandering, running away, and staying out late at night.' The impact of periodicity which appears to affect a vast amount of a woman's life, compels them to 'roam the streets accosting strange men in fantasy' and 'outbreaks of temper are exceedingly frequent'.

The onset of puberty was an especially dangerous period. At this point, both over- and under-developed girls are prone to deviant sexual behaviour. Over-developed 'maidens are dangerously alluring to the eye of the opposite sex; inwardly they are apt to accumulate an unusual store of sex-emotion pent up within themselves.'[132] Pent-up emotion may vent itself in two contradictory directions, causing 'bold, brisk, and animated creatures, fast in action and forward in behaviour' or 'inert and easy-going sluggards, limp, lazy, and languorous, dreaming all day on cushions like a cat, and prowling around in the evenings to steal or solicit because they are too indolent to work.'[133]

He also saw sexually active young women as extraordinarily dangerous. They were viewed as a threat to community morality and to the reputations of 'innocent' adult males. Not all delinquent girls were of this 'dangerous' nature, but for those who were 'hard work and physical exercise' was recommended. The views of William Healy, the prominent American psychologist, were invoked, 'tempters of the opposite sex, purveyors of disease and spreaders of vicious knowledge among their friends and casual acquaintances' should be subjected to a course of asceticism under medical segregation. For the most dangerous of this type, 'segregation must be advocated . . . if only to protect society.'[134] Female delinquents who were not dangerous only required temporary segregation in training colonies operated like a 'normal family . . . with grown house parents . . .'[135]

Burt's proposals did not have an apparent and immediate effect on reactions to women in prisons. They did, however, influence the work of Grace Pailthorpe who focused specifically on delinquent women and girls and had a profound impact on official thinking about women prisoners. Results of her research on 223 women and girls confined in prisons and preventive rescue homes were published in 1933 in a Medical Research Council report and in a popular book, *What We Put in Prison*.[136] Both works are remarkable in their unswerving commitment to a bio-psychological approach and in the degree of ignorance of the lives and problems of working-class girls and women.

The women and girls she subjected to investigation were, like Burt's delinquents, imprisoned for minor offences such as, 'pilfering . . . asocial behaviour, running away, staying out late, insubordination, violent temper, bad companions . . . sexual irregularities including prostitution, promiscuity, and obscene conversation.'[137] Biological factors were seen as the main determinants of this deviance and crime:

> Where society's demands have been set out, it has been for the purpose of emphasizing a norm, serious deviation from which is an indication of deficient adaptation capacity on the part of the individual to his surroundings, therefore, of a biological deficiency.[138]

Deficient biological development was revealed in underdeveloped immoral sentiments and various psychopathologies. She claimed that 84 per cent of the women and girls in the sample were lacking in sentiment development and over 93 per cent of the adult women she examined suffered from some form of psychopathology, '. . . either by psychological arrest in development, or through maladjustment and mental conflict, or through incipient psychoses.'[139] These women and girls are not offenders or 'malefactors' they are 'sick persons' who '. . . should be regarded in the same light as people suffering from the various contagious fevers.'[140]

Working-class women, she claimed, were lacking in sentiments, self-deceiving, and unable to form lasting and significant perceptions.

> They adopt the clap-trap of their particular class, but it is mere imitation, it never takes the permanent form of dispositions and sentiments . . . Their pseudo-sentiments can be put on and off as easily as the powder and paint they affect on their faces.[141]

The language of early twentieth-century psychology played a significant role in Pailthorpe's proposals, yet these conceptions were heavily laden with moralistic perceptions; 'They have reached an elementary standard of cleanliness, the lowest that would be tolerated by the society in which they move.'[142]

The 'solution' for the deviance of these women and girls was mainly in the application of psychological corrections ideally applied at an early age. Pailthorpe thought that early education might make a difference, but it must be based on the middle-class ideal of 'co-ordinated character training'.[143] Delinquent girls and criminal women would also benefit from 'permanent and temporary' segregation. Her ideal approach would involve extended 'Psycho-analysis [as] . . . the only radical cure for all psychological mal-adjustments.'[144] For women described as passive mental defectives, prone to promiscuity resulting in pregnancy, permanent segregation could be useful but sterilization would be best since it would allow them some freedom.[145]

A central clearing station must be established on the 'lines of an infectious hospital' in order to determine the particular moral ailments.

> In fact, there should be instituted a number of small laboratories where the investigators represent the several different schools of psychology . . . Those in charge should be given hunting grounds from which they may select their cases, and the subjects chosen should, from that time onwards, come under the sole guardianship of the investigator.[146]

Using these 'hunting grounds', psychologists would then be able to apply an experimental method in order to 'discover the actual value, as judged by results of each individual school of psychology.'[147]

In the work of Pailthorpe we reach the end of one era and the beginning of the next. Her work represents a clear and acknowledged link with the early bio-psychologists such as Burt who identified unique sexual and biological characteristics as the roots of criminality. These perspectives were in turn linked to the physiognomic and evolutionary approaches that preceeded them. The early bio-psychologists such as Maudsley, Tredgold, Ellis and Burt shifted the focus to women's sexuality and biology. Facial features were no longer seen as indicators of criminality; instead women's innate biology was thought to be the cause of crime. For some, this was because women were overly masculine, for others because they were compelled by periodicity. Criminal women were seen as outside the boundaries of the ideal, chaste, cloistered Victorian woman and in need of unique, individualized treatment. Theories focusing on the innate features of women in general provided the prevailing orientation to female criminality in the first half of the twentieth century. In the United States such studies often emphasized body types and feeble-mindedness, in Britain, faulty sentiments and psychopathology were thought to play the prominent role in criminality.[148]

Only a few observers offered alternative proposals. The British prison chaplain William Douglas Morrison provided an extraordinarily interesting socio-economic account of female criminality in which he noted the relationship between economic activity and opportunities for crime.[149] Even he, however, invoked Victorian conceptions of the cloistered woman, deploring the recent entry of women into the public world of politics. For him, the recent suffrage agitations contaminated the minds of others, and 'political leagues and other female organisations of a distinctly militant character' lowered the instinctive moral nature of women.

One of the strongest challenges to the prevailing view of female criminality and the nature of the prison system came from Mary Gordon, the first woman inspector of prisons. Writing in 1922, after she retired from the service, she observed that there was little difference in the nature of criminality of men and women. She rejected the widespread use of imprisonment and described local short-term institutions as an 'expensive absurdity', a 'bad joke'. Imprisonment for women had become the machine envisaged by Bentham, with little interest or concern in the problems and emotions of prisoners. Prisons operated to produce the model prisoner, *'Discipline of a rigid, mechanical, repressive kind is over her everywhere, and she had, before all else to become a good and obedient prisoner.'*[150]

Gordon's most vehement criticisms were directed at members of her own profession of medicine. She described the usual patient/doctor relationship as one based on mutual respect and 'absolute freedom' of the patient to begin or end consultation. Inside prisons doctors act as 'punishing officials' and a patient has 'no right to his own confidences and secrets'. An integral feature of a doctor's work involved a direct collusion with penal discipline. This occurred in various ways when, for example, he '. . . carries out the "cat and mouse" regulations [force feeding of suffragettes], decides if they are fit for work, dietary punishments, solitary confinement and corporal punishments and is a witness to hangings.'[151] In all these respects and others, Gordon saw doctors as having '. . . the heaviest hand over the prisoner.'[152] Despite these criticisms, her solution for the penal system was remarkably similar to Pailthorpe's, involving the introduction of more medical and psychological expertise. What was needed was '. . . a scientific clearing and sorting house for convicted persons, with proper places of treatment provided . . . [so] that the doctor's work would soon become all important . . .'[153]

Critics such as Gordon and Morrison were rare. Few experts within the penal system offered alternative conceptions of women prisoners and the causes of their crime or challenged the operation of prisons. It was apparently becoming increasingly difficult for those within the prison system to criticize it. Morrison was dismissed from the prison service for his observations. The new reigning orthodoxy on the imprisonment of women saw all or at least the majority as emotionally disturbed and in need of treatment. It never seems to have occurred to such observers that the criminalized political actions of the suffragists were rational political acts requiring careful planning and coordination, or that the 'pilfering' of working-class women could be based on a reasoned assessment of their impoverished circumstances. For the new positivistic behavioural scientist, women, and to a lesser extent men, were ruled by forces beyond their comprehension and/or control. The economic, social and political accounts of women and girls who committed crime were ignored or transformed into phobias, complexes and neuroses.

Pailthorpe's work was a watershed in the British perceptions of the crimes and penal treatment of women. With the encouragement of the Prison Commissioners she brought the issue of psychiatric treatment of women into the public arena. Her research and efforts were instrumental in the insertion of psychiatric and psychological professionals into prisons for women through the appointment of the first medical psychotherapists in 1939 and the first psychiatric social worker in 1946.[154] Despite the creation of fresh theories and the appointment of new professionals, no new prisons or regimes were created strictly for the treatment of women in the first half of the century. The major new developments included a rather abortive experiment with institutions for habitual inebriates, the creation of the borstal system in 1908 and the introduction of open prisons in the 1930s.[155] None of these were primarily intended for women. The creation of unique penal institutions for women offenders based on these strong bio-psychological and therapeutic perspectives would not occur until the 1970s with the building of the new Holloway prison in London and Cornton Vale in Scotland.

6

Therapy and Discipline

The conception of women prisoners as intellectually deficient and emotionally disturbed gained increasing support from penal professionals and observers of the penal scene. By the 1960s most discussions and publications about women in prison reiterated such a position as if it were an iron law. In the early 1960s the prison official Michael Wolff claimed that most women prisoners and borstal girls were of an 'exceptionally low calibre' or 'mentally disturbed'.[1] John Camp's officially sanctioned account of women in prison, published in 1974, followed a similar vein. According to him the 'great majority of women offenders need some form of medical, psychiatric or remedial treatment. . . . "[2] Joanna Kelly, governor of Holloway Women's Prison from 1959–66, claimed that most women were of 'low mentality or emotionally disturbed' and that staff had to deal with '. . . a body of women of whom a large proportion are warped and thwarted.'[3] She was pleased to report that the prison department had taken steps to assess these deficiencies and provide 'treatment'. Increasingly women were being remanded to Holloway for medical, psychiatric and psychological reports involving 'progressive matrices, vocabulary tests and the I.S.B. tests' as a means of determining the 'most suitable treatment'.[4] The needs of the 300 women in Holloway were, she believed, being met by a professional staff including forty nurses, a full-time psychologist and social worker, two part-time psycho-therapists, part-time physiotherapists, chiropodists, dentists, gynaecologist, and optician. These examples illustrate the almost unquestioned conception of the needs of women prisoners, based on the assumption that they were emotionally disturbed and mentally deficient, assumptions that were firmly rooted in nineteenth-century views of women criminals.

In the remainder of the book we will consider the imprisonment of women in Britain today and explore the way the nineteenth-century legacy has played a part in the development and operation of prisons. In this chapter we will analyse the way conceptions of women and therapeutic ideals have shaped the development and operation of the two newest prisons for women and consider how women's prisons are still primarily geared to principles of discipline and punishment despite the rhetoric of therapy. In the remaining chapters we will consider other aspects of the regimes in these prisons, such as work and education, and the way the demands of discipline affect the relationships between the prisoners themselves and between prisoners and staff.

In the last decade there have been two major developments in the prison system for women in Britain, the rebuilding of Holloway prison in London during the 1970s and the building of Cornton Vale prison in Scotland in 1975. Analysing some of the policy documents preceeding the opening of these new institutions helps reveal the legacy of past policies and beliefs and explain the modern form of women's prisons and contemporary thinking about the female prisoner. Following them into the prisons themselves helps elucidate the actual practices in prison regimes and the daily life of a prisoner. It must be remembered that neither of these prisons was intended to house a particular type of female offender, with both prisons serving large geographical areas and broad sections of offenders. So whatever the aims, ideals, and practice of these institutions, they may be assumed to be based on beliefs about the nature and needs of women prisoners in general.

Planning the New Prisons

There was a surprising lack of published material produced while these institutions were being conceived and established. In both cases, the existing material relies heavily on, or is the product of, internally produced data, and presents a consensus view of all aspects of the imprisonment of women. No independent research was commissioned or even drawn upon in the plans and there is no evidence of debate or conflict. Although a decade or so later, a parliamentary sub-committee taking evidence on women and the penal system could find very little agreement among prison staff, inmates, academics, or clinicians,[5] this was not evident in the planning of the new institutions.

In preparation for the opening of Cornton Vale, a working party was set up to make recommendations for 'the treatment and training of female inmates in Scotland'. The membership of the working party included: administrative members of the prison department, the governor and principal officer of Greenock (at that time the main women's prison in Scotland), the consultant psychiatrist who had worked at Greenock for years, and an academic in social work who had conducted research on borstal girls at Greenock. Papers were submitted to the working party, and a report which is essentially a policy document for Cornton Vale was circulated.

Several points emerge clearly from this document. Firstly, there is an almost unstated and certainly unsubstantiated assumption of psychiatric morbidity among the prospective Cornton Vale population. It is stated as a matter of fact that

> . . . in any institutional setting for women or girl delinquents, because of the very high incidence of psychiatric disorder and emotionally disturbed personalities there are always likely to be more people who appear to require individual therapy than are able to get it . . .[6]

From this assumption, the other main emphases of the report logically follow. Indeed, nine pages of a sixteen-page report are devoted to the supposed psychiatric needs of women in prison.

Thus, the 'hospital' is conceived as the hub of the prison. The report states that

> [the new institution] will have its own hospital with both in and out patients. It has been planned to maintain an appropriate environment for inmate patient care, where personnel management, development of personal and working relationships and development of educational programmes may revolve around the individual care of the patient.[7]

This hospital, the report states, 'will be unique in its facilities for the management and treatment of personality disorders.' In such a scheme, the psychiatrist, of course, has a key role

> . . . the professional function [of the psychiatrist] is not only to discuss cases, to try to interpret behaviour and help in the management of all inmates (whether 'psychiatric' or not) but is also to be involved in a more general way in discussions of policy, and should have suggestions and advice to give about all policy matters . . . a psychiatrist will either be directly or at least marginally involved in the assessment of every case.[8]

Various devices are employed to co-opt all aspects of the regime under the rubric of treatment. For example, Cornton Vale is presented as a 'therapeutic community', defined in the broadest possible way, the assumption being that once this has been stated to be the case, everything that happens must be therapeutic.

> . . . the therapeutic community simply means trying to establish a total regime in which everything is geared towards the therapy and rehabilitation of the individual, and where the negative aspects of institutional life, which can undoubtedly exist, are either completely eliminated or reduced as far as possible. Therapeutic community developments in fact have taken place in certain penal institutions and in certain approved schools . . . and conditions of security have been considered to be of great value and in themselves made a useful contributions to the therapeutic community development in relation to the treatment of hardened offenders.[9]

'Security' had been defined in terms of its therapeutic value – indeed, this is the only context in which the discipline system is discussed. There is no other mention of it at all in the entire report. And discipline staff are to be mainly therapists;

> It is very important to emphasize that psychiatric treatment as such cannot be separated from the total care of the resident of the institution. Hence it is very important not to think exclusively in terms of individual treatment being carried out only by psychiatrist, social workers, or psychologist. In fact, this is a situation in which many members may have a part to play.[10]

Similar themes emerge from papers and statements relating to the redevelopment of Holloway. In July 1968, the Prison Department set up the Holloway Project Group with representatives from the Prison Department and the Department of Health and Social Security in order to 'work out and develop the basic principles of the scheme.'[11] The Home Office Research Unit was asked to make a study of the number of children belonging to women received into Holloway during 1967 and their family circumstances[12] and was given access to information collected by Gibbens of the Maudsley Hospital for his medico-social survey of women received into the prison.[13] By December 1968, James Callaghan, the then Home Secretary, stated in answer to a parliamentary question, that the main feature of the programme to re-shape the system of female penal establishments in England and Wales was to demolish the existing prison at Holloway and build an establishment that was basically a secure hospital. The central features would be medical and psychiatric facilities, and normal custodial facilities would comprise a relatively small part of the establishment. Moreover, the new Holloway was to be designed so that, if and when it was no longer needed as a prison, it could be handed over to the National Health Service and used as a mental hospital.[14]

It is worth considering Gibbens's work in some detail since it was significant in the deliberations of the Holloway Project Group. In 1967, Gibbens sampled every fourth woman who entered Holloway, including those remanded before or after conviction as well as those sentenced to imprisonment. His aim, like those of Pailthorpe and Burt before him, was a 'medico-social survey' of imprisoned women. His methodology is more or less unexplained, except that we are told each woman was interviewed by a social worker, and a proportion of the sample was given a 'psychiatric assessment' by Gibbens himself. The findings are hardly elaborated from table form. Before embarking on a description of his study, Gibbens offers some generalizations about the nature of women offenders, among whom 'psychological and social disturbance' is common. On the subject of young offenders, he relies heavily on the work of Cowie, Cowie and Slater[15] concluding that 'clinically a high proportion of wayward girls are obviously seriously disordered psychologically'. Gibbens' categories of 'abnormality' among women include physical ill-health, mental ill-health, history of in-patient treatment, suicide attempts, alcoholism, venereal diseases, current pregnancy, and past or present prostitution. Many women in Holloway, he states, suffer from 'personality or behaviour disorders', and 'the heavy load of physical and mental illness and abnormality makes a women's prison into something approaching a secure hospital.'[16]

In another paper based on a sample of women remanded in Holloway for medical (psychiatric) reports, he admits that, currently, psychiatrists may have little or nothing to offer people with 'personality disorders' (which are undefined). In only 9 per cent of the large number of women remanded for medical reports did psychiatrists recommend a psychiatric disposal, such as committal to a mental hospital or probation with the condition of psychiatric treatment. For a large group (53 per cent of the whole sample of those categorized by Gibbens as suffering from 'personality disorders' which 'included a wide range from the moderate to the severely psychopathic'), the doctors had to advise that 'treatment was unlikely to be available or helpful.'[17] Some of these women, we are told, were remanded more than once during the year, 'as if the magistrates were reluctant to believe that nothing could be offered.' By saying that treatment was unlikely to be 'available or helpful' Gibbens implies that no effective 'treatment' for 'personality disorders' is known. However, discussing this group of women in his more general paper, he says,

There is a less seriously disordered group [than those confined in special hospitals] for whom variations of assistance, support, persuasion, pressure and even compulsion for a time, are required. These problems will only be resolved when there is a closer and more flexible liaison between prisons, hospitals, and community services, and this will take some time. But it may come about first in relation to women offenders.[18]

This vague statement is the only thing approaching a policy suggestion, and the final sentence presumably refers back to an earlier observation that 'the new Holloway prison is designed, in fact, as a medically-oriented establishment.'[19] It seems that from the outset, the Holloway Project Group only wished to consult research supporting their pre-conceived ideas and these appear to continue in the vein of psychological and physiological explanations that had come to dominate the thinking at that time. The Radical Alternatives to Prison (RAP) pamphlet *Alternatives to Holloway* points out that until the beginning of major rebuilding work in 1971 'no plans had appeared nor were there published research data or documents to support either the fundamental policy changes [to a therapeutic system] or the maintenance of the old policy of secure confinement of women offenders.'[20]

The Therapeutic Ideal

Therapy was the dominant theme, and was presented as the central purpose of both Holloway and Cornton Vale prisons. Three linked sets of beliefs have contributed to the importance given to 'therapy' in the planning of contemporary women's prisons: the view that women *per se* are more mentally unstable then men;[21] the long-standing assumption that women offenders are by definition mentally disordered, or at least acting out of (stereotypically female) character;[22] and the view, also strongly evident in the nineteenth century, that women prisoners are more 'difficult' than men prisoners, that is that they react to imprisonment itself in a more extreme and more neurotic way than do men.[23]

In some quarters these three statements have acquired the status of unquestioned assumptions and they are certainly treated as such in the background to the development of Cornton Vale and Holloway. Such research as was referred to, and that was scant, itself used these assumptions as its starting point.[24]

The implications of the broadness of definition of mental disorder among women in general, women offenders, and women in prison, are that women in prison are *triply* mad, and that unlike men in prison, all are in need of treatment. At the same time as Holloway and Cornton Vale were being established as 'therapeutic' institutions to serve the supposed needs of unselected populations of women offenders, the psycho-therapist of ten years' standing at Wormwood Scrubs men's prison stated that 'Psychotherapy can be of benefit to only a limited number of [male] prisoners, even by using group and community therapy methods . . .'[25]

It is a truism that 'therapy' and 'discipline' are necessarily conflicting goals. One of Giallombardo's theses in her work on women's prisons is that 'Formal organisations that attempt to maximise both punishment and treatment oriented goals will be characterized by internal conflict.'[26] However, a corollary of the belief that all women prisoners are mentally disordered seems to be that anything that is done to women in prison may be defined as 'therapy'. The Cornton Vale Working Party Report[27] does, in fact, use the words 'therapy', 'treatment', and 'training' interchangeably, and this verbal sleight of hand is as nothing compared, as will be seen, with what happens in practice.

For both Cornton Vale and Holloway, there seems to have been a reluctance to deal with the questions of discipline, security and punishment that have always formed a major part of the prison regime, or perhaps there was an assumption that these questions would become irrelevant within the new therapeutic environment.

Discussions about both Cornton Vale and Holloway are marked by a linguistic ambivalence. Prisoners are 'inmates' or 'residents'. The prison is an 'institution', a 'therapeutic community', or a 'hospital'. Cells are 'rooms'. The hard fact of physical containment seems difficult to reconcile and the ambivalence also appears in the appearance, if not the purpose, of the architecture. For example, Faulkner, a Home Office official, describes the plans for the new Holloway as follows:

> Only a part of the site will have a conventional perimeter wall. Where possible, the buildings will themselves form the perimeter (with suitable security precautions), and in this way it will be possible not only to make the fullest use of the limited area available, but also to avoid the forbidding appearance of a security wall along the front of the site. Within the perimeter, the buildings will be grouped around a green to give an open aspect while preserving a high degree of supervision.[28]

A prison officer interviewed at Cornton Vale described the perimeter of the prison in this way; 'the wire fence surrounding the institution in no way spoils the view, but provides us with just about the right amount of privacy'. This is in contrast to nineteenth-century prison architecture which produced awe-inspiring forbidding fortresses uncompromisingly dedicated to punishment and discipline.

Building for Therapy

Cornton Vale is the only purpose-built penal establishment for women in Scotland. It is situated in Central Scotland, outside Stirling and within a forty-mile radius of Dundee, Edinburgh, Glasgow and Perth. All convicted women and young offenders in Scotland and almost all those remanded for background reports, or awaiting trial or sentence, are held at Cornton. A few women are remanded in the female wing at Aberdeen, Dumfries and Inverness prisons. The prison opened in April 1975, and became fully operational the following year. Most people, seeing Cornton Vale for the first time, do not realize that it is a prison; it merges into the contemporary landscape. It has been variously described as like a housing estate or holiday camp, or university campus. It consists of low white clusters of buildings set among neat gardens. The bars at the windows are designed to look decorative rather than functional and the perimeter fence is unobtrusive wire netting.

Within the perimeter fence, the prison complex consists of an administration block, a 'communal' block, housing the workshops, laundry, kitchen, gymnasium, education unit and library, a health centre, a recently added chaplaincy centre and five blocks in which different categories of prisoners live. There is room for 219 women, though it is rarely, if ever, full. Outside the fence are staff housing and a staff restaurant.

The residential blocks are known throughout the prison by their code names. The remand block (Romeo) contains all women detained on remand and has 41 rooms. The prison block (Papa) has 55 rooms for adult convicted women. The secure block (Sierra) has 27 rooms for adults undergoing 'assessment' at the beginning of their sentences and those women deemed to require a more 'secure' regime. The borstal block (Bravo) has now changed, but during the research contained 55 rooms for young women between the ages of 16 and 21 undergoing a two-year period of borstal training. After November 1983, borstal training was phased out, and all under 21s are now classified as young offenders. The young offenders' block (Yankee) has 41 rooms for under 21s.

Each residential block is divided into 'family units' consisting of seven single rooms along two sides of a corridor. One of the rooms is larger than the rest, designed to accommodate a mother and baby. Each room has its own wash-hand basin, bed, table and chair. Women have a room each and rarely is there a need to double up. There is a bathroom area in each unit containing bath, shower, wash-hand basin and toilets. There is also a store-room, kitchen, and living/dining room in which all meals are taken. The staff offices are at the end of the corridor between the individual rooms and the unit's communal facilities.

Everywhere in the prison is immaculately clean and polished. Walls are painted white and the untraditional prison windows let in plenty of light, and the constant sight of the world outside. The kitchens are modern and well equipped and the living/dining rooms comfortably furnished with round table and chairs, easy chairs, coffee tables and bookcases. Each room is connected by a two-way speaker to the Administration Block. All the blocks except Papa have electronically locking room doors, which means that as long as there is no technological breakdown, women have access to night-time sanitation. With a request through the two-way speaker, the room door can be electronically unlocked and left open for eight minutes. The inmates of three of the Papa block units have keys to their own rooms. But women occupying the other five units in Papa block have no access to toilet facilities during the night. Since being given a key is a privilege granted after some time, it is one that many adults serving short-term sentences are never given.

The old Holloway, built in the mid-nineteenth century for male prisoners, had a looming facade modelled on Warwick Castle, with towers and a massive gate. Behind the facade, it was a typical example of a Victorian prison, with long wings and tiny cells. Redevelopment began in 1970, and as with Cornton Vale, a group living plan was adopted as the basic unit. Women live in units of 16, each unit having some communal space. Within the units women live in single rooms or four-bedded dormitories.

Holloway has room for 500 women, but unlike Cornton Vale is often overcrowded. Situated in North London, it is the Remand Centre for the South Midlands and South-East of England and is the closed prison for the whole of the South of England. It is composed of various 'wings' including the psychiatric wing, the mother and baby wing, the drug addiction wing, the punishment wing, the hospital wing. There is also an occupational therapy centre, an education centre, a gymnasium, and prison officer's quarters. The intention was to classify prisoners according to the treatment they needed.

These designs were to embody new approaches to the confinement of women based on the assumptions of the policy papers. However, much of the discussion in the Working Party Report for Cornton Vale and in the papers relating to Holloway is at best unclear and at worst meaningless. For example, labels such as 'mental disorder', 'emotional disturbance' and 'personality disorder', are used with abandon, and in ways that are ill-defined or undefined. Cornton Vale is described as a 'therapeutic community', although the necessary conditions proposed by the coiner of the phrase, Maxwell Jones, are all absent.[29] We are told there will be 'group therapy' and 'group counselling' at Cornton Vale, the former apparently to deal with 'deep-seated emotional problems' and the latter 'with less serious ones'. The content of such sessions is unspecified.

Thus, in the thinking behind the design of the new women's prisons, female prisoners were defined as a group qualitatively different from male prisoners; they were mentally ill. Their prisons were to be hospitals for treatment. However, the confusion, unexamined assumptions, and ambivalence of language became very obvious when we looked at what happened in practice in terms of 'therapy' and 'discipline' at Cornton Vale Prison.

Therapy in Practice

As we have described, the Working Party Report saw 'therapy' as the main aim of Cornton Vale, and throughout the decade since it opened this has been reiterated in official statements. In 1977, the then governor of Cornton Vale stated at a symposium on prison architecture that 'Our brief was to create an institution totally geared to treatment – using this term in its widest sense.' In 1982 the Prison Inspectorate's report on Cornton Vale began thus:

> In the relatively short period of six years, Cornton Vale has successfully achieved most of the objectives identified by the Working Party. . . . The drive and determination of the Governor and enthusiastic support of members of staff have made the concept of a caring community within a secure perimeter a reality.[30]

However, having spent a great deal of time in the prison observing daily life, and conducting lengthy interviews and discussions with

prisoners and staff, we will present a more detailed account of dail
life in the prison and medical, psychiatric and social work practic
that would suggest an alternative evaluation.

As we have described, the Working Party Report represented th
Health Centre as the potential hub of the prison, and th
psychiatrists as playing a key role in the prison regime. The 'aims' o
the Health Centre as they appeared in the working Party Repo
were as follows:

1. To investigate offenders suffering from behaviour which may
    call for a psychiatric approach and require observation in a
    special unit.
2. To investigate the mental condition of offenders, the nature of
    whose offence suggests mental disorder.
3. To explore the problem of emotionally disturbed inmates and
    to provide treatment or managment to which they might
    respond.

It was 'to provide accommodation for those inmates who b
reasons of their behaviour are considered to be requirin
psychiatric investigation or treatment.' Yet no terms were defined
there was no elaboration of what 'treatment' meant and th
distinction between the first and third 'aims' of the Health Centr
was unclear. In fact, although the Health Centre had been designe
so that it would be a self-supporting complex and had enoug
single rooms for nine women, these rooms had never been used
Instead, those for whom this complex was probably intended sper
much of their sentences languishing in the punishment cell
During our period of observation, there was a debate between th
nursing sister in charge of the Health Centre and the priso
administration about opening up the Health Centre rooms an
staffing the centre with prison officers. The sister, who disagree
with much prison policy, refused as she felt that unless staffed b
trained nurses the Health Centre would inevitably become a
extension of the punishment cells. This impasse kept the room
empty until towards the end of our period of research, and whe
the sister left, the rooms were promptly staffed with officers dealin
with a small group of 'difficult' women on a daytime basi
According to the Inspectorate Report, this is still the curre
situation as a 'shortage of suitably trained medical support staff ha
not made it possible to operate the centre as originally envisaged.'
This statement, we would argue, reflects the reluctance of th
prison department to engage civilian staff whose ideas abo
'treatment' may conflict with prison practice.

Psychiatry and Drama Therapy

Cornton Vale had more psychiatric resources than any other Scottish Penal establishment, and twice as much as the former women's prison at Greenock. In addition there were the services of visiting general practitioners and of a team of social workers. There were four visiting psychiatrists who each did two sessions a week. There was one psychologist in attendance two days a week, and at one time, a drama therapist worked in the prison one day a week.

However, the roles of these professionals were far removed from that envisaged in the Working Party Report. All women were seen on admission, except those sentenced for 24 days or less for unpaid fines. One purpose of this was to identify individuals for transfer to mental hospitals. This, of course, could also happen at any time during a sentence. Some women were seen periodically throughout their sentence by psychiatric staff. This has been optimistically described by a Cornton Vale psychiatrist as a 'limited programme of psychotherapy'. There is also a certain amount of 'group therapy.' In addition, the psychiatrists described their function as 'explanation and reassurance to staff' and 'occasional intervention in prison regime'. We shall look at each of these areas of activity in turn.

There seemed to be two main categories of prisoners who might be seen after the admission interview and/or on some periodic basis, namely those with a previous record of psychiatric treatment (in-patient or out-patient) and those in prison for particular sorts of crimes, notably violence and neglect, injury, or killing of a child. As one woman convicted of child injury put it, 'They assumed I was mad because of the case.' There are some crimes, it seems, that a woman must be 'insane' to commit. A few individuals established a strong personal relationship with a psychiatrist, using him as a confidante, and most found them pleasant on a personal level. However, on the whole, the women we interviewed did not find contact particularly helpful. The five women who had already experienced stays in mental hospitals, and were singled out for psychiatric treatment, mostly had very negative feelings about psychiatrists and the effectiveness of psychiatric treatment. Three of the five had a history of discharging themselves from mental hospitals and the two convicted of culpable homicide of a child both rejected psychiatric treament, having found it unhelpful.

Group therapy as conducted by the psychiatric staff consisted solely of one session a week led by one of the psychiatrists. This was available only for borstal girls and young offenders during their six-week assessment and at the beginning of a long sentence. Almost without exception, the girls we interviewed described it as useless, and our observation of several of these sessions revealed why. The group of about six women met in a large, rather comfortless, room with chairs arranged in a circle. Open discussion in these groups was impossible because of the constant presence of a prison officer, which meant that the institution and staff could not be criticized, language had to be restrained, and there could be no undue show of emotion. The prison officer was not there as a participant in group therapy, but as a guard on proceedings. Statements made by women that went counter to approved Cornton Vale morality, such as 'I don't like working', drew conventional replies from the psychiatrists during these sessions. There were many embarrassed pauses, broken by polite conversation from girls rescuing a sticky social situation. Typical comments about the values of these sessions were 'It's just a skive – you just sit there and don't say anything,' and, 'Dr X's groups are alright, but there's an officer there, it makes you feel as if you don't want to say anything.'

It was predicted that one of the psychiatrists' functions would be 'explanation and reassurance to discipline staff and occasional intervention in prison regime.'[32] However, our discussions and interviews with discipline staff revealed that, on the whole, they saw psychiatric staff as lacking in understanding of 'grass roots' problems. The main opportunity for communication between psychiatric and discipline staff occurred at weekly staff meetings at which discussion of individual cases, as well as other matters, took place. All grades of prison staff were present, and the meetings were inhibited affairs directed by hierarchical prison etiquette. We observed that basic grade officers obey this etiquette, speaking only when spoken to. It was difficult to imagine any meaningful communication occurring between psychiatrists and officers in such a situation, since they were in no way meeting as equals. Rather, pronouncements were made by one group (the psychiatrists) and listened to submissively by another. Linked to the whole question of 'explanation and reassurance to discipline staff' was the issue of 'intervention' in the prison regime. Prison regimes, based primarily on security, are inflexible, and only exceptionally did intervention occur. On these rare occasions, the manner in which suggested policy was carried out usually ensured that while the letter of the law might be followed, the spirit was not. A prime example of this, which we describe in detail at a later point, was the intervention of a psychiatrist to ensure that a borstal girl could keep her baby, born during her sentence. She was allowed to keep her baby with her but under such rigid conditions that the point of mother and child being together was negated.

It is, of course, arguable whether 'therapy', and 'counselling' fail because they are in themselves mostly ineffective strategies,[33] and therefore their application at Cornton Vale is inappropriate, or because they are carried out in a deficient manner. Studies conducted in the California prison system suggest that both group counselling and individual psychotherapy *can* sometimes be of use if continued in a stable group for a long time – conditions not met with at Cornton Vale.[34]

One obvious way of gauging the value of therapy is what, if anything, prisoners feel they gain from it. While most of those interviewed thought that the individual and group therapy offered by the psychiatrists was of little benefit, this was not true of another form of 'group therapy' which occurred at Cornton Vale. During the six-week assessment session, borstal girls and young offenders serving nine months or more attended a weekly drama therapy session. The drama therapist had fought, according to her account, a hard battle to exclude officers from these sessions although they had been invited to participate as members of the therapy sessions. No one had taken up this invitation, and drama therapy was regarded by the staff with almost uniform hostility and suspicion, although one or two members of staff acknowledged that if the girls themselves felt they gained something then it was worth retaining. Staff suspicion arose from their own exclusion and from the knowledge that there were no restrictions on what was said or how it was said in these groups. More specifically, the girls swore and criticized the prison regime and staff. According to staff, these sessions were disruptive since girls returned from them 'high' and were difficult to control. It was certainly true that the atmosphere of the drama therapy sessions was completely different from the usual suppressed atmosphere of the rest of the prison. In this sense, the sessions could be construed as 'disruptive'. On the other hand, they offered a rare opportunity for the expression of emotion and airing of grievances through techniques of role-play and the acting out of situations. Many girls echoed these sentiments.

> That's the only place where you can let your feelings out. I feel a lot better afterwards.

> Dr's groups are good but E's [the drama therapist] are better. We should get to have her the whole time. The staff think she's a

> crackpot but it's them who are. You can relax there and get things
> off your chest.

Not everyone felt positively about drama therapy. Some people
rejected the whole idea of airing problems in front of other people.

> I don't think the groups do much good. I don't like talking about
> my problems in front of other people.

A few agreed with the officer's estimation of drama therapy.

> Her groups are a lot of rubbish. People jump about and swear all
> the time. They never do it anywhere else.

> People go there just to abuse and swear. She tells you it's a safe
> place and you can do what you want, but you've got to learn to
> control yourself, so what's the point.

One important example of a girl who felt she'd been very much
helped by drama therapy was a borstal girl convicted of child injury.
Because of her offence she met with a great deal of hostility from
other girls, culminating with her 'cracking up'[35] during her
assessment period after a campaign of abuse from fellow inmates, led
by one particularly dominant person. For 'cracking up', she met
with the usual reaction and was put on report, and because of her
'uncontrollable' behaviour and 'for her own protection' was placed
in a punishment cell, in solitary confinement. The offending girls
had also been placed on report, which turned out to be yet another
cause of hostility. At the same time, the officer's report of these
incidents acknowledged the girl's need for help rather than
punishment, and so she was referred to the psychiatrist whom she
found 'not helpful'. Confinement in the punishment cell had been a
traumatic experience. Shortly afterwards, all the girls involved
(including the victim) had attended a drama therapy session and a
great deal of hostility was openly expressed. Instead of being
instantly suppressed, it was used to open up and air the whole
situation. The girl who had been the object of aggression had found
this a turning point in her relationship with other prisoners.
Although she felt that because of her crime she would 'never be
popular', she felt that from this date her life in prison became at least
tolerable. The aggressors said that as a result of the drama therapy
sessions, they had gained a great deal more understanding of why the
girl had injured her child. Many felt that by providing a legitimate
situation for the release of tension, incidents which would otherwise
have resulted in discipline reports were avoided.

Medical Care

The doctor was a local general practioner (GP) who attended the prison daily. There were complaints from almost every one we interviewed about access to the doctor.[36] Although the procedure was the same as for social workers, requests for social workers were rarely questioned by prison officers but requests to see a doctor were very often met with questioning (Why? Can't it wait? etc.). The Health Centre nurse constituted a further similar barrier and people often felt that they were being 'fobbed off' with the nurse when they really needed to see a doctor. A typical comment was 'They say "Doctor'll think you're daft". Then you have to get through the nurse.'

In some cases, it seemed treatment which depended for its administration on prison officers was not carried out. In one case, a woman said,

> I saw the gynaecologist and he said I was to wear cotton underwear. I put in a request for it fifteen weeks ago, but I haven't got it yet. You get granted a thing but you don't get it.

Many people complained that they were not taken seriously.

> It's a contrast with outside. They don't seem to bother. They don't take you seriously.

> I went three times for sickness and stomach aches. He just said grow up – there's nothing the matter with you.

> The doctors are terrible. They answer you before you've finished telling them what's wrong. They assume it's your imagination when you've really got something wrong with you.

The rate of GP consultation was about twice that of the average community. It seemed clear that many of the complaints which prisoners took to the doctor could be connected with the extreme stress suffered in prison, for example, eczema, asthma, migraine, ulcers, rashes. In addition, there was a large number of self-inflicted injuries including friction burns and sewing machine needles inserted into flesh.

The women perceived the medical reaction to their health problems as labelling of all symptoms as 'imaginary' and based on the assumption that their motivation was to get off work and 'attract attention'. Overall, prisoners did not feel that their complaints were treated seriously, and thought that there was a risk of their symptoms being misdiagnosed and that conditions stemming from stress and anxiety were discounted. 'Demanding attention' was not regarded as a legitimate plea for help, and once behaviour had been labelled in this way, it was assumed that the correct reaction was to ignore it. However, there are two reasons why this reaction may be particularly misplaced at Cornton Vale. Firstly, doctors are traditionally people to whom others take problems and confide intimate details to be held in the strictest confidence. This becomes a very significant element in the transactions between doctor and patient in the collusive atmosphere of a prison. Secondly, direct airing of grievances and frustrations stemming from the institution itself was not only discouraged, but punishable. Indeed, this was true of any strong expression of emotion. Given such repression, it may be that 'presenting' problems of the sort taken to doctors should have been taken very seriously, particularly when they become manifest as self-injury. The doctors were a natural focus for problems, but despite the rhetoric of therapy they did not appear to exploit their role in order to help prisoners, and the prison regime did not encourage such 'therapeutic' forms of contact.

Social Work and Legal Advice

Another service available to prisoners was that offered by the team of four social workers. During our period of research, the team was a very efficient one. Reports were kept absolutely up-to-date, and problems were dealt with quickly. Prisoners obtained access to a social worker by putting in a request to a prison officer and they were usually met the same day. Most of the women interviewed appreciated the speed and efficiency of the social work team, and there were no complaints about access, or delay in having problems dealt with.

While social workers were seen to deal with practical problems which had some tangible solution, many often had strong emotional content as well, such as problems concerning children in care. The sort of problems that women said they had taken to a social worker fell into four broad categories. First, problems connected with imminent release, such as accommodation, employment, eligibility for an NFA, a 'no fixed abode' grant. Second, practical problems occurring outside, such as the payment of insurance stamps or rent. Third, problems to do with legal and court matters which may or may not be related to the original offence, such as appeals, pending cases, divorce proceedings, custody proceedings. Fourth, problems with family outside, such as contact with children, children in care, marital relationships, general family relationships. In our interviews and discussions with prisoners, it seemed that social workers were perceived as being there to deal with practical problems to do with their life outside, which, because of their confinement, they could not deal with themselves. As one woman said, 'You're very dependent in here on people like that because you can't do anything for yourself.' In fact, many of the things that social workers did for prisoners, they could very easily have done for themselves if they were given even slightly more self-determination. At the same time, the fact that people were rendered so helpless clashed with a favourite tenet of social work philosophy, that people should be encouraged towards self-help. This led to 'token' self-help, for example where a prisoner was physically made to write a letter dictated by a social worker, and the characterization of prisoners as intrinsically helpless, rather than as rendered so by the institution. Furthermore, the training and philosophy of many social workers have encouraged them to regard clients' problems as 'presenting' rather than 'genuine'. This could lead to a failure to recognize the reality of problems that affect prisoners, particularly where these lay in a field outside traditional social worker expertise.

This was particularly marked with regard to legal problems, with an apparent failure on the part of social workers to recognize prisoners' needs for proper legal advice. Whether or not prisoners got such advice depended almost entirely on their own, or their family's, awareness of such need. For example, we spent one morning with one of the social workers seeing five women newly admitted on remand. All were asked whether they had a lawyer and whether he or she had been or would be notified. If they had no lawyer, there appeared to be no provision for getting them one. They would then have to depend on the duty lawyer at court when they got there. The question of appealing against remand in custody was never raised, even though it was difficult to see why any of the five women in question had been so remanded. All were trivial charges except one who hadn't been charged at all. Three of the women had been charged with fairly minor theft and one with defrauding the Department of Health and Social Security by not declaring her earnings as a cleaner. The case of the woman who had not been charged was not followed up in any practical way by the social workers, although the soical worker did say she was inclined to believe the story since the prisoner's husband had a building business and they owned their own house. Three of the five women were employed, and very anxious that their employers shouldn't know they were there, and two had pre-school children for whom they had to make sudden and makeshift arrangements. Also in the area of legal advice, several interviewees reported a tendency not to encourage inmates to appeal against their sentences even when they felt they might have a good case.

The general discounting of the relevance of legal expertise seemed to stem from two factors. Firstly, the rigidly hierarchical structure of Cornton Vale discouraged any challenging of the decisions of authority. Once made, it was the function of the institution to carry out decisions, not to question them. Secondly, the conception of Cornton Vale as a 'therapeutic' establishment encouraged the view that women had been put there 'for their own good'. The crime itself and the justice of the sentence were less relevant. While this second factor fitted naturally with much of the philosophy of social work, it might be thought that there would be conflict inherent in the first for 'professionals' trained to work usually in less hierarchical and more self-critical situations. This did not seem to be so, both because of an ability, already noted, to construe almost *anything* as therapeutic, and because of the particularly collusive adaptation of the social workers to the prison, an adaptation that went under the guise of 'good communication'.

There are some general comments to be made about the different aspects of the so-called therapeutic regime just described. We shall look at the deficiencies in the psychiatric help available, at the implicit view of 'personality' held by the prison staff, and at the varying adaptations made by groups other than discipline staff to the prison regime.

There were various problems in the way that psychiatric help was dispensed at Cornton Vale. It seemed that the psychiatrists defined need for help in terms of criminal and mental health history and not in terms of the stresses of imprisonment *per se*. In addition, there was the problem of referral. In the community, the usual pattern is that you are sent or taken to psychiatrists. In prison, as in the community, referring yourself to a psychiatrist is often seen as defining yourself as mad. Similarly, prisoners tended to reject other people's definitions of their need for psychiatrist help, and as part of the rejection, could see no point in the contact. It is interesting to note that the women we interviewed who, for example, *requested* social work help were by and large satisfied with the outcome, whereas those who were its unsolicited recipients were dissatisfied. The forms of therapy defined as the most successful were those where a definite task was to be done, (such as learning relaxation techniques, or role playing a particular situation suggested by the drama therapist), which did not require the prisoner to initiate action.

However, the main block to whatever genuine help might be possible through therapy or treatment, is the overall tone of prison policy which officially denies that the crime 'matters' and thus denies the need for grief or guilt relating to it, the blocking of any criticism of prison policy or personnel, and the meeting of any sort of emotional outburst with suppression and/or punishment.

While it might be assumed that a proposal for any institution attempting to effect radical change in people might rest on the most solid theories of social behaviour available at the time, there was no reference anywhere in the Working Party Report to any theoretical foundations for the proposals. Nevertheless, observation of the way in which the daily routine at Cornton Vale operates indicates that some sort of tacit working conception of 'personality' did emerge.

This conception of personality was at its most explicit in the operation of the 'grade system' – which was the basis of the borstal system, but also used for long-term young offenders. The grade system is essentially a crude behaviour modification regime based on a mixture of punishment and reward. It is inherited from the mark and progressive systems of the nineteenth century and as such is deeply embedded in prison regimes. During the course of an indeterminate borstal sentence, girls progressed from Grade III to Grade II to Grade I, after which they were given their liberation dates. Borstal training was for two years, but could be completed in a minimum of about a year, depending on the speed with which one progressed through the grades. Girls were then released on licence/parole for whatever was left of the two years. As can be imagined, this was a powerful incentive for girls to attempt to do whatever may have been demanded by the regime. An assessment booklet was kept on each girl. 'Behaviour'; 'attitude to staff', 'attitude to girls', and 'cleanliness' were assessed by staff at regular intervals by a tick put in an appropriate column – very good; good +; good; fair +; fair; poor. Girls were shown these 'assessments' and they were considered at the monthly staff meetings at which it was decided whether or not a girl should go up a grade. Going up a grade meant primarily getting nearer the gate, but it also involved privileges such as television, record player, later bedtimes, being allowed to wear trousers, more money, and less staff interference.

The use of pre-selected one-word assessments and the actual categories of behaviour to be assessed represented, in telling shorthand, the view of personality held within the prison and what the prison regarded as the 'right' reaction to imprisonment. Categories for assessment (which bear striking resemblance to those proposed by Fry), that is 'behaviour', 'attitude to staff', 'attitude to girls' and 'cleanliness' were all to do with outward manifestations of emotional and mental state and the implication was that it was only the outward manifestations that mattered or indeed existed. What counted as 'good', 'fair' or 'poor' could be guaged from the comments of the girls and women and of prison staff, and from prison social work reports.

'Good' behaviour and attitudes seemed to rest on a phrase 'keeping things nice' which cropped up continually in conversations and interviews with prisoners on the topic of coping with imprisonment. Thus, one woman said of the psychologist, 'She's the only person here who doesn't stop you saying how you feel. The staff won't let you – you've got to keep everything nice for them.' 'Keeping everything nice' meant not expressing how your really felt, but presenting a bland image. A borstal girl commenting on the grade system said, 'They tell you to be yourself. When you are, you get into trouble.' Two further comments typify how the grade system operated in the view of the borstal girls and young offenders: 'To get your grade, you have to watch your attitude, not have a carry-on and treat all staff the same' and 'You have to like the staff, or not show that you don't.' Borstal girls and young offenders emphasised the aims of the grade system as being to encourage and reward quiescence and conformity and self-suppression. Supporting evidence of this was found in social work reports in which the comments of prison staff at grade promotion meetings reappeared as unquestioned fact in social work reports, for example in the following cases:

> This girl has come on by leaps and bounds since her admission. She has a slight temper, but seems to be able to control it now.

> Good reports for everything. She is seen as a good influence. After a long discussion among staff, it was decided that she was too forward and could do with another month before promotion.

> Very good effort again. She is trying to improve but still likes the last word. She is loud but this is probably quite natural in her home background. (Medication recommended to quieten her down).

Social worker reports of their own interactions with prisoners supported the view that expression of emotion was not encouraged. Constant cheerfulness appeared to be demanded. One social worker reported of a prisoner

M. would hardly talk at all. She would not smile and snarled at me, "don't feel like smiling". I decided not to wait to be scowled at – and left her glowering, having made it clear that it was not part of my duty to try to coax spoilt brats into better moods.

This fear on the part of staff of confronting emotion was articulated by one prisoner who said of her social worker.

She'd die if I said I had a problem. She's very nice, but a barrier goes up when I really need her.

Few members of prison or non-prison staff challenged the way in which the prison regime worked, but instead they found modes of adapting to the regime. One mode of adaptation was that adopted by the social work department within the prison. It was known as 'good communication' and was extolled by the 1983 Inspectorate Report:

Relationships and communications between the unit and the Regional Social Work Department on the one hand and with senior management staff, and all departments within the establishment on the other are quite excellent. The measure of understanding and integration which has been achieved represents the ideal arrangment and reflects great credit on all members of staff in the social work unit and all departments in the establishment.[37]

Relationships were indeed acknowledged as 'excellent' by both officers and social workers. It was obvious from prison records, and it was claimed by both groups, that a great deal of information about prisoners was shared. Prisoners' fears and feelings about lack of confidentiality and invasion of privacy appeared to be well grounded. Prison officers were present at visits, and censored all mail. Information gathered in these ways was freely passed to social workers as is shown by the following extracts from social work reports, all of which were based on the reports made by prison officers of conversations overheard at visiting times:

J . . . told her visitor that she was not pregnant. Mr H. asked me to check as this would influence the decision regarding a visit with her boyfriend [this was because under 21s were not allowed visits from boyfriends unless they were the father or about to become the father of their child].

I was told by Prison Officer X that her boyfriend wants her to have an abortion.

I inquired of staff to find out what kind of visit M. *really* had with her husband, and learned that because she was on report, she had not had her visit with the others, but on her own with an officer

present. I spoke to the officer and got rather a different version of
what the husband told her.

While there was great concern that no information about anyone
or anything should leak from the institution to the outside world,
there was a total lack of confidentiality with regard to prisoners
among some of the staff within the institution. Descriptions of
prisoners as 'manipulative' and 'devious' were common, but within
a system where prisoners felt they could never trust staff to respect
their privacy, devious behaviour may have been the only defensive
weapon left.

There were only two explicit staff challenges to the regime while
we were there. One was the nurse who refused to let the Health
Centre rooms be opened up to be staffed by prison officers. The
other was the drama therapist who steadfastly, and in the face of
constant hostility and attempts by prison staff to undermine her, ran
her drama therapy groups according to her own beliefs about the
value of clearing tension and opening up issues of contention, rather
than by the prison standards of containing and suppressing them.
Both these individuals were drawing on different conceptions of
'therapy' than those in general currency in the prison. Significantly,
neither the nurse nor the drama therapist is there any longer, and the
latter has not been replaced.

Rules, Discipline and Punishment

The prison rules provide the framework of control and security in
every prison. They are essentially what makes a prison a prison, and
makes each prison part of a system which is both homogeneous and
highly centralized. The prison rules are the same for young and old,
male and female, northerners and southerners. They cover a wide
range of behaviour, from swearing to escaping, and infringement
may result in a variety of punishments from forfeiture of smoking to
loss of remission. It is against this backcloth that any claims that a
prison is 'really' a 'therapeutic community', 'hospital' or whatever
in which individual treatment does or could take place must be seen.

Neither the Cornton Vale Working Party Report (WPR) nor the
Holloway papers make any mention of the discipline system. The
WPR mentions 'conditions of security' only in terms of their
supposed therapeutic value. What these 'conditions of security' are
is never spelled out. But it is salutary to realize that what it can boil
down to is solitary confinement for giving tobacco to a friend. The

Inspectorate Report also had little to say on the subject, devoting only one paragraph of a thirty-page report to it, which went as follows:

> considering the personality disorders apparent in many inmates, reports for indiscipline are not unreasonable and the individuals concerned who appear in the orderly room are dealt with in accordance with the regulations. The inspectors detected no signs of tension among inmates.[38]

It is telling that the Inspectorate Report accepted as natural a link between 'personality disorder' and reports for indiscipline, accepting as a matter of course that these should be dealt with 'in accordance with the regulations'.

While the discipline system seems to have little significance for the makers of policy, it is a different story for the prison officers and the prisoners. Many women at Cornton Vale said that for them the worst thing about imprisonment was the fear of being put on report for an offence against prison discipline, and this is hardly surprising, given that the prison rules and their application dominate and direct relationships both among prisoners themselves and between prisoners and staff. According to the prison rules, certain forms of behaviour are prohibited or proscribed. Many of the prohibitions of prison life do not apply in ordinary life. The rules were exercised with wide discretion, which could become in prisoners' eyes omnipotent power by prison staff.

As we have shown, conventional wisdom has it that women, while committing far fewer crimes of violence than men outside prison, once imprisoned behave more 'violently' than men. Women are consistently punished and put on report more frequently than are men for offences against prison discipline as documented in the annual prison reports. This had always been attributed to women's 'hysterical nature', their worse reaction to confinement, because of intrinsic female characteristics. An alternative explanation, as we suggested in Chapter Four, may lie in differences in the rigour with which the prison rules are applied to women. Greater readiness to put women on report for behaviour which would be tolerated in a men's prison (for example, swearing), and because of this, greater tension, generating its own 'incidents', may be the results of such a policy of close control of female behaviour. A recent report[39] by the National Association for the Care and Resettlement of Offenders shows that women prisoners are punished for disciplinary offences twice as often as men. In 1984, each woman was punished for an average of 3.3 offences. It was predicted that when women's prisons

became more treatment-oriented, meeting the supposed real needs
of women in prison, the number of disciplinary offences would drop.
This was the implication of Faulkner's discussion of indiscipline in
Holloway.[40] Smith predicted similarly that 'when the women prisoners are moved from Manchester to Styal, it will not be surprising if
the number of offences reported against discipline decreases
considerably . . .'[41] This did not prove to be the case. 'Punishment'
levels have risen both at Holloway and Cornton Vale since
'treatment' oriented regimes were introduced.

When women's recalcitrant or rebellious behaviour in prison is
commented on, it is often scathingly noted that it is 'hysterical'
rather than 'threatening'. Faulkner's comments are typical,
labelling women as 'inadequate' even in the way they break rules;

> . . . there are few [women prisoners] who could be described as
> professional or hardened criminals and very few need a high degree
> of security. There may be waves of hysteria or demonstrations of
> aggression – towards themselves, towards property, or towards each
> other or staff – but few women have the resources or the wish to
> organise a major disturbance or a serious attempt to escape. Those
> who are violent in prison are not usually violent outside and then
> violence is commonly an outburst which reflects an inability to
> express themselves in other ways.[42]

Women's behaviour in prison is defused and devalued by being
construed as due to their own inadequacy rather than a legitimate
response to a repressive regime. However, it is in this area of
behaviour, which to the ordinary person denotes, for whatever
reason, mental distress, that the most obvious contradiction between
the 'therapeutic' ideals and actual prison practice occurs. The WPR
and the Inspectorate Report devote pages to the 'mental disorders'
of women prisoners but do not mention the fact that such behaviour
as attempted suicide, self-injury, and 'cracking up' are routinely
dealt with through the disciplinary system.

The most telling aspect of this contradiction was the reaction to
the most 'disturbed' behaviour by imprisonment in the punishment
cells. They are a feature of all prison regimes but they are not even
mentioned in the Working Party Report, the Inspectorate Report, or
the official annual reports of the Scottish Home and Health Department. Neither does the prison appear to keep proper internal records
of their use. Nevertheless, 'going down the back' was a feared and
hated feature of life at Cornton Vale, and it was not a rare occurence.

Infringement of the prison rules is dealt with by means of the
report system. Prisoners can be 'put on report' for a very wide range

of offences. The main categories are: refusal to work; bad or indecent language and disrespect; assault; committing any nuisance; having, giving or receiving forbidden articles; damage to property; attempted escape; escape and absconding. The offences are far-ranging and such terms as 'disrespect' and 'committing any nuisance' are obviously capable of wide interpretation. The main punishments were: forfeiture of remission or loss of grade; loss of earnings; loss of association at work and exercise; loss of association at recreation. Other punishments such as deprivation of mattress and deprivation of visits were technically available, but seemingly never used at Cornton Vale.

Once an offence was committed, the report procedure began. An officer told an inmate that she was on report and hence confined to her room until she appeared before a governor, usually the next morning. If someone was put on report over a weekend, they did not see a governor until Monday morning. Several officers were present at what constituted a 'mini-trial'. The prisoner on report was escorted in by two officers: if under 21, she had to remove her shoes, apparently in case she decided to throw them around. The reporting officer read out her statement. Other statements may have been read by other officers. The prisoner was asked if she wished to say anything and the governor then pronounced judgement.

Prisoners and staff had very conflicting views of the discipline procedure. All staff interviewed felt it was a fair system, fairly operated. The one complaint was that sometimes punishments were insufficiently harsh. The interviewer's questions about 'prisoners' rights' were not understood. It was assumed that prisoners were always guilty of the offences for which they had been reported, and that all offences committed threatened the 'discipline' of the institution and therefore must be punished.

Prisoners, on the other hand, were critical of several aspects of the system. They felt it was operated with a lot of discretion on the part of staff. The offences are so wide-ranging and poorly defined that they could be used by members of staff to victimize individuals, or as release for their own tension. Appearance before the governor was described as 'a great performance about nothing', 'worse than going to the sherriff court', 'more like a High Court' and felt most of the time to be quite inappropriate to the offence. The main complaint was that with all the paraphenalia of court-like formal procedure, there was very little justice in the system. It was quite unheard of for anyone to be found 'not guilty' of an offence they'd been reported for. It was felt that the officers' word was always accepted and a lot of people felt it was not worth even attempting to say anything in their own defence.

Examination of the discipline records supported these feelings. There were no cases where prisoners had called witnesses in their own defence, and there were very few written statements from prisoners which were usually in the form of apologies. Thus, the column in the disciplinary records headed 'prisoner's statements in answer to the charges' either was left blank, or had the reported comments of officers such as 'she made long excuses that she had things on her mind'; 'she had nothing to say but her attitude was appalling'; 'she said she was sorry for breaking the rules'; 'she agreed with the statement – a very limited girl'. This was in contrast to accounts of offences and procedures given by the prisoners interviewed and often corroborated by others, in which the offence was frequently seen as the reasonable result of an accumulation of incidents for which there was a reasonable explanation.

Moreover, officer's 'evidence' often included statements (good or bad) as to the general behaviour of the prisoners – statements which clearly affected the severity of the punishment meted out. For example:

> Prison Officer X said in support that Jean had until now maintained a good attitude.

> Officer Y said that Mary was lazy in the units.

In such an impoverished environment, the punishments employed were powerful, encompassing as they did both an attack on material living standards and degradation. The discipline system as a whole provided the most overt means of the close control of the victims of an authoritarian and repressive regime. This was clearly illustrated by the following accounts written by prison officers of the events leading to the putting of a woman on report. The sort of events described below are everyday features of life in the prison and are in no way extraordinary.

Through the report system, close control could be exercised over details of daily life. Thus, getting up, getting dressed, tidying your room, going to work, coming back, preparing and eating meals, conversation, and so on, were subject to continuous scrutiny which was stressful in itself and could also result in punishment. In the following three examples taken directly from prison discipline records, the issue was initially, at least, clothing, and concerned adult women.

Prison Rule:
'disobeys any lawful order or refuses or neglects to conform to any prison rule or regulation'
and part 8
'leaves his [sic] cell or place of work or other appointed place without the permission of an officer.'

> . . . the marginally named[43] inmate who had just returned to work asked me if she could go to her unit for her cardigan. I checked with Sierra and Senior Officer Miss M. said that as Janet Murphy was not doing outside work, she had no need of a cardigan. She then refused to work and walked out of the cook-house without permission. I informed Sierra of the incident. Janet is now on report.

Prison Rule:
'disobeys any lawful order or refuses or neglects to conform to any prison rule or regulation.'

> I was on duty in Papa on Thursday at 8 a.m. Work parties were being called. Dorothy Brown was told to put on a cape as it was raining. She refused not once but three times. I told Dorothy she could not go out without one. She said that she would not go to work. I informed her that she was being placed on Governor's report.

> At approximately 4.55 p.m. whilst in Sierra, I asked the marginally named if she had her tights on. She ignored me and proceeded to walk to the dining-room table. She sat down, lifted her plate, banged it on the table and shouted, 'Yes, I bloody have.' She then grabbed the plate and threw it against the food hatch where I was standing, smashing the plate. She stormed out of the sitting-room and Miss S. and myself escorted her to the strong cell. I then informed her she was on Governor's report.

In the next two examples people were put on report for not making a bed properly and refusing to open a window. One might ask if this is inculcation of domestic skills, therapy or discipline and punishment.

Prison Rule:
'commits any nuisance.'
'in any way offends against good order and discipline.'
'is idle, careless, or negligent at work, or refuses to work.'

> At 7.50 a.m. on 20th May I was on duty in Bravo Unit 7. While checking the rooms for cleanliness and security I had occasion to call Sarah Thompson back to her room to remake her bed which was very untidy looking. As she pulled back the top cover of the bed it was revealed that she had not straightened the sheets, far less

tucked them in. The bed was in fact unmade and the top cover only thrown over.

I placed Mary Roberts on report for refusing to open her window in order to air her room. Mary was given a further opportunity but stated her window was remaining closed because she was frozen.

Lack of choice was a feature of life at Cornton Vale, both with regard to small issues such as whether or not to wear a cardigan, and large issues, such as work. In spite of the much vaunted, but hollow 'job application' system (see Chapter Seven), several people claimed that the only hope of a change of job was to get put on report for offences at work or refusal to work, in which case a change might be considered, albeit at the cost of a punishment. Merely asking and putting your case in a reasonable way was unlikely to be successful.

Related to this – and ironic, given the very high rate of sick leave among officers at Cornton Vale – was the impossibility of prisoners ever taking time off work except for certified sickness. This was particularly unfortunate for those serving long sentences, who got almost no holidays other than Christmas, or any other break from routine. Thus,

> At approximately 8 a.m. the marginally named prisoner refused to go to work as she did not feel well. I told her she would see the doctor, as it was up to him to say if she could go to bed or not. At approximately 9.15 a.m. I went up for Roberta to go and see the doctor. Roberta refused to get dressed properly, banged her wardrobe door saying, 'I don't want to see the fucking doctor.' I informed Roberta she was on report.

The following example illustrates the rigidity of the Cornton Vale regime, in its inability to allow the smallest degree of self-determination to a lifer, incarcerated for many years who was supposed to be being 'rehabilitated' (e.g. by being taken out to help with the Women's Royal Voluntary Service luncheons once a week) for imminent release.

> The marginally named inmate was not out of bed by 7.30 a.m. She would not have her breakfast with the other inmates but started making her own breakfast at 7.50 a.m. just as medicines were called. She was called upon three times but still proceeded to her room and started to eat her breakfast. On arrival at the health centre she would not stop uttering and swearing. On return to Sierra Unit 4 Jean started to make another cup of tea and took it to her room. She was informed that this was not allowed, that breakfast was finished and she should have it at the same time as other inmates. She started shouting and said 'she would do as she

wants and no officer would tell her what to do.' She said that she was going downstairs to complain to the principal officer. On going downstairs Miss H. asked Jean to go a message and she refused to take cleaning materials to clean her room, saying 'she would clean her room when she wanted to.'
I then informed her she was on Governor's report.

The report system enabled the control by staff of relationships between prisoners and between themselves and prisoners. Ordinary gestures of friendship such as the giving and receiving of gifts were denied. Interference in relationships between prisoners was zealous.

> At approximately 6.25 on the 29th September, 1980, I was escorting inmates from Papa block to the Health Centre for medication. As we were proceeding downstairs I saw the marginally named prisoner give Ann Burnett a roll-up. On returning to the unit I asked her what she gave Ann but she denied giving her anything. Catherine kept shouting 'Oh come off it.' Her tone of voice was angry and her behaviour insolent.
> I informed her she was on Governor's report.

Attempted suicide and self-injury were automatically reportable offences, being categorized as assault. While to the lay person these indicate a disturbed state of mind requiring treatment and understanding rather than punishment, in Cornton Vale the common explanation was 'attention-seeking behaviour' for which the apt reaction was 'denial of attention' by locking up in solitary confinement in a strong cell 'to cool down'. This was also the reaction to any sort of physically violent behaviour such as plate-smashing, clothes-tearing, even 'excessive' shouting and swearing. Thus, behaviour which in psychiatric terms would be regarded as classically 'symptomatic' of stress and anxiety (whether this emanates from the individual, the institution or whatever) was treated at Cornton Vale at face value as a discipline problem. While removal to the strong cell could be preceded by attempts by staff to 'talk through' the situation, the strong cell was an inevitable stage in the procedure, as was punishment after appearance before the governor. One attempted suicide by a lifer at the beginning of her sentence when she had just had her appeal turned down, resulted in her removal to the strong cell. The governor admonished her and told her she would 'give her another chance'. This particular admonition (a telling off without further punishment) was widely regarded by staff as an example of the humane and flexible attitude at the prison.

While this suicide attempt was treated reasonably seriously, most cases of self-injury were not. The following officer reports reveal an impassive attitude to self-injury, and an overriding concern with damage to prison property.

> Whilst I was on duty today in Sierra Officer J. and myself were doing room checks. At approximately 11.35 we entered the marginally named inmate's room and found Helen lying on her bed. I noticed blood on Helen's floor and also on her cardigan, and on investigation found that she had cut both her wrists. I covered both her wrists and told Officer H. to phone the Health Centre. Helen was removed to the Strong Room and I informed her that I was placing her on Governor's report.

Her punishments were one day off smoking and three days' loss of earnings. No medical or psychiatric evidence was offered.

> At approximately 6.56 p.m. I had occasion to enter Teresa's room with the evening medication. When I tried to open her door I had to push the door and I saw blood all over the floor. I called for Officer C. and we went into the room. Teresa had placed her chest of drawers and chair behind the door and she was under the bed. She had cut her arms and legs and we wrapped towels round her arms and escorted her to the segregation unit. The nurse was notified and I told Teresa that she was being placed on report. When Teresa was questioned as to what she cut herself with, she told me she had used a salt cellar and that the rest of it was on the window sill.

Self-mutilation is also a common event in Holloway. Cookson,[45] writing in 1977 a generally unenlightened and unenlightening paper on self-mutilation in Holloway, turned up a rate of 1.5 incidents a week. While she put her main emphasis on the women's mental state, she also referred to the 'sensory deprivation' of the punishment block as a contributory factor. By the end of 1983, a campaign had been launched by a new organization, Women in Prison, to bring to light conditions in Holloway's psychiatric wing, where in recent months two women had tried to gouge out their own eyes – one successfully – and a third had attempted to cut off her breast with a broken light bulb. In a second outbreak, there were twenty-four incidents in a three-week period when women on the wing either mutilated or tried to kill themselves.[46]

Conditions on the psychiatric wing in Holloway have been graphically described among others by a Holloway art therapist who resigned in protest at the conditions in the prison;

> . . . women are sent to C.I. [the psychiatric wing] because they are thought to need treatment. Instead they find a regime aimed primarily at containment. C.I. and the punishment block are very

similar . . . they look the same and its very much the same regime. The women are locked up all the time and have their meals shoved through the hatch. The cells are indescribable. You'd hesitate to keep animals in there. . . . Gradually deprived of furniture and clothes – either as punishment or in an attempt to control them – women can be left with just a blanket, crouched naked in a corner, refusing to wear the stripdress in protest.[47]

Despite the behaviour involved, the punishment block represents the end of the continuum of discipline and punishment. At Cornton Vale, both Yankee and Sierra had punishment blocks which are used for the entire prison population, and not just the residents of Yankee and Sierra. In both cases they consisted of two 'silent' cells and two 'strong. The cells were quite empty except for a mattress brought in at night. Food had to be eaten in the cell, off the floor. There were no windows and no colour. Once in the cell you could hear or see nothing of the outside. An acrid smell pervaded these units. A few people categorized as 'highly disturbed' spent almost their entire sentence in them. While under prison rules no-one could be kept there longer than twenty days at a stretch, they could spend repeated periods of several weeks there. Some individuals slept in these cells, but went out to work during the day. Records as to who went to the cells, why and for how long, were not satisfactory. Such records had only been kept over the last year. The column for 'reasons' was only filled in (and then not consistently) for the first six months that records were kept. The way in which these cells were used was therefore outside the operation of the formal discipline system and of even the dubious protection that this might afford to prisoners. In the year during which our research was conducted there were 75 admissions to the 'back' cells, with 53 different individuals involved (nearly 50 per cent of the whole population). The usual time spent there was one to three days, though some were there for much longer. The usual reason was removal after a particular sort of offence (assault of an officer, assault of another inmate, damaging room, etc.) for one or two days before the report was heard. Some officer accounts will give an idea of the context of removal to the punishment cells – apart from attempted suicide or self-mutilation.

> This girl had torn some clothing. . . . She was taken to her room and her chest of drawers, chair, and daily clothes were removed. While attending to inmates in the back cells, I heard voices and I discovered Suzanne shouting our of her window, "These bastards have just been in my fucking room and removed all my fucking stuff." I reported to Miss W. the conversation I had heard and it

was decided to remove Suzannne to the strong room. Suzanne walked to the strong room but once in refused point blank to remove her nightdress and put on a strong dress.

Of the sixty women interviewed, twelve had spent some time 'down the back'. They described events that led to incarceration down the back as 'cracking up'. When tension gets too much, you crack – you start shouting, swearing, damaging furniture, people, yourself. A sixteen-year-old girl described her experiences.

> A lot of people crack up after four months of a two year Borstal sentence. I was in my room one day when I heard the ice-cream van outside. It brought back so many memories – the next thing I knew I was in the silent cell. I'd pulled the radiator and wash hand basin off the wall and smashed a cupboard. I was down the back for two weeks. It's like being deaf and completely removed from the world. There's hardly any light and you can't hear anything. No one can hear you either. At night you get a mattress. During the day there's nothing but stone walls and a stone floor. They hand in your food and bang it down on the floor. That's the only human contact you get. The back cells do more than anything else here to harden people's attitudes. It was definitely a turning point for me – I thought if they're going to treat me like an animal, I'll behave like one.

An 18-year-old girl in prison for injuring her child had 'cracked up' after six weeks of torment from the other women because of the nature of the offence. She refused to go to work because of fear of the others and started 'shouting and bawling'. She spent seven days down the back. These are a few of the comments of individuals who had experienced the punishment cells.

> When you're locked up, you get plenty of time to think. The trouble is you think all the wrong things.

> The reason for crack-ups is tension – people getting at you. It's the individual versus the system. You're put in the back cells till you see the Governor. It's a bad way of dealing with it. They see it as attention-seeking, but it isn't. You have to use a chamber [pot] down there and put on a strong dress [a restricting canvas garment]. I felt as if I was going off my head.

> There's two girls permanently down the back. They don't get a room. I've cracked up. It's usually from thinking about outside. I've been down in the cells about four times. It's freezing. You get your meals on the floor. You don't get a mattress during the day. You're there until you see the Governor, usually about two days.

> A lot of folk crack up. They put them down the back. I cracked up once. I assaulted an officer and smashed up my room. I was put down the back that night and the next day. You just sleep all the time.

A lot of people crack up. Tension builds up. They get shoved down the back. I was put down the back cell in Sierra when I was in Romeo. I was there for a week. It's awful – you wear a funny dress and they fling your meals in.

Lots of people crack up. There are crack ups about once a month. It's always the same people. It's usually because of their personality. I've felt like cracking up but I haven't. I've got a wee doll in my room that I can batter about. When people crack up, they start flinging furniture about. It can be catching, then you get a whole crowd of them down the back. People are *always* put down the back if they crack up. The most they stay there is about 28 days. Sometimes it's combined with CC [confined to cell] in which case they're there all the time except for exercise.

Conclusions

For ideological and historical reasons, certain assumptions have been made about the nature of women in prison. In establishing new penal institutions for women, little proper research was conducted or referred to as to ascertain the actual needs of women prisoners. Instead, they were characterized as 'disordered' and 'disturbed', to be 'treated' in therapeutic settings.

In the background reports and papers and in more contemporary discussions, women in prison are frequently described as suffering from 'personality disorder'. The term although widely used has proved impossible to define.[48] From the outset, psychiatrists themselves have denied it as a psychiatric category and denied the efficacy of psychiatric treatment, and moreover have stated this in direct response to sentencing policies that recommend psychiatric treatment for offenders.[49] Nevertheless, it was somehow assumed that women's prisons in their new role as thoroughgoing psychiatric establishments would be the appropriate setting in which women with 'personality disorders' could be treated.

The ideals of therapy and the notion that women prisoners are mentally ill or disturbed dominated the planning and architecture of the new prisons, while the issues of punishment and discipline were almost completely ignored. Although it may have been believed that since therapy and discipline were basically incompatible, the earlier regimes of discipline would be completely submerged under the new approach, this has clearly not happened. The new ideology has been adopted, the new professionals put into place and the new buildings constructed, but a prison remains. Indeed, the therapeutic approach has actually enlarged the net of discipline and woven it still finer by extending surveillance and control to even the most intimate and mundane aspects of daily life.

While therapy itself has remained relatively undefined, and what is practiced under its name does not appear to have worked, it has had the effect of expanding the behaviour subject to control and thereby tightening and intensifying the conditions of confinement, resulting in more discipline and punishment for women than would otherwise exist in a prison regime. For example, under the name of therapy, it is seen as important to be 'nice', as opposed to not being bad, and women may be disciplined for failing to do something good rather than for actively doing something wrong. Thus, self-effacement and propriety can become required behaviour, and conversations, attitudes and motivations are scrutinized for compliance and managed so closely that the women are left with little of themselves under their own control and outside the therapeutic regime or beyond the domain of discipline.

Gender assumptions have been vital in the development and implementation of such a regime. The therapeutic model has played only a minor role in most men's prisons: by committing crimes they are not labelled as mad or mentally defective, and the scrutiny of their behaviour under confinement is less all embracing. We would suggest that the nexus of therapy and discipline contains the dual and often contradictory expectations of women in society at large. Because they are not generally seen as independent, self-motivated individuals but rather as biologically or emotionally driven, medicine and psychotherapy are the obvious answers to any form of independence or deviance. The successful outcome of therapy is in re-establishing the characteristics of a good woman, i.e. dependence, compliance, caring for others rather than themselves, and so on. Deviations usually result in pressure to comply and/or punishment. Hence, a female who does wrong even in the slightest detail must be made into a proper woman (who by definition does not do wrong) and this can be achieved through a therapeutic regime that seeks to reach even the most minute behaviour or motivation. Should this fail and the woman not approximate to the minutiae of the ideal (which seems inevitable) these infractions become subjected to the equally extensive system of discipline and punishment. Within the prison, the two have become even more entwined and extended even further into the daily life of the women.

7

Work, Training, Education

In spite of the conception of Cornton Vale as a 'therapeutic community' and of its inmates as in need of treatment, we have seen that very little time is actually devoted to 'therapy'. What then do the prisoners do all day? Most of them spend most of their day in work. Indeed, prisoners are *required* to work, and refusal to work is a punishable offence under prison rules. Under 21s may spend a small part of their day in 'education', while adults may attend evening classes. These, of course, are the activities that have been traditionally regarded as 'rehabilitative'.

Great significance has been ascribed to 'work' in prisons. As we have already shown, in pre-capitalist societies the penality of confinement as a deprivation of liberty did not exist. Writers such as Rusche and Kirchheimer,[1] and Melossi and Pavarini[2] have considered imprisonment in terms of the relations between modes of production and modes of punishment. They have located the prison as a specific form of punishment within the emergence of capitalist social relations and the development of generalized labour. It is this development which, they argue, produces a regime of punishment based on the deprivation of liberty. The aim of such a system is not only to punish, but to reform in terms of the demands of capital, to produce disciplined workers. Melossi and Pavarini's work in particular rests on what they see as both symbolic and actual links between the growth of the prison and factory systems. Women do not figure in any of these historical and theoretical expositions either as prisoners or as ordinary members of society.

The development of both the concept and the role of the woman as the guardian of home and family may have both reduced female inclination and opportunity for criminal activity, and/or made Courts reluctant to imprison women.[3] This reluctance may stem from the feeling that, although a prison can be compared to a factory

159

and can be said to have some of the functions of a factory, it cannot be compared to a home and its functions. Far from being *intrinsically* able to teach women how to be ideal wives and mothers, it is more often seen as *intrinsically* destructive to such relationships. However, as we have seen, women criminals have been widely conceived as 'sick' and in need of treatment. If a prison cannot really be a home, perhaps it can be a mental hospital. At the same time, women prisoners remain a very marginal part of a highly centralized system designed for men. The same prison rules, which decided essentially how a prison is run, apply to men's and women's prisons, and contemporary regimes are surprisingly similar.

This has led to a deep ambivalence on the topic of what women *should* do in prison, and to a relative silence on the part of policy makers and social scientists on the subject of women's work in prisons. As we have shown, work has always been an integral feature of prisons for women linked to moral ideals, the demands of the institution and sometimes those of the external labour market. In this chapter we shall begin by looking at these issues as they affect women's prisons now, and then consider what women actually do in prison and how this compares with regimes in men's prisons. We shall discuss in detail the nature of work and educational programmes in the prison and examine how they provide an arena for close control of the aspirations and behaviour of women prisoners.

Views about Work, Training and Education in Women's Prisons

Most social scientists and observers writing about women in contemporary prisons have had little to say about work, training or education. This is true of sociological studies, of radical campaigning documents, of theoretical work about women and crime, and of policy documents.

Three important sociological studies of women's prisons conducted in the United States in the 1960s and 1970s generally ignore these aspects of women's lives in prison. Ward and Kassebaum's book, about Frontera, California concentrates entirely on the sexual relationships between women.[4] Giallombardo, in her book about the Federal Reformatory for Women, Alderson, West Virginia states in the preface: 'My purpose is to examine the prison from a sociological perspective, that is as a system of roles and functions'.[5] What these roles and functions might be in the case of women prisoners is often assumed by Giallombardo. The chapter dealing with work is headed 'The treatment goal and the primacy of maintenance.' Work is dealt with in terms of this supposed conflict. Ideally, in the perfect women's prison, work is treatment. The conflict, as Giallombardo sees it, is between work as 'treatment' and the demands of institutions for upkeep and security. The 'treatment' we are told, 'comes principally of employment and teaching good work habits'.[6] Thus, it would seem that the conditions to be treated by work are 'idleness' and 'not knowing how to work'. Compared to men's prisons, the work of women prisoners is disproportionately concerned with the domestic upkeep of the prison. If the treatment is housewifery, the sickness, it is implied, is being an inadequate and incompetent housewife.

Comparing men's and women's prisons, Giallombardo notes that there is more 'made' work (of a domestic nature) in women's prisons, more 'productive' work in men's prisons. According to Giallombardo, this is merely a realistic response of 'prison officials' to the differing attitudes to work that men and women prisoners bring with them to prison. 'The male is oriented to look upon work as a meaningful activity in career terms, and this fact is recognised by prison officials.'[7] What is more, Giallombardo claims, prison work reflects the reality of the outside world '. . .It is apparent that much of the 'busy work' in the prison designed to keep the female inmate occupied, is not unlike many of the tasks that women perform in carrying out a home-making role'.[8] The implication is that women outside prison are under-occupied, spending their time on trivial tasks whose only purpose is to fill time. Men, on the other hand, in prison and outside, are engaged in important and purposeful activity.

If regimes in men's and women's prisons are different, there are obviously other factors involved than the 'demands of the institution'. Giallombardo presents these 'other factors' as prison reaction to inmates' attitudes and ignores the obvious ideological issues involved. She does not look at the facts available about women's lives outside prison nor at the specific backgrounds (in terms of work) of the women in the prison she studied.

Heffernan studied the women's Reformatory at Occoquan, Washington DC, which ceased to exist as a women's prison shortly after the research was completed. She looked at a population with a wide span of offence types and a variety of sentence lengths under a mixed security system. Her aim was the systematic analysis of an inmate social system, and she developed her perspective from prisonization studies of men's prisons.[9] Prisoners, we are told, spent seven hours a day working. The type of work was limited. Short-termers worked in the kitchen, in the mending room, in the dormitories, or did 'yard-work'. Long-termers did these jobs too, but might also have worked in the laundry, the power-sewing room, doing clerical work, or housekeeping for the superintendent and the staff.

Heffernan analyses work entirely from the point of view of prisonization, that is, difference in attitudes and responses to work in what she had defined as different 'types' of prisoners both in terms of their criminal careers outside prison and their adaptation within it. There is no discussion of the almost entirely domestic or quasi-domestic nature of the work, or of what work women did before entering prisons, or how far what they do in prison fits them for life outside.

On the subject of education or training, neither Ward and Kassebaum nor Giallombardo had anything to say at all. Heffernan has one paragraph, which does not even incorporate a comprehensive list of what was available. We are told merely that there was ' . . . a choice of couses in English, History, Mathematics, Current Events, Art, Typing, Shorthand and so on . . .'[10]

Carlen, in her recent study of Cornton Vale Prison,[11] does not deal with work, education, or training in the prison as topics in their own right. They are discussed, as they occur incidentally in discussion of the prison as a system of social control, but they are not seen as important elements in that system of control. The case histories of her sample of interviewees contain no details of their work or educational experience. This is interesting in that one of Carlen's main themes is the over-emphasis of domestic and particularly maternal roles in the processing of who goes to prison. It would seem that she is not only illustrating this process, but in a sense, subscribing to it in her choice of the 'selected details' of prisoners' lives.

Interestingly, the few radical campaigning documents concerned with conditions in women's prisons in the UK make little or no mention of work or training opportunities. For example, there is nothing on this subject in a pamphlet entitled *Alternatives to Holloway*.[12] Similarly ELWAP (East London Women Against Prison)[13] published a manifesto based on demands smuggled out of Holloway by prisoners. While this document makes a demand for full-time educational facilities, again there is no mention of work. In the

United States, on the other hand, women prisoners have apparently successfully challenged their exclusion from work release and work training programmes on constitutional grounds in a series of lawsuits brought mainly under the 'equal protection of the law' clause of the fourteenth Amendment of the Constitution.[14]

Where the effects of traditional theories about female criminality on actual criminal procedures have been considered, for example by Chesney-Lind, prison regimes themselves have not been studied.[15] Carol Smart, however, provides a starting point in her general statement about women's prisons.

> Most regimes employed in penal institutions for female offenders are typically those which reinforce the sterotypical traditonal sex role of women in our culture. Inmates are usually given the opportunity to learn to cook, sew, and do other domestic tasks, and in more liberal regimes, they may be able to learn to type or take education courses.[16]

Smart suggests that women are not perceived as potential 'bread-winners' and as such there is no need for them to acquire money-earning skills. In her view, one of the aims of such programmes is 'feminization' and this can be partly attributed to the identification of female criminal behaviour with 'masculinization'.

Failure to consider the needs of women prisoners for work and training is evident in the official government papers which discussed the setting up of Cornton Vale[17] and the rebuilding of Holloway. While a great deal was said about therapy and treatment, very little attention was paid to work and training. Where these are mentioned, they are considered primarily for their supposed therapeutic value. In 1968, the Chairman of the Holloway Project Group discussed the new prison in terms of three main themes, none of which included work. Work is mentioned almost incidentally in the last of the aims,

> . . .To construct a community with which she can identify herself and within which she can form relationships . . . There will throughout be an attempt to develop her resources in any way which seems likely to help her in the future – by improving her ability to communicate, *by giving her practical skills which might help her to earn her living* [our emphasis], by encouraging sparetime interest which will keep her occupied during her leisure time, and by letting her know where in the community she can look for help if she needs it . . .[18]

There is one further paragraph devoted to work, the key phrase of which is 'the work provided will be regarded as having a therapeutic rather than an industrial purpose'.[19] The scope of the proposed work is limited. Women on remand who choose to work and the 'most disturbed' women will do 'bag-making, handicrafts and simple assembly work which will not suffer if it has to be interrupted.' The 'more capable' will '. . . help with gardening, maintenance, laundry and general domestic work in the establishment, but there will be no attempt to reproduce industrial conditions or to set industrial targets of production.[20] At the same time as the planning group for Holloway was ignoring the whole area of work, the prison services in the UK had defined reform as training, and training equalled work. Beginning in the late 1960s, increasing emphasis was placed on productive industrial labour linked to ouside contractors.[21]

Similarly, the education and training proposed for women were limited. Academic education was recommended for those of school age and for 'those who can benefit from it'. What this would entail was not stipulated. 'Vocational training' was envisaged as 'domestic cooking, laundering, use of domestic appliances, home decorations, domestic dress-making and soft furnishing.' Faulkner states that 'all these subjects will provide useful skills to women who have been unable to make an ordinary home for their families and some will help them to obtain employment after release.'[22] The only employment that springs to mind is as low-paid domestic workers. The aim to produce 'good housewives' is clearly stated, and it is implied that successful family life depends on women's domestic skills.

Fitzherbert, in her discussion of the redevelopment of Holloway, points out how therapy has subsumed both work and education. 'The distinction between work and education will cease, all daytime activities being devised for each individual from whatever course will be most therapeutic, be it art, machining, or physical education.'[23] The Working Party Report on Cornton Vale includes just one paragraph on education and one on work. The paragraph on education reads: ' . . in addition education should be taken and social training in health and hygiene should be included in the curriculum.'[24] 'Training', it is proposed, is part of 'treatment'. Thus, 'Many parts of the total treatment regime are in fact often referred to as training, for example, educational and vocational training, training for freedom, physical and recreational training etc.'[25] The main proposed work opportunities, that is kitchen and laundry work and the machining and manufacture of garments, are listed under the heading 'Programme for developing social skills.' Women's needs are envisaged in the following way, 'Individual programmes . . . will be designed to fit women and girls for the responsibility of life whether it may be in the sphere of work or domestic living and rearing a family within a community.'[26]

The confounding of language in all these discussions is significant. 'Training' and 'education' are 'therapy'. 'Work' is 'social skills'. the way in which the term 'therapy' is used has already been discussed. If working in a laundry is acquiring 'social skills', it is never explained how this is so or why it is important; one suspects that it is an ideological gloss for the wider purpose of meeting the demands of the institution while continuing to define everything as therapy. There is an assumption that women have the *option* of working or staying at home, and that it is the acquisition of domestic skills which is of prime importance. Remembering in particular that these papers are proposing an ideal (not describing what might have turned out to be a disappointing reality), the scope of the work opportunities proposed is extraordinarily limited, in fact almost entirely housework on an institutional scale. Little thought is given to education or vocational training. It is implied that 'training' for the limited work available is acquired 'on the job'.

Women's Work in Scottish Prisons

Over time there seems to have been little change in what women actually do in prisons in Scotland. In 1847, occupations in the newly established Perth women's prisons were reported as 'embroidery, Berlin woolwork, shirt-making, common sewing and weaving.'[27] In 1940, Smith states, the occupations of the prisoners varied little from those which had existed before the First World War. Between 1946 and 1951, women in Duke Street prison in Glasgow 'continued to be employed mainly on domestic work.'[28] They made clothes for men and women prisoners and laundered prison clothing, bedding and a variety of articles such as towels for government departments. Younger prisoners spent the day doing domestic work, and embroidery and dressmaking in the evenings. In 1957, in Greenock, 'prison work was very much the same as that provided formerly at Duke Street' although 'more modern sewing and knitting machines were installed in the workroom.' The education programme included literacy, home-nursing and child-care, dressmaking, cookery and budgeting . . . 'so that [the prisoners] would be more competent in looking after their homes on liberation.'[29] This dreary domestic tale, Smith regards as a triumph, for 'In Scotland – as in England and Wales – it was at last acknowledged that women prisoners should be returned to society trained as efficient 'housewives' rather than as efficient 'housemaids'.[30] Thus, the main transformation from past to present prison training was the ultimate purpose of domestic work, to be used in one's own home as a wife rather than in someone else's as a maid.

In recent annual prison reports for Scotland, education, vocational training and occupations are discussed separately. There is no division by sex, and it was necessary to refer to the 1982 Prison Inspectors' Report on Corton Vale to confirm to what degree these official prison reports are in fact reports on the male prisons. Before discussing these reports in detail, two general points must be made about them. Firstly, the men's and women's system are generally similar enough to be discussed as one in the official reports.[31] Secondly, what is really being discussed in the official reports is men's prisons. Women in prison are insignificant, of no account – they hardly alter the statistics one way or another. Official reports have very little to say about education. There is no breakdown of what courses are offered, how much time is made available or how many people have access to education. The paragraph devoted to physical training and recreation is effectively a description of what is available for male prisoners. As there is no breakdown by institution, it is impossible to know how widely available facilities and courses are. Indeed, very few of the activities listed are available at Cornton Vale. It seems to be assumed that women are less in need of outlets for physical energy than men. The end result is certainly greater physical suppression for women, which may be a contributary factor to reportedly high levels of tension in women's prisons.

None of the vocational courses of the various industrial training boards is available to adult or Under 21s at Cornton Vale. While such facilities are available at only a few adult male prisons, they are available more or less across the board in young offenders' and what were borstal establishments for males. The following vocational courses are offered to at least a few male prisoners: general construction, painting and decorating, hairdressing, upholstery, carpentry and joinery, domestic applicance servicing, radio and T.V. servicing, fabrication and welding, mechanical engineering, motor vehicle mechanics, vehicle bodywork repairs/paint-spraying, bricklaying. However, the number actually doing these courses is small. Only 12 percent of a total male prison population of around 5,000 get any accredited vocational training during the course of their imprisonment, and only four per cent get any qualifications in any one year.[32]

The sections of the annual reports dealing with actual work in prison tell a similar story. Forty-one occupations are listed, in which the thirteen different sorts of work available to women prisoners are subsumed. Fifty per cent of male prisoners are employed in twenty different sorts of manufacturing enterprise ranging from woodworking, general engineering and heavy textile manufacture to bookbinding, upholstery and simple assembly work. In Corton Vale, 33 per cent of the women are employed in the only manufacturing enterprise – garment production – many of these on unskilled tasks of cleaning up or packing. The rest of the entire Scottish prison population, male and female alike, is employed mainly on various domestic and institutional tasks providing upkeep and maintenance for prisons. Even here, a much wider choice is available to male prisoners who may work within their institutions as blacksmiths, carpenters, electricians and plumbers. While not many male prisoners are employed outside their prisons, in the case of female prisoners the proportion is even fewer (indeed, none at all between 1976 and 1982).[33]

Can one conclude in the light of this evidence that there is no need in our women's prisons for emphasis on challenging work, training and education, either because women in prison are already well qualified to earn their living, or because the supposed emphasis on domesticity is sufficient for the life they will lead on release?

The Relationship between Female Criminality and Women's Work

These questions have been brought very much to the fore in the recent academic and public controversy about the changing nature of female criminality and its relationship to changes in their employment and social status. In separate works published in the mid 1970s, Adler[34] and Simon[35] both claimed a significant rise in the female crime rate in the United States since the 1960s. Both linked their different arguments to the women's movement. Adler attributed a supposed rise in the amount of violent crime committed by women to psychological changes in women due to increased 'liberation'. She said, 'It is a disturbing side effect . . . of the steady erosion of the social and psychological differences between men and women.'[36] This sort of reasoning lies squarely in the tradition of criminological work on women. As Box and Hale put it:

> A supporter of feminism might regard women's social existence in our culture as bad enough without their collective attempts to achieve liberty and equality being viewed pejoratively as

criminogenic. Yet, historically, it is just this irony that has haunted the imagination of male criminologists . . .'[37]

And Alder has indeed attracted criticism[38] similar to that levied at criminologists such as Lombroso, Thomas and Pollak, Konopka, Cowie, Cowie and Slater (who are not, incidentally, all male).[39]

Simon, on the other hand, claimed a rise primarily in the amount of property crime committed by women. This she attributed to higher and different levels of employment by women, giving them the opportunity to commit certain sorts of property crime not previously committed by women.

Both authors have been attacked on statistical grounds. Other criminologists have re-analysed their data using more stringent and appropriate forms of statistical analysis and have found that the supposed rise in violent crime (relative to male rates) is non-existent.[40] Moreover, while there has been a rise in property crime, the sort of crimes being committed do not support Simon's argument, being for the most part trivial, and not usually primarily related to the workplace.

Perhaps most importantly for future directions of analysis and research are the questions raised about the accuracy of Simons' and Adler's portrayal of the current social and economic position of women in general, and, by implication, of convicted women. Here we see a picture of the conditions of work changing very little for women, most of whom work in low-paid jobs which are limited, sex-segregated and insecure.

The General Household Surveys and census reports for Britain show that large numbers of women, both married and unmarried, are in paid employment and indeed, most women go out to work for a large part of their lives.[41] At the same time, recent levels of registered unemployment among women have risen, demonstrating that for many women, full-time domesticity is no longer voluntary. The preliminary results for 1983 of the General Household Survey show that 56 per cent of the female population were engaged in full- or part-time work and six per cent registered as unemployed. Among the sub-group of married women, the percentage working was actually slightly higher (57 per cent) though more were engaged in part-time work. A further four per cent were registered unemployed, a figure that definitely underestimates the true number of married women looking for work since many do not bother to register.

The jobs that women do outside the home are often similar to those they do inside it. Hakim, in the research done for the Department of Employment, looked at occupational segregation by gender and discovered that more than half of employed women in Britain work in only three service industries.[42] Seventeen per cent in the 'professional and scientific' category are typists, secretaries, teachers and nurses. Twelve per cent are employed in 'miscellaneous services', such as laundries, catering, drycleaners, launderettes. A quarter of employed women work in manufacturing industries. Half of these women are concentrated in only four industries – food and drink manufacture; clothing and footwear; textiles; and assembling electrical goods. This kind of concentration is not found in male employment, where no single industry contains more than ten per cent of the male workforce.

In spite of the Equal Pay Act, 1975, women's earnings as a percentage of men's have fallen slightly in the last few years and the average gross hourly earnings of full-time employees over eighteen years of age is now 73.5 per cent.[43] An important factor in this differential is the basic structure of occupational segregation by gender, which by allocating men and women to different jobs determines the rewards they are likely to receive.

With this in mind, Miller, questioning both Adler's and Simon's particular analysis of the economic factors relevant to changes in women's crime rates, has suggested that the particular social and economic positon of women when related to broad socio-economic events (such as the Depression of the 1930s and the current recession) might be a more fruitful line of enquiry than those of opportunity suggested by Adler, Simon *et al.*[44]

One question on which all those who have written about women in prison are agreed is their poverty and lack of earning skills. Velimesis has reviewed in detail research in the United States on the 'characteristics of incarcerated females' and lists those about which there is some agreement.[45] Foremost is that before imprisonment women have mostly held poorly paid jobs requring few skills, and have been the main breadwinner for themselves and their children. Velimesis points to the failure of prison programmes to meet the needs implied by these findings. Chapman, again looking at the US, concurs with Velimesis,

> The data available from prison studies provide the basis for most descriptions of the woman criminal. Such data suggest that the average women prisoner is young, poor, black, with limited education and skills, the head of a household and the mother of several children. . . .'[46]

Greenwood makes a similar point to Chapman in describing women prisoners in Britain, although in the absence of published information about the class, race or level of education of prisoners, she has to rely on American studies to do so. She also emphasizes the similarity on these counts between male and female prisoners.

As stated earlier, no thorough-going research of the nature and needs of the female prison population in Britain was undertaken before the rebuilding of Holloway and the opening of Cornton Vale. However, Box and Hale have tested Greenwood's[47] suppositions about the relationship between female emancipation and crime with statistical data for England and Wales for the years 1951–79. They reached the conclusion that

> Social circumstances common to both men and women are more important in accounting for these types of crime than a sex-specific factor such as female liberation; indeed not one of our four indicators of liberation was related to female property offences.[48]

Nevertheless, it must be borne in mind that, with all the sophistication of the statistical analysis, the chosen indicators of 'female liberaton' were crude, and in their crudity demonstrate the problems involved in the so-called measurement of such concepts. Despite these particular limitations, their conclusions provide a better explanation of female criminality than do those of Adler and Simon. They, like other commentators, maintain that such an explanation lies more in economic marginalization than in female emancipation.

Prison Work Histories and Experiences

Looking in this light at employment histories of women in Cornton Vale, it would seem that they are fairly typical. Of the girls admitted for borstal training during the year of our research, all had been unemployed except four who had worked as a barmaid, a stitcher, a machinist and a boxmaker. Of the 131 young offenders who were admitted during the year, twenty-five had been working just before admission in the following jobs: clerk, packers, sales assistants, homehelps, nursery attendant, machinists, waitress, factory workers, barmaids. Four had been school students, and four-full time housewives. Of 38 adults admitted during one month, 14 described themselves as housewives and 13 as unemployed. The rest included a teacher, cleaner, boxmaker, machinist, sales assistant, clerical assistant, chicken killer, two hairdressers and two barmaids. These records reveal that those girls and women who had been employed were mostly doing low-paid unskilled jobs. Many had been unemployed prior to imprisonment.

Moreover, these records, dismal as they are, probably give an over-optimistic picture since it emerged in the interviews that those having a job on admission had not necessarily had it more than a few days, and did not necessarily have any more stable employment record than those recorded as unemployed. This was particularly true of the borstal girls and young offenders.

Of the 19 adults interviewed, all had worked at some time in the past, typically in factories, at cleaning jobs, at seasonal hotel work and as shop assistants, but then were unemployed just before admission to prison. Three had not worked since they had children and others had stopped work in the past to bring up children. Of the nine women who were employed at the time of imprisonment, three had formal work qualifications, namely Higher National Certificate in hotel management, nursery training certificate and a qualification as a State Enrolled Nurse, and had been working in these areas. Four had held the same job for at least six years as secretary/book-keepers, a bar steward, and a school cleaner. The other two women had been unskilled factory workers.

Of the eighteen borstal girls and young offenders interviewed, only two could be said to have had a stable employment record. One had always worked since leaving school in a jute mill and a factory. The other had been a trainee florist for two years. Of the others, three had never worked at all and thirteen had worked for very short periods (a few days, weeks, or months) with long spells of unemployment in between. Typical jobs were seasonal hotel work and shop and factory work. Only one girl had any work or educational qualifications. But she had had a string of jobs and was in borstal for fire raising at work.

Descriptions of how time was spent while unemployed belie notions of emancipated girls forming rampaging criminal gangs as described, for example, by Adler. Their activities tended to be isolated and homebound. Some typical accounts of their lifestyles were,

> I used to go down to my granny's, do the shopping and take my nephew to nursery school. I did a lot of housework.

> I didn't want to work. I just wanted to be around the house, but I got bored, then I had the kid. I had her through drink. I was alone all day with the baby – I'd stick her in the pram and go down to the shop and get some Carlsbergs then I'd come back and drink them.

> I just stayed in bed half the day. Then I'd sit in the house.

> I used to hang about at home. I helped a lot with my nieces.

Looking at women's experiences in prison, how far did Cornton Vale seek to make good these obvious educational and work skill deficits? In terms of the range and type of work available, there was little at Cornton Vale that was not a direct legacy from the past, involving maintenance of the institution and some production. For example, the most recent figures available show that out of a population of 87, nine were undergoing assessment and were not available for work. Of the remaining groups, 27 were employed in the two production workshops (adults and Under 21s) and a further four worked in the Training Office. Almost all of the remaining 47 were employed in maintaining the institution. Of these, the largest group, 13 women, spent their day cleaning the units. Others were employed cleaning the administrative block, working in reception, the Health Centre, the kitchens, laundry, grounds, and staff restaurant. One women was employed in 'home produce', involving the sale of prison produce such as vegetables, home backing and so on.

Most of the work available outside the production workshops was to do with the day-to-day running of the institution. Almost invariably, it involved following rigidly set routines, with no opportunity to take initiative or responsibility or make decisions. Cleaning tasks in the units were to be done in a particular way, in a particular order, often different from the methods women themselves used in their own homes, and the same was true of kitchen and garden work. Working in the laundry involved the use of industrial machinery and the laundry dealt with washing from other institutions as well at Cornton Vale.

The only forms of employment offering any real training leading to skills which would be recognised and might be applied outside prison were work in the office and more importantly in terms of numbers, in the two production workshops. The adult production workshop manufactured industrial overalls, hospital theatre gowns, catering gloves, and, for the prison service, dresses for prisoners. The Under 21 workshop made shirts for male prisoners and bags for outside contractors, but its main function was 'cutting' for outside contractors. Not all areas of production involved skilled work (for example, packing and cleaning up). 'Training for Freedom' which is supposed to mean work experience outside the prison for those nearing the end of a long sentence – and usually does for men – almost always involved work in the staff restaurant (which is technically ouside the prison gates by a few yards if not outside the prison regime).

The classification of prisoners into certain categories directed (and limited) the choices of work, education, training and recreation which were available to them. Classification made it impossible to generalize about the daily regimes experienced by inmates. Classification has long been a feature of prison regimes, and the categories employed in Cornton Vale were traditional ones of sentence length, age and perceived competence. Thus, those women serving short sentences were denied certain privileges because of the length of their sentence. If they worked at all they were given menial jobs such as institutional cleaning which didn't pretend to do anything other than fill time. In addition, no one was entitled to 'association' between the hours of 6.00 p.m. and 8.00 p.m. until they had completed three months of their sentence. As this was when evening classes occurred, adults serving short terms were effectively barred from vocational education, as well as being relegated to the worst jobs. It should be remembered that short-termers form the bulk of the prison population.

There was a further division between the young prisoners (Under 21s) and the adults. Until November 1983, borstal girls and young offenders on long sentences were committed for 'training'. Such girls almost always ended up in 'production', since this was the only work which was seen as setting out to train and lead to the eventual acquisition of specific skills. Educational provision was made on a day release basis for Under 21s who also had six-week 'assessment' and 'citizenship' periods at the beginning and end of their sentences.

The route to one's position in the prison was through assessment, not a particularly meaningful exercise, given the limited options. 'Assessment' was a much vaunted part of the Cornton Vale regime, the basis, it was claimed, of 'individual treatment'. The Working Party Report on the subject of assessment said,

> This involved a broader concept than 'investigation' or 'diag-nosis'. It is rather an attempt to build a comprehensive under-standing of the individual personality. It embodies the individual's history, her present situation and her future potential. It is a skilled process which involves the combination and co-operation of a number of disciplines.[49]

In 1977, the then Governor of Cornton Vale, said at a symposium on prison architecture,

> We are totally dedicated to provide for the needs of the individual. The establishment of these needs requires an assessment involv-ing all disciplines from staff, supporting staff, and visiting

professionals. Assessment is only good if it is ongoing and discussed with the individual concerned.

The assessment procedure did not in practice appear to meet these aims. Firstly, it seemed not to apply to the adult population at all. Only those admitted for borstal training and young offenders serving sentences of six months or over underwent assessment. An assessment group lived in one unit in the young offenders' block and was supervised throughout the six-week assessment period by the same staff. They did not mix with other women during this time. One member of staff was responsible for writing a report based on her observations of the individual at the end of the six weeks. The young women on assessment were responsible for cleaning the unit. Each day they went to the 'assessment room' in the central block where they made draught-excluders and teddy bears under the supervision of the assessment officer. Once a week they had an hour of 'group therapy' with one of the psychiatrists, attended also by the assessment officer and one other staff member, and at one time they also had a weekly hour of 'drama therapy'. During the six weeks, the following assessments were done: psychological (IQ and apititude tests); educational (reading, writing and arithmetic); production (assessment in the garment factory); office (typing and clerical); and psychiatric assessment.

At the end of six weeks, there was an 'induction meeting' between the deputy governor, the registrar governor for the Under 21s, a prison social worker, outside social worker, assessment officer, unit officer, teacher, and psychiatrist, and their reports were presented. It was difficult to see any results or purposes of this assessment procedure. No educational decisions were taken, as a further six weeks of 'continuing education' followed automatically, at the end of which all girls were placed either on 'O' level (equivalent to American High School) or remedial courses – rendering individual assessment totally unnecessary. According to their sentence, they almost always went to the young offenders or the borstal block and inevitably in the least privileged grade and unit. Job choices were extremely limited, and what people did eventually was probably as much to do with the needs of the institution as anything else. One purpose assessment did fulfil was to sort out potential trouble-makers and forewarn staff about 'handling' them.

Those prisoners perceived by the prison as the least capable, that is, the women allocated to the secure block and the Under 21s who were regarded as particularly difficult, did 'home-making' (housework) and were not given 'proper' jobs unless there was no one else to do them. This is curious, given the importance supposedly placed on training for domestic life. In the words of one interviewee, 'Sierra people only go to work if they run out of Papa people.' That is, those from the secure unit who were usually defined as the least capable only had employment when no one was available from the non-secure adult blocks. These women were allowed to attend clases during the afternoon – a ragbag of so-called 'educational and social skills'.

Prison work differs radically from work outside.[50] Although the actual work may in many cases be the same, the social context in which it occurs is so different as to alter the whole meaning and purpose of work. From the point of view of the prison staff, economic objectives, rehabilitation, the inculcation of certain moral values and security all jostle as overt or covert aims. The general context is one in which the workers are utterly powerless, lacking any of the normal rights that workers have. In this context, work may become another arena for control and the exercise of the discipline system. From the point of view of the prisoners, the main purposes of work are the relief of boredom, respite from the extremely tense relationships with discipline staff, and the earning of meagre wages. In this setting even the smallest sum of money can be very valuable for purchasing what might be seen as necessities outside (such as tobacco and refined soap) but become luxuries inside.

Thus, there was little general agreement as to which were the 'best' jobs. Different jobs or aspects of jobs could be valued for different reasons, by different people. Jobs in the public parts of the prison such as the administration block and the staff canteen might be prized for the illusion of freedom they give. With some jobs, such as those in Reception and in the administration block, there was the possibility of picking up news. Work in the gardens ensured fresh air and the physical freedom to move around. A clear case of the inversion of work values and one which illustrated the changing meaning of time in prison was the prizing of jobs with long and unsocial hours (more money and less boredom). Such jobs were those in reception, the central kitchens, and the staff canteens. Absolutely crucial to a positive evaluation of a job was the character of the supervisor (whether civilian or prison staff). While the character of the supervisor is important in outside employment, inside prison it assumes vital significance given the powerlessness of prisoners to take any action against an unfair supervisor to change their job, or to demand different conditions. For example, because of the popularity of the prison officer who was in charge, women enjoyed working in the laundry in spite of the low pay and uncongenial nature of the work. The qualities of a good boss were first and foremost fairness, of great importance in the highly discretionary prison system where prisoners feel they have little or no possibility of countering injustice. Secondly, within the often impersonal system, a boss who 'treated you like a human being' was highly valued.

On the whole, people said they liked their work with the exception of 'home making' and work in the 'cutting room' (the Under 21 workshop) which was regarded as unbearably boring. Some people liked work for its more relaxed atmosphere than that of the units. This was largely a result of different sorts of relationships with work staff, whether civilian or not. As one woman said, 'I like my work (looking after the maintenance men's office, making their tea, etc). I like the staff, they'll give you a fag and talk pleasantly to you.' Work, unless extremely unpleasant, was regarded as a more interesting way of passing time than being locked in one's room or sitting about in the units, but it was not usually thought to be interesting or valuable in itself.

In the prison setting, and in the absence of all the normal rights that workers have, the work situation clearly became another arena for control. This was clear when the issues of pay and job allocation were considered. Deprivation of pay in some areas of work could be imposed as a punishment without even recourse to the formal discipline system. In fact, within the formal discipline system, loss of pay was the most common punishment. It is impossible to discuss a set scale of pay at Cornton Vale. When we conducted our research, the basic pay was 64p a week. The average was 70–80p, and the maximum anyone in our sample received was £1.47. The amount of pay depended on a number of factors. 'Work' was better paid than 'home-making'. Bonuses could be paid for extra work done in production and in the laundry. Whether or not bonuses were available depended not only on individual capacity, but also on whether extra work was coming into the prison. Some jobs, such as those in the central kitchen, the staff canteen and the reception yielded more hours of work. Within limits, it was up to the supervisor how much people earned. Some supervisors were more generous than others. For example, it was generally recognised that the gardener, the maintenance men and the supervisor of the Under 21s factory paid well. In the Under 21s, officers were able to deduct from or add to the pay of people employed in home-making for things like 'behaviour and attitude' while working. People got small increments as their sentence progressed, although these were not completely predictable. They were supposed to occur every month, but did not always do so. Finally, women could lose pay as a punishment for having been put on report. Again this was the most common punishment.

This all added up to a system in which no one was sure what they were entitled to, and in which almost no one's pay could be compared with anyone else's. The pay was uniformly regarded as 'terrible' and insufficient for the things that prisoners had to buy themselves – such as soap (other than abrasive prison soap), tights, make-up, letters (other than the one per week supplied by the prison) and most important, tobacco. Everyone smoked rollups – the most that the majority of people could afford per week was half an ounce of tobacco and a packet of papers. Pay, and loss of pay, were thought of largely in terms of tobacco. Pay used to be given on Monday and is now given on Friday, as staff found prisoners becoming unmanageable during long, boring, tobacco-less weekends.

In spite of a much-vaunted system of 'applications' for 'advertised' jobs there was in fact little choice of jobs allowed either initially or during the course of a sentence. A further disincentive to changing jobs was that when you changed jobs, you started again at the basic rate of pay. In response to this apparent rigidity, women employed subtle methods to attempt to change employment as a simple request to do so would usually not be met. For example, it was widely recognized that refusing to go to work and being put on report could result in a change of work.

Other methods of achieving a job change also illustrated that the staff reserved for themselves decisions as to change of work. Almost the only way that a prisoner could get a change of work was to engineer a situation in which staff would take a decision in the direction she required. To do this, women sometimes put to use the stereotypes held of them as neutrotic, hysterical, and unstable. One woman said,

> You have to be subtle about it [changing work]. I managed to convince the doctor I might cut my wrists with the scissors if I had to stay there. The real reason was that I didn't like it. Refusing to work doesn't work because staff are afraid everyone'll start doing it if they give in to it.

Another woman said, 'I was in the cutting room. I hated it. I kept asking to be moved; eventually I was because the doctor said it was affecting my nerves.' However, a second woman's similar attempt did not work. 'I wanted a change from the cutting room. I tried to make them think that because of my offence [attempted murder], I couldn't be trusted with scissors, but it didn't work.' Some women reported that repeated unsuccessful attempts to do certain types of work were refused for no reason. They implied that straightforward requests for change of work were useless.

> I'd have liked to work in the cookhouse. I've put in for the cookhouse six times but it was refused for no reason. I wanted to go in for catering. They asked me what I wanted to do when my Borstal report was taken, but they didn't take any notice.

> I requested to see the Governor after two weeks asking for a move. I've still had no reply. The only way you get what you want here is if you act stupid.

Women were dubious about the 'rehabilitative' value of work in prison. Most people had no definite ideas about what, if any, work they were going to look for once they were released. No-one expected any help from Cornton Vale in finding a job. Some people felt that far from improving their job chances through any extra training, prison had harmed them, both through stigma – 'Perth Infirmary laundry doesn't like Cornton Vale girls' – and through deterioration of skills while they were there. Even when people enjoyed the work itself, it rarely made them want to look for that sort of work outside, even when they recognized that their experience in Cornton Vale might help them in getting a job.

> I don't want to see another laundry. I used to like going to the steamie – not any more.

> I'd have to be really desperate to go for a machining job. It would bore me silly.

The few women that had jobs to go to had invariably got them through relatives. Those who had a stable work history usually wanted to return to the same sorts of jobs. Otherwise, when people mentioned jobs in the future, they were usually of the waitressing or cleaning type.

Many felt that they weren't being taught any skills, particularly those working on the units, those cleaning in the central block and those in certain areas of production work such as packing. Even where there was training potential in a job, such as the kitchens, it was felt that this was hardly exploited at all.

> Cornton Vale doesn't give you a proper training. You're just thrown in and left to get on with it. You don't get taught anything properly.

There's no job here that rehabilitates. Not like men's prisons where you can get training in plumbing and carpentry and things. Here you just get told what job you're going to do. Some people get put in the factory because they already know how to machine – if they're silly enough to say so. They should have proper courses here – say an hour a day of typing or nursing.

Some people suggested training that they would have liked and felt it might have been possible to arrange, such as nursing, catering, hairdressing. They felt there should be more links between education and work. Others felt that nothing Cornton Vale could have offered in terms of work and training would have made any difference since it didn't fit their own amibtions for the future.

Cornton Vale opened new doors for a few women and made them think of their future in different terms. One borstal girl who had not worked previously at all really enjoyed it and had become very skilled at machining and intended to get a machinist's job when she left. Two women who had held responsible jobs for a long time and were serving sentences for embezzlement saw the necessity for retraining since they wouldn't again be able to work with money. One, who'd been a book-keeper improved her typing and shorthand skills. The other had been given a job in 'home produce'. This involved baking cakes, biscuits, etc. which were sold to the staff. On the basis of this, she had decided to do a catering course when she left.

Training and Education

As has been pointed out, there was no work training other than that occurring 'on the job' The Education Department described in the Inspectorate Report as a 'purpose build Further Education Centre' had the potential, in terms of space, staffing allocation and so on to meet vital needs, but did not do so. It was hampered by the stereotypes held about women in prison, particularly their presumed lack of intelligence, by the narrow and conventional interpretation of what constitutes education, and by their mistaken notion of the future needs of women.

Few of the women interviewed had formal educational qualifications, and in this they were very probably like the general population of prisoners in Britain. The question of general intelligence and potential is obviously a different one. As we have seen, women in prison have been constantly characterized as stupid, although such studies as have been made of the IQ levels of women prisoners (with all the drawbacks and deficiencies of such studies), would suggest that there is little difference in term of intelligence between women in prison and the general population. Certainly, it is a stereotype held dear among prison staff, and is indeed essential to their concept of their charges and to the sorts of relationships they have with them. The idea that prisoners may be intelligent is one that most prison staff find theatening. Over-riding evidence of intelligence will usually be counteracted by the characterization of that individual as 'mad' or devious. Thus, the governor said to us 'we don't really have any intelligent inmates – except X, but then she's hardly a normal girl.' The implication was that 'normal' prisoners were unintelligent. One woman of obvious ability had to fight for a very long time, with the support of a visiting psychologist, to be allowed to do an Open University course, and she continued to be treated with scepticism by prison staff. An assistant governor faced with a request from the mother of a borstal girl who already had all the 'O' grades offered at Cornton Vale, to do courses in Biology and Geography, wrote in her report of this interview, 'What does she think this is – a finishing school', and the education officer herself concurred with this line of thought.

'Non-vocational' courses included everthing that was not part of an exam syllabus. This was 'remedial' and 'continuing' education, basically the '3 Rs' taught in an unimaginative and limited way, using conventional school material. A course known as 'The Family and the Home' operated for approximately two hours a day. This was for those mentioned already who were deemed incapable of 'proper' work. Under its rubric fell health education, food and nutrition, fabrics and fashion, and 'community involvement'. 'Community involvement' entailed visiting speakers from a variety of bodies such as the RSPCC, the Salvation Army, Marriage Guidance, the Police, and Women's Aid.

Vocational courses, for the most part, were 'O' grade syllabuses and were even more limited than the non-vocational courses. They included Arithmetic, English, Home Economics (in two parts, food and nutrition and fabrics and fashion) and Ordinary National Certificate in Business Studies. Occasionally Higher Grade was taken in the same subjects, and there has been one Open University student.

All Under 21s received some daytime education and could go to evening classes as well. Adults who were not working in the living units (that is, who went 'out' to work) could only go to evening classes. These were not available to those serving sentences of three months or under since 'association' between the hours of 6 p.m. and

8 p.m. was a privilege granted only after three months of a sentence had been served.

Most of the women interviewed who were taking one or more 'O' grade (six adults and fourteen Under 21s) felt that the number of hours a week allocated to each course was not really enough, particularly as the courses lasted less than a year, and individual standards varied greatly. None of the adults interviewed relished the prospect of taking exams. Some had suffered the ignominy of not being considered good enough to take the exams.

> I'm doing the courses, but I've got no brains to sit the exams.

> I was taking 'O' grade cookery. I wasn't good enough, so now I just go to the classes.

> I enjoyed the English class until we started working for the 'O' grade.

Several women felt they were pressured to take exams.

> I didn't want to take the exams, I just wanted to brush up on my English. But you can't get out of it. It's held over your head that it'll be bad for your parole if you do. I was told I couldn't say no. It was the same making sweets for the sales and Christmas concert. I didn't really want to do anything but I was pressured into doing the make-up.

Defending the presentation of women for 'O' grade exams, the Education Officer claimed, 'They like getting certificates, even if it's for a fail. They won't have had certificates before.'

The range of subjects was limited. One adult prisoner was planning to live in France on release and would have liked to learn French. She had asked about this, was told that something would be arranged, but heard nothing more. Three of the Under 21s would have liked to do science, history and geography. Two of these girls wanted to train as nurses on release and needed more 'O' grades, but one repeated courses she had already passed before coming into Cornton Vale, saying 'I just took them again to break the routine and use my mind.'

A major problem was that Cornton Vale followed an ordinary academic year in the organization of its 'O' grade courses with courses beginning in September and ending in May. Unless a woman began and ended her sentence at the right time of year, she could miss part of the course and/or not be around to sit the exam. If women left before the date of the exam, even if arrangements were made for them to sit the exam in their home town, exam records showed that they were not very likely to turn up. Four of the Under 21s interviewed said that they would be out by the exam dates and did not intend to sit the exam.

We have seen that in the realm of penal philosophy/policy theory 'work' in women's prisons is rarely considered. In sociological and psychological studies on women in prison, it is similarly ignored. Despite the rhetoric of rehabilitation and domestic skills, prison work remains an essential part of the regime, primarily intended to maintain the institution and produce commodities. The work and education opportunities available to women are a marginal issue. Official reports are about men's prisons, where the admittedly limited opportunities are still considerably broader than what is available to women. In place of considered policies there are implicit, and sometimes explicit, conceptions that the needs of male and female prisoners are different. At the same time, the actual situation of women (for example their domestic responsibilities, poor educational qualifications, and lack of money-earning skills) demonstrate a need for appropriate training and educational facilities. They also suggest an explanation for the rise in female crime rates in a time of economic depression which is rather more plausible than those theories that hinge on the rise of feminism.

In terms of the educational work and training opportunities available the emphasis which predominates implies that the failure of women prisoners is their failure as wives, mothers and housekeepers. Educational and work opportunities are on the whole presented as a means to improving women's performance in domestic roles, not as worthwhile ends in themselves. In practice they appear to be related more clearly to the maintenance of the institution itself than to either the domestic or economic needs of the women. This orientation, taken with the widely held stereotype of women in prison as stupid, has meant that work and educational opportunities at Cornton Vale are generally restricted, unimaginative and inappropriate.

Finally, the system of classification, job allocation and discretionary levels of pay all afford powerful methods of control of prisoners by prison staff.

8

Relationships

As we have seen, disrupted or non-existent family relationships in the past have been seen as highly relevant to explanations of female deviance and criminality. 'Good' family relationships are regarded as crucial to the stability of women's mental health, which has also been regarded by many as a factor in the criminality of women.[1] Such thinking has formed part of the philosophical and policy background of the new prisons for women. It has been regarded as being in the *nature* of women to need such relationships, and acknowledged that the social position of girls and women renders them more dependent on their families for identity, status, a sense of worth and so on.

One corollary of this is that modern prisons for women, in their therapeutic guise, claim to be concerned with 'relationships' or rather their simulation in the prison setting. Another is the self-fulfilling sentencing policies which suggest that women whose relationships are disrupted may be more likely than others to receive a sentence of imprisonment, the dual motivation being punishment for being less 'adequate' women, and cure in institutions which claim to be concerned with 'repairing' relationships.[2]

Visitors to Newgate Prison after Elizabeth Fry's work had begun there noted that 'This hell on earth' where only a few months ago abandoned and shameless women affronted their eyes now appeared like 'a well-regulated family'.[3] Two hundred years on, the architecture of Cornton Vale had as its stated aim the social organization of prisoners into small 'family' groups, within which 'family type' relationships may be encouraged. The Working Party report stated that

> at the new establishment, all inmates will be housed in units of seven or multiples of seven, each with its own dining/recreation area and small kitchen . . . this design will enable a family or group atmosphere to be created within each unit.[4]

The Scottish Office Inspectorate duly reported, ten years after the creation of the prison, that the 'central principle in the planning of Cornton Vale was the creation of small living units for a maximum of seven inmates,'[5] described later in the report as 'family' units.

Relationships between Prisoners

The physical division of prisoners into groups of seven was the principle means by which the prison sought to organise and control its population and, at least in theory, to create the kind of family-like intimate relations considered to be so important for rehabilitation. As stated earlier, there were five accommodation blocks, each composed of four, six or eight units. Each unit had seven bedrooms, lavatory and bathroom area, kitchen and living/dining area. In this they approximated living conditions outside. However, each unit also had an office which was always staffed. More ominously, an integral part of the living accommodation in two of the blocks (the secure block and the young offenders'), was used as the punishment area.

Based on unit living, 'homemaking' was the method by which it was claimed that housewifery skills would be learned in a 'family-like' context. It was implied that the role of the homemaker inside was like the role of 'mother' outside. The duties of a homemaker varied from unit to unit. The remand block excepted, food supplies for breakfast and supper were issued to units on a weekly basis. The 'home maker' for each unit was responsible for preparing and serving breakfast and supper. In some self-catering units, the raw materials for the main meals of lunch and tea were supplied and the homemaker prepared them as she wished. In most units, however, main meals were provided in containers brought to the units from the central kitchen. The term 'homemaker' actually referred to the person who stayed in the unit, rather than going 'out' to work. She may have been responsible for cooking daily meals, or merely for making tea and toast, morning and evening, and doing routine cleaning as instructed by prison officers. In the former category were those who were doing a stint on homemaking as part of their so-called training while in prison. The latter were 'homemaking' because they were considered incapable of doing anything else. Women were of course acutely aware of the distinction, and their feelings about ' 'homemaking' varied accordingly. Thus, when homemaking involved making decisions as to what dishes to prepare from the materials available, a responsibility for getting meals on the table at a particular time, dealing with the responses, negative or positive, from the other women in the unit, they could also enjoy rising successfully to the challenge even though they often feared taking on the role of homemaker. On the other hand, being confined to the units to be engaged in routine cleaning and tidying under the close surveillance of unit officers was regarded as boring, pointless and time-wasting.

There were two sorts of assumptions involved in the claims that were made for the value of 'homemaking'. First, that it was *appropriate* training. That is, that the recipients needed and wanted it and that it would be of use to them in the lives they would lead on leaving prison. Second, that the form in which it was offered was effective – that is, enough like 'outside' for what was learnt nd experienced to be relevant. As the first points have already been discussed, we will only consider the second.

Warning bells ring at the language used. 'Homemaking' is a self-conscious term and is not a word that ordinary women would ever use to describe their ordinary activities. And, indeed, when we looked at 'homemaking' at Cornton Vale, it became obvious that the elements which give housework and caring for a family its meaning are missing and that what happened at Cornton Vale was merely a hollow simulation – based on domestic tasks.

Decision-making is of course an essential aspect of running a home: of budgeting, of when to do what, of what to cook, of balancing the many demands made, and often of the demands of paid work as well. Yet, obedience, not decision-making was the skill learned. There was a 'right' way to do everything, and the prison officers knew the way. There were routines established by others that must be followed in the same manner and at the same time each day. Because there was not really enough work to do, routines of extreme boredom and triviality, bearing no relationship to what people do in their own homes, have been established. For example, books are individually dusted everyday; floors are polished three times a day.

Most essentially, in the outside world, 'home-making' is to do with people. In prison, 'home-making' is conducted in a context where a group has been involuntarily thrown together and is constantly changing in composition. Where there are no emotional bonds between the people involved, the heart is taken out of the process. At Cornton Vale, the least essential parts of the whole process have been emphasized. Just as 'going out to work' was a simulation, so was 'homemaking'.

However, unit living fulfilled functions other than those of bogus homemaking and bogus relationships, although no claims were made for their therapeutic effects. The splitting of women into small units made for easy physical and social control. Women had few opportunities to form any sort of relationships with people not living in their unit. There were no meetings of the whole community (apart from religious service) as advocated by the Working Party Report. The composition of the individual units was controlled by the prison staff, and could be changed at will. As one women said, 'They split up good units because they're too pally.' There was a constant intrusive presence of prison officers in the units, and a continual monitoring of physical movement, behaviour and conversation.[6] In addition, each room was electronically linked to the central office. There was literally no privacy anywhere.

One result of the constant monitoring and manipulation of the composition of the units was, ironically, the failure of people in them to form strong relationships with each other. As one long-termer said, 'In my unit there's no sense of community – everyone leads a very individual existence. In the evenings, the sitting room's often empty because everyone's in their own rooms.' Sociological studies of prison populations have suggested that among some groups, and in certain conditions, strong bonds of solidarity may form between inmates. Studies of long-term women prisoners in the United States found that many women formed 'mock families' while in prison to compensate for the loss of their outside relationships.[7] While no such phenomenon has been observed in British women's prisons, such studies as have been conducted have taken an entirely different approach, by looking at the individual characteristics of female prisoners rather than at the social organization of prisons. Such a prison culture, with strong relationships forming between prisoners, did not appear to exist at Cornton Vale. Indeed, it would take extraordinary strength to resist the degree of control, surveillance and manipulation directed at preventing the foundation of such bonds or at breaking them once formed. Add to this the shifting, short-term nature of the prison population and the women's own attitudes to their sentences and their fellow prisoners, and there is little atmosphere is which personal relationships can flourish.

Of the adults we interviewed, all except one said that it was very difficult to make good friends in prison both because of the nature of the regime and because of their own and other people's attitudes to imprisonment. Most women felt that their 'real' life was outside: 'I'm friendly with the girls in the unit, but they're not like friends at home . . . I wouldn't want to make close friends with anyone.' In addition there was a strong sense of shame and stigma which made people unwilling to form lasting relationships with fellow prisoners;

> No-one has close friends here except possibly long-termers who pal
> up with one particular person. I want to forget this part of my life.
> People say they'll see people after – but they don't.

Under 21s also said that it was not easy to form friendships inside but on the whole they felt it was the nature of the regime more than their own feelings about being in prison that was the cause. Most of the Under 21s, in contrast to the adults, intended to stay in touch with one or two people, although girls out on licence[8] were not supposed to see other borstal girls. It was pointed out that social workers usually turned a blind eye to this and it was very rare for someone to be recalled for this reason. Friendship within the prison was sometimes a question of maintaining relationships that pre-dated the sentence. All the borstal girls and young offenders interviewed except two already knew some people from outside. One girl knew eight people from her old List D school![9]

Young and old alike felt that the nature of the regime itself militated strongly against the forming of friendships. Choice of companions was severely restricted. Claustrophobia, tension and lack of confidentiality were features of such small groups – 'you can't trust the lassies here – things come back to you.'

Specific features of the particular regimes affected the sort of relationships that could form. For example, among the Under 21s, the grade system was used to control and manipulate relationships. Members of different grades were not supposed to 'fraternize' with each other. An 'ideal' borstal girl, who got her grades and therefore was released in the shortest time possible from Cornton Vale, had certain sorts of relationships with her fellow inmates. She got on with everyone, but was not too deeply involved with anyone. In some people's view, the system encouraged a degree of selfishness, as well as militating against certain personality types:

> To get your grades, you've got to mix with everyone. It goes better
> for you then. Some lassies are very quiet. This goes against them.
> You have to be friendly but not too friendly.

and

> It's difficult here. Everyone's out for themselves. It you want to
> get on, people could pull you back. Some people hold themselves
> back on purpose so they can be their friends.

Other aspects of the regime such as parole and release on licence were seen too as encouraging selfishness,

> Everyone's bound up with their own self-interest. They don't want you to get close. They tell you so much, but there's a barrier all the time. Being in here has made me selfish. I wasn't before.

In the view of most prisoners, parole made people selfish, interested only in their own release, and reluctant to do anything that might delay it. They felt that parole was used quite mercilessly by staff, and dangled like a carrot in front of prisoners to keep them in line. In addition, some prison rules seem to be aimed at preventing the ordinary gestures of sociability, of giving and sharing. Rules that forbade the offering of tobacco, or even of a match, implied that committing such acts was to be involved in racketeering. This is just one example of the way in which the most negative interpretation possible was put on the most ordinary human behaviour.

Prisoners and Officers

Relationships between prison officers and prisoners were envisaged by the Working Party Report as a lynchpin opf the whole concept of Cornton Vale as a therapeutic establishment. The report states

> It is very important not to think exclusively in terms of individual treatment being carried out only by psychiatrist, social worker, or psychologist. In fact this is a situation in which many members of staff may have a part to play. . . . She (the inmate) may begin talking freely about herself and her problems to this member of staff, who in fact then begins to play the role of therapist.. . .[10]

However, there is little in the prison officer's training to prepare her for such a role, and little evidence of it in daily life at Cornton Vale even though the prison was well staffed. In 1981, there were 138 prison officers, of whom 17 were male and 121 female. On the day of the 1981 prison inspection, there were 120 prisoners. Significantly prison officers are referred to as 'discipline' staff (as opposed to 'civilian' staff such as instructors, social workers, teachers) and indeed the prison rules form the basis of their training and of their work.

Prison officers tended to have different reasons for joining the prison service. Often these had little to do with 'relating' to prisoners. Different reasons for joining the service, along with different sets of regulations and training, naturally presumed very different attitudes to prisons and prisoners. The reasons the prison officers we interviewed gave for joining the service fell into three broad categories. First, there were those who were bored with their current job, usually clerical or factory work, and wished to 'work with people'. Such people usually found the job satisfying and saw it as a step-up from their previous jobs. One such officer who said,

> I felt that I'd had a lot of problems in my own childhood and early part of marriage and had come through them, and so I'd have something to offer these women. I went in as a knight in shining armour.

A second category were ex-forces people who saw their career as having been in the forces. They tended to see the prison service as a less efficient version of the army, and the job in general as a step down – for example. 'After the army, I was shocked by the chaos, lack of communication and lack of need of anything between the ears.' Last were those people who gave very practical reasons for joining the service – such as needing somewhere to live because of homelessness after divorce or the death of parents:

> It's a free roof and light. I sold the house in Glasgow when father died, and I had to think of somewhere to go.

> I'd come from the country and I needed a living-in job as it wasn't the done thing for girls to get flats.

Such a range of reasons for joining the prison service would suggest the importance that training specifically geared to women in prison might have played. However, training involved a six-week residential course at the officers' Training College, Polmont, followed by twenty-six weeks on the units in different parts of the prison. The six-week course was exactly the same as the course followed by officers in men's prisons and there was no special course for the borstal. It was concerned with prison rules, police/court routines and the filling in of official forms (for example, for the reception of prisoners). Noticeably lacking was any mention of relationships, counselling, and coping with distress. Most officers expressed general satisfaction with the training which they described as 'very thorough', 'a good grounding'. Most people did feel that six weeks wasn't long enough – although they were not envisaging any radical change, since they usually added 'eight weeks would be better'.

Cornton Vale was supposed to be unique in providing its own ongoing training, mentioned as vital in the Working Party Report. However, most of the staff interviewed had little or no ongoing training. While we were there, there was no training officer and the job was about to be re-allocated and reduced to a half-time job. Until then, the training officer had been a woman with little formal education but with twenty-four years in the prison service. She reiterated that 'all training pertains to prison routines' and stressed her own lack of qualifications and the fact that she drew almost exclusively on her own experience in the prison service. For principal officers, extra training consisted entirely of increased familiarity with the prison rules and standing orders. The training officer was completely unsympathetic to psychiatric approaches, and she accused the psychiatrist of being unaware of the implications of their treatment for 'full-time handling'. When asked whether she thought this sort of thing should be included in officers' training, she said 'that's not part of an officer's work, and if they'd wanted to be mental nurses, that's what they would have done.'

The extremely narrow scope of the training, with its almost exclusive emphasis on prison rules and routines, underlined the authoritarian nature of the prison officer's job both in relationships with prisoners and in their place in the prison hierarchy. Relationships with prisoners were in fact guided by the prison rules. It was the officer's job to monitor behaviour, conversation, and relationships for possible infringement of the rules, and to perform the random body and room searches that were such a hated part of prison life. At the same time, the prison rules are so framed as to yield the possibility of, but not the necessity for, controlling every aspect of prisoners' behaviour. Considerable discretion was exercised by prison officers in their execution, and prisoners found that the inevitable inconsistency and unpredictability that resulted were hardest to cope with in their relationships with officers. As one woman said, 'every staffs' got different rules. Some bring you sweets – some dub you up [in the punishment cells] for nothing.'

An important source of ambivalence in officer/prisoner relationships lay in the actual structure and organization of Cornton Vale. Because of the unit system, prison officers and prisoners were forced into very close and constant contact with each other, different entirely from the sort of contact between officers and prisoners for example in a gallery or hall where there is at least the chance of anonymity in numbers. While the ideology of modern women's prisons suggests that the officer is the prisoners' friend and therapist (leaving out the possible conflict between these roles), the actual operation of the prison through the prison rules underlined by the officers' training promotes an authoritarian mode. A good illustration of the ambivalence of the prison officers' role, and how relationships with prisoners varied, was the contrast between young offenders' and adults' views of prison officers. Staff were moved at frequent intervals between the prison blocks, including Under 21s and adults, so the women interviewed from the various blocks were discussing the same staff.

When asked, 'Do you have any close friends here?', several of the Under 21s volunteered the names of staff. Of those who said they had friends among the staff, a majority said they would like to keep in touch with them afterwards and only four said they would not take personal problems to them. The 'friend/confidente' relationship was institutionalized in the Under 21 section through the 'chum' system. This was a system whereby girls were encouraged to seek out one particular member of staff as a confidante. Not all girls had 'chums' or thought that they were a good thing, but the majority of those interviewed seemed to have a special relationship with someone. A common attitude was to make general derogatory comments about the staff as a whole, excepting the 'chum' – such as 'I've got one friend [staff]. Apart from him, I take them or leave them', and, 'I pretend to like them all so I can get on. I'll write to one of them – he's helped me a lot. I like him because he talks normal and not snooty.' Many people really valued their 'chum'.

> My chum's like a big sister. I regard her as a friend not a member of staff.

> I would tell her anything. I trust her and I know it doesn't go any further.

Other girls took an attitude more like that of the adults interviewed:

> It's a job, someone's got to do it. They encourage you to go to them with your problems. I don't because I don't trust them. You know that everything's discussed with everyone.

Among adult prisoners, however, without exception the attitude to the staff with whom they were forced into intimate daily contact was one of indifference.

> They don't annoy me. I don't annoy them. Sometimes they come and sit with you – then you can't talk about what you want to.

> If you don't bother them, they'll not bother you . . .

Relationships with officers were described as a 'game' where you communicated with them just enough to avoid being put on report for ignoring them. At the same time, unpredictability and lack of confidentiality meant that there was little trust and a large element of fear in staff/adult relationships. A commonly expressed feeling was that officers did not regard them as individuals, but treated them as one of a (sometimes subhuman) herd.

> I assumed once they got to know you they'd realise you weren't really part of the criminal element – but they don't, they just treat everyone the same.

> We're not human to them. But we're not robots who can be told 'do this, do that'.

Suspicion was the hall mark of relationships between prison officers and adult prisoners. In a situation where power appeared to be all on one side, staff described prisoners as 'manipulative', the label invariably attached to oppressed individuals, the powerless, and the frightened to whom it is often the only strategy available.

Such relationships were also not rewarding to those who held the power. The Prison Inspectorate Report for Cornton Vale may state that 'the morale of the majority of members (of staff) is excellent',[11] but the signs of stress among staff were obvious. The sick leave rate among staff was extremely high, and dependence on nicotine as marked as among prisoners.

Family and Friends

We also examined relationships between prisoners and their family and friends – the connection between their lives inside and outside prison. We discussed what happened to women's relationships with their children at the time of imprisonment and afterwards, and the actual mechanisms – letters and visits – through which prisoners maintained their contact with the outside world. The fear of contagion and contamination so evident historically was still seen to be a predominant influence in the attempts to manage women's relationships with the outside world in 'decontamination' rituals evidenced at points at which the two worlds met.

Mothers and Children

Women as mothers have specific experiences of the penal system. Mothering has been assumed to be women's central role and so much importance is attached to it that judges, magistrates, sheriffs or juries may be influenced when she is living with her dependent children. Indeed, the need of children for their mothers and the pain suffered by women separated from their children is the main plank in the Radical Alteranatives to Prison plea for alternatives to prison for women.[12] While sentencing practices have not been studied systematically, Carlen in her interviews with sheriffs felt that this was the case. Sheriffs interviewed made comments such as: 'If she's a good mother we don't want to take her away. If she's not a good mother, it doesn't really matter.' A corollary of this approach may be a positive willingness to send 'proven' bad mothers to prison both as punishment and cure. Another sheriff said:

> One often finds out, when inquiries are made, that the women have left their husbands and that their children are already in care. In those cases it may seem a very good idea to send them to prison for 3 months to sort themselves out and to see what the Governor's and the staff's skills can impart to them.[13]

Not much is known about the parental responsibilities of women who go to prisons, or the effect of imprisonment on children and their relationships with their mothers. Gibbs, looking at a sample of women received into Holloway in 1967, found that 42 per cent of the dependent children of those women had not been living with them at the time of their imprisonment.[14] No information was sought as to the reasons for separation or what contact continued to exist between mothers and such children. Of the remainder, imprisonment affected their living arrangements (which were all that were considered in the study) in a variety of ways. For example, 21 per cent continued in the same family situation, 11 per cent went to live with a known adult (usually a female relative) and 23 per cent went into local authority care. Single parents were particularly vulnerable to having their children taken into care upon imprisonment and this happened to half of these children. In addition, cohabitees and stepfathers very rarely maintained parental responsibility once the mother of the children with whom they had been living was imprisoned. Finally, two of the women in Gibbs' sample who had babies under one year old took them into prison with them.

On the women in our sample at Cornton Vale, 9 per cent had adult children, 16 per cent had no children and 65 per cent had children under 18. There were 24 dependent children. Of those women with dependent children, 47 per cent had been looking after their own children; and the children of 17 per cent of the women were looked after by close relatives. The children of the rest had been in local authority care (foster parents, children's homes, List D schools) for some time and this did not change.

For children being looked after by their mothers at the time of imprisonment, a range of other arrangements were made which were related both to the original domestic and family situation of the mother and the crime committed. In half of these cases, the children were looked after by other female relatives (sisters, mothers, grown-up daughters). These children were not in the care of the local authority, and those relatives were not classified as foster parents. In all the cases, the women were living with a man before arrest, although most were not legally married, but in no case did the man care for the children after arrest. In three cases, the man and woman had been jointly charged, convicted and imprisoned at the same time. In one case, the child in question was the granddaughter who was returned to her natural mother upon the imprisonment of the grandmother.

In the other half of the cases where children had been cared for by their mothers before imprisonment, the children were taken into local authority care, and lived either in children's homes or with foster parents. In these cases, imprisonment resulted from a domestic situation which threatened the child either directly or indirectly, including one case of child injury, two cases of killing of a sibling, and one case of violence between the adults in a family. In all these cases the woman had not been living with the father of the children at the time of the offence. The pattern here was one of dependent children living with their mother/parents before a crime involving some form of violence in the home who were then taken from the home and placed under the care of local authorities rather than with relatives.

What happens to women's relationships with their children when they enter prison? Chapman has reviewed rehabilitation programmes for women offenders in the United States, many of which are focused on 'parenting' or have it as an element in a broader programme.[15] While stressing that such programmes are not generally available, she does cite some interesting examples, including alternatives to incarceration, which take the mother out of an institution and give the children back to her in a community-based facility, visitation policies with overnight and weekend visits, and local foster-care programmes where the children live with families in the locality of the prison and have frequent visits with their mother. All these are conducted in the context of general rehabilitation programmes including counselling and parenting courses. At Cornton Vale, there were no special arrangements of any kind to facilitate or mend relationships between imprisoned mothers and their children, despite the claim to help its inmates to form stable relationships and improve the ones they had. Among those who had not previously been caring for their children none had any contact with their children during their sentence, although in two cases women heard about their children from their soical worker. In all these cases except one, there had been some contact before the sentence, ranging from very infrequent to daily involvement. Two of these women had no visitors at all during their imprisonment, which they attributed to the shortness of their sentences (in each case three months) and the distance relatives had to travel for the sake of a twenty-minute visit.

Of the category of women who had previously cared for their children who now lived with relatives, all the children were seen at nearly every visiting time. There was one exception, and this was a case where the mother kept in very regular letter contact with her children, but did not want to see them as they had been told she was working away from home. All of this group expected to resume the care of their children on release.

The whole question of contact in the case of those children recently placed in local authority care was problematic since in every case it was a situation which threatened the children that had brought them into care and their mothers into prison. In all cases it was highly questionable whether the mother would ever resume care of the children. In two cases where a sibling had been killed by the mother, there had as yet been no contact between the other children and the mother (after six months and one year respectively). In three other cases, children had been brought by a social worker either monthly or at very infrequent intervals. In all these cases, the women said they would have liked to have seen more of their children. In these cases, decisions about contact between mother and child were seemingly taken completely by social workers. They brought the children, usually outside ordinary visiting time, and visits occurred outside the usual visiting area. The women interviewed felt extremely threatened in this situation, and often felt they had been treated peremptorily. One young woman, imprisoned for injuring her child, said that she felt pressured by her social worker to sign a form giving parental rights to the local authority without really understanding the implications. She did not know what access rights, if any, she had and was told by the social worker she could see the child when she had 'settled down'. She had seen her only once in six months and felt bitter that the social worker had not even kept her informed by letter about her child. She also felt that the Cornton Vale social worker was in league with her home social worker to keep the child away from her and to keep her in ignorance about the child.

Another long-term prisoner described in similar terms the pressure put on her to sign a parental rights form, and said that this sort of situation was quite common at Cornton Vale. She objected to the wording on the care form that she was 'unfit' to look after her children and fought to have it changed to 'unable'. She claimed that you couldn't depend on the prison staff for correct advice, and she also felt that her children's social worker and the Cornton Vale worker were in conspiracy against her, that her wishes as regards the children had been deliberately flouted, and that she was continually at a disadvantage with them. She had been granted access three times a year, but as long as ten months had sometimes passed between visits. A clause had been written into the access agreement that access was to be allowed as long as the children 'were not unduly upset' by the visits and this woman felt that this was interpreted in a capricious and arbitrary way by the social workers. In one of the cases described in the social work reports, there was 'trouble' over the signing of the parental rights form[16] and the woman involved 'kept insisting' that she wished to attend the Children's Panel where a decision would be made about her child's future. It was implied by the social worker that such insistence was out of place.

Obviously there was a very real dilemma here in that the relationship between the mother and child was the reason for imprisonment, and the whole future of the relationship had now been put into question. In such cases, social workers may have felt that protecting the child's interests inevitably involved acting against the wishes of the mother and ignoring her needs. In addition, in contrast at least to declared policy in other cases, the 'crime' which brought the mother into prison was kept continually in the forefront in dealings with her, and very explicitly so when her relationship with her children was considered. Nevertheless, when looking at social work reports there did seem to be some substance for the prisoners' feelings that social workers were sometimes conspiratorial, evasive and even uncaring when dealing with their cases.

In one case, a mother of four, pregnant with a baby later born in prison, was imprisoned for child injury. Initially, two of the children were fostered and two were in different children's homes but eventually, all were moved to the same children's home. Mrs Hill was admitted in the autumn. According to social work reports, she immediately requested to see a social worker to ask whether she could see her children and was told that she would get a visit before Christmas. The prison social worker reported in January that Mrs Hill was 'peevish' because the outside social worker had not yet brought any of the children, and in February, that 'Mrs Hill did express a little spurt of resentment that she had never had the promised visit from her children.' The outside social worker said that she could not bring more than two of the children, as she couldn't manage them in the car, and although the mother was asked which two she would like to see, the decision (not the same as the mother's) was eventually made between the social workers. At the end of March the social worker was explicit in her reports about the stalling techniques. 'The fact that the outside social worker would prefer this during school holidays makes it easier as that will push it on till after the end of June.' The visit was arranged for July, nine months after Mrs Hill's imprisonment, and strict timing was planned and observed. 'Mrs Macmillan [the outside social worker] asked if the escort [a prison officer] could be told precisely as to the length of the visit and conclude it firmly when time was up.' The same escort was present throughout the visit with the children and gave a highly critical [of Mrs Hill] account of the visit to the Cornton Vale social worker, condemning Mrs Hill's behaviour during the visit, and her relationship with her children.

Another case was that of Mrs Craig. She had a long history of in-patient psychiatric treatment and her children were in care. In this case, the Cornton Vale social worker seemed to comply with the assessment of the Children's Home matron. Mrs Craig was making constant requests to see her child or at least have a photograph of her.

> I telephoned [the matron] who said that she felt a request of this kind would *not* be in the interest of the child. The question of photographs is rather an expensive one but she will look to see if she has any snaps of Amanda and if so will forward what she has. Matron would not consider having a photograph taken specially for Mrs Craig. Apart from the cost involved, Mrs Craig only shows interest in Amanda when she is in custody.

In those cases where the children of a prisoner were not taken into care, but were looked after by relatives, they were subject to the standard formal and restrictive visiting regulations and conditions. No special concessions or arrangements were made for children; nothing was done to help mothers, children, or other members of the family cope. There were no activites provided for children. They could not be with their mother in a relaxed, quasi-normal situation and they had to sit, like adult visitors, on one side of a table, behaving well and quietly under the constant surveillance of prison officers. For older children this was arduous, for young children an impossibility, particularly following what was usually a long and tiring journey.

Mother and Babies

Some babies stay in prison with their mothers. While this is considered extraordinary practice in the United States, in the United Kingdom it is on paper at least an accepted part of the official regime.[17] There are mother and baby units at Holloway and Styal, with places for eight and fifteen babies respectively, up to the age of one year. At Askham Grange open prison, children may live with their mothers until they are two or three years old.

At Cornton Vale, the mother and baby rooms (one in each unit of seven) were a much advertised feature and we were told that children were allowed to stay until the age of two. Officially, women had the choice of keeping their young children with them but the practice was somewhat different. Women were, in fact, strongly discouraged from keeping with them babies born while they were in prison, or from bringing babies and infants in with them. There was only one baby in the prison while we were there. He was the child of a young woman serving a borstal sentence who had fought very hard to be allowed to keep him, and only succeeded eventually by enlisting the support of professionals within the prison. She also successfully fought a battle to breast-feed, and somehow managed to survive the very harsh regime imposed upon them both which meant living in isolation in the mother and baby room. The baby was not allowed in the communal parts of the unit, such as the living-room, and the reason given was 'security'. She was urged continually to hand her baby over to her mother to look after, but managed to resist this pressure. Feeding times, rest times, exercise times were rigidly prescribed by the prison, apparently common practice in women's prisons. Fitzgerald and Sim report that

> Even in the mother and baby units at Holloway . . . regimentation is the characteristic feature. Generally reserved for women who give birth while in prison, life in these units is as regulated for the babies as it is for the women. Mothers, for example, cannot decide feeding times, and no-one picks up the babies between feeds.

There are also no provisions for children in prison to be taken on outside visits.[18]

The pressure we observed being applied to the young borstal woman was also, according to the evidence of social work reports, applied to others. For example, when one woman's baby was born in prison, she kept him for some months, and expressed her wish to continue to care for him. We gained the distinct impression from the social work reports that there was a slow and deliberate gathering of evidence against her to justify the eventual taking of the baby.

> Superficially he looked fine and his clothing was clean, but in the little important bits – his ears and the creases in his neck and elsewhere – there was room for improvement.

> The staff wonder if the mother is beginning to resent the attention he receives.

Aspersions were even cast on the character of the baby, described at the age of two months as 'a greedy child'. The baby was finally taken with very little warning or preparation, to prevent a 'fuss' being made by the mother. This illustrated, among other things, the characteristic policy of employing short-term repressive measures, to avoid and deny emotional confrontation.

Whether the policy of keeping babies and infants in prison with their mothers is a good one is arguable. It is often presented as a humane policy and one which can encourage 'good mothering'. However it seems in fact that the 'needs' of mother and child are sacrificed to the 'needs' of the institution and at least one governor of a women's prison, James Anderson of Styal prison would like to see almost all imprisoned mothers of new-born babies paroled as soon after the birth as they are fit to leave hospital.[19]

Children already in Care

The Home Office has stated that:

> To send a woman to prison . . . is to take her away from her family; her children in particular, may suffer from this deprivation, which can lead to the break up of the home even where there is a stable marriage. When a man is absent from home, it can be kept going by his wife if she is provided with sufficient money and general support. But when it is the woman who is absent, the husband is often unable to cope and unless there are relations who can take on the housekeeping and care of the children, the home may have to be broken up and the children scattered either into the care of the local authority or to different relatives.[20]

However, looking at studies of women in prison, it is clear that in many cases a prison sentence does not come as a bolt from the blue disrupting a previously stable situation. The high proportion of already separated mothers and children may reflect sentencing policies, the propensity of criminal activity to go hand-in-hand with a generally disrupted lifestyle, or both. The reasons for imprisonment may have a lot to do with a woman's perceived failure as a mother, explicitly so in cases of child injury but also in cases where children are already in care.

Those children already in care before their mothers were imprisoned had no contact at all with them while they were in Cornton Vale. Since in every case there had previously been some, or a great deal of contact, this must have represented a deterioration in their relationships. As we have described, relationships between mothers and their children put into care as a result of the mother's crime, were extremely sporadic and difficult. In general, the attitudes of prison staff towards women whose children were in care, in particular where child injury or death had occurred, were that such women have not only proved themselves incompetent to look after their children, but are also devoid of feeling for them. If they expressed a wish to see their children or objected to signing parental rights forms, this was construed as 'peevishness' or 'awkwardness'. This was of course easier than dealing with raw emotions of grief and guilt. The situation of imprisoned women whose children were in care was one of extreme powerlessness, and it appeared to be a situation which Cornton Vale fostered.

While making claims to be a therapeutic environment in which relationships may be forged or mended, what happened between women and their children provides the most telling example possible that this was not so, and illustrates with clarity the failure of the prison to deal with the reality confronting the women.

Friends and Relatives

Relationships with children outside prison and with other relatives and friends are maintained by means of letters and visits. The sending and receiving of letters and the arrangements made for visits are enmeshed in rules and regulations, the exercise of which is often discretionary and may thus become another weapon in the prison's armoury of control. Adults were allowed to correspond with anyone, except people in other prisons. This rule could be waived in the case of a special relationship, such as husband or parent. Correspondence between prisoners and ex-prisoners of Cornton Vale was not allowed.

Under 21s were only allowed to correspond with relatives. Cousins, aunts, etc. would be checked out by social workers, and for this reason prisoners often did not request to write to them. Letters could not even be received from friends, and prisoners were not allowed to write to explain why they could not correspond with them. There was enormous resentment in the whole Under 21s group that they were not allowed to correspond with friends. Letters were allowed from boyfriends only if they were defined as 'co-habitees'.

Everyone was allowed one letter a week to send out. Extra letters had to be bought although these were a privilege that could be granted or refused at the discretion of the governor. All mail in and out was subject to censorship. The censoring of mail was not a specialized task; but one done by an officer who happened to be on duty. If we were present in the office while mail was being read, we would frequently have bits read out. Letters were handed to prisoners without the envelopes. When we asked why, we were told 'In Greenock [the women's prison before Cornton Vale opened] there was a paper shortage'! Women were not allowed to keep more than a few letters in their room at a time. They were removed and stored with their property. Censorship in and out took three forms: first, rules about who letters could be written to; second, content was scrutinized with regard to security including not only blatant risks such as escape plans, the sending in of drugs etc., but also mentioning any other inmate or member of staff in any way which might identify them, and criticizing any aspect of prison regime or staff and so on; third, letters must not 'upset' the recipient. Bad news, depression, or anger was censored out of letters.

Between them the second and third categories ensured that there was very little of importance to prisoners that could be discussed in letters. In addition, the knowledge that letters were going to be read by a third party was in itself a very inhibiting factor, particularly when women knew that what they wrote and what was written to them could at best be freely communicated between members of staff and other people working in the prison, and at worst be held up for public comment or even ridicule.

Women generally held negative views on censorship:

> I don't think it should be done, especially letters coming in. You imagine them laughing at what's in the letter. They say things like 'You tell your friend less of that bad language or she won't be allowed to write in.' There's personal things in letters. Officers

speak of it in front of everyone about the contents of your letters. They asked me about my sister's hysterectomy and they could only have known that from the mail.

My letters out have never been stopped, because I don't really write anything. My letters are very dull. I write letters about nothing. You can't express yourself – not at the visits either. You just keep everything nice. I wouldn't want to worry them anyway, especially my husband.

Every letter's the same. You can't write about your feelings, you just write about work.

You'd like to put down a lot of things that you can't. You just tell a lot of lies. You say you're getting on fine and not to worry. But they can't stop you criticising the place once you're out.

It used to bother me – it doesn't any more. I've got used to not being able to write things.

Several people gave specific examples of things which had been censored.

My letter to my aunt didn't go out – because I criticised the doctor and said he was more like a vet.

There was a section in my grandmother's letter which was scored out. I think it was about my friend.

I wrote an angry letter to my father about not coming to see me because he was too busy with his bird. I told him he ought to grow up. I had to rewrite it nicely.

Sometimes letters were held back, and people were not told why, or even who they were from,

There's one letter that came for me that's been held back for five weeks. They never have time to tell me why. I think it's from my Granny.

Criticisms of food, members of staff, and other inmates were all quoted as reasons why letters had had to be rewritten. One letter written in pencil had to be rewritten in ink. These sorts of constraints were applied as much to adults as Under 21s.

Special requests by Under 21s to write to relatives who did not belong to their immediate family and boy and girl friends were subject to extensive checking, long delays, and peremptory judgements where staff seemed to start from the assumption that 'cousins' and even 'grandmothers' were really criminal associates.

A month ago, I requested to write to my cousin. I've not heard yet.

I asked to write to my girl friend. The social worker said no – she's a bad influence on me.

I had to request to write to my granny. Then a social worker had to check her.

One borstal girl who had not had contact with her family since she had been in prison was also refused permission to receive letters from her 'undesirable' boyfriend.

My aunt and uncle are mad. They haven't written or visited since I've been in. They feel I've let them down. I wrote to my brother and my mother when I came in but they haven't written back. They won't let me get letters from my boyfriend – they say I should forget him.

As one young offender pointed out, the overall effect of these restrictions is that the rules stop you keeping up your friendships.

Visiting is another important aspect of maintaining relationships but one that is also made difficult by the prison regime. The regulations surrounding visiting are complex, and often subject to the discretion of the governor, with the result that prisoners often do not know their entitlement to visits. Statutorily, a convicted prisoner is entitled to one visit a month. Visits vary in frequency and length from one institution to another and from one time to another within the same institution, and may be allowed more often than once a month, according for example, to the availability of staff. Visits may be made by a prisoner's family or friends with the permission of the governor. Prisoners send their prospective visitors a visiting order which must be handed in at the gate when the friends or relatives arrive. At Cornton Vale, discretion was sometimes exercised over who was allowed to visit and when. For example, a newly admitted young offender was deemed 'not ready' for a visit from her twin sister, which was held over as an eventual reward for 'good behaviour'.

At Cornton Vale, prisoners were usually allowed fortnightly visits. Visits were 'open' – that is prisoners and visitors were not physically separated and visits took place in the visiting room, which was laid out with separate tables and chairs, prisoners sitting on one side of a table, visitors on another. Drinks and refreshments were available from a Women's Royal Voluntary Service trolley. Prison officers were posted round the room at very frequent intervals, every conversation and every movement made within their hearing and their sight.

Everyone agreed that visits, although open, lacked privacy.

> I don't feel at ease. There's far too many officers in the room – there's more officers than visitors. They hear every word you're saying. There's no time for tea – often you don't get the full twenty minutes.

> They're certainly not private. You can't get talking. There should be more and they should be longer. It's a very long journey just for an hour.

> I'd like to see more of them [her two children]. It's very upsetting. The officers listen in and you can't be soft with them around.

> There was an officer who was listening to what I said, and she questioned me afterwards about what I'd said to my mother.

> The officer was laughing and joining in the conversation. She didn't even go so my husband could kiss me goodbye. [This was a room-visit when prisoner was ill.]

The general arrangement was felt to be inhibiting and the effect depressing.

> It's like when you're in hospital. An hour's enough. You run out of things to say.

> My mother and sister have come three times. I've decided not to have any visits now as everyone gets too upset and I feel really depressed afterwards.

However, the most disliked feature of visits was the strip searching that occurred before and after visiting. Several women said that in their opinion the benefits of 'open' visiting were outweighed by the degradation and humiliation of the body searches. While prison staff believed that prisoners 'got used to it' and that searching was an essential part of an 'open' visiting policy, most women in fact found body searches increasingly hard to bear, and felt that they were conducted with unnecessary disregard for personal dignity.

Body searches did not occur only in conjunction with visiting. They could be made at random, or more often after some contact with the outside world or with the wider community of prisoners, for example on return from a 'pv' (privileged visit outside the prison with family to which a few women near the end of long sentences were entitled), or coming back from work in the administration block. Although there were obvious practical reasons for conducting searches after some contact with the outside world, searching at these times served a symbolic function of reaffirming imprisonment, shame, and lack of status in the same way the very formal procedure of a 'mini-trial' for dealing with disciplinary offences served to remind prisoners of their original trial which resulted in imprisonment.

> You get searched before and after visits. I was pulled out and searched in the middle of a visit because I moved my hands quickly onto the table.

> After visits you get strip-searched. They went through my hair and said they were looking for hash! I said 'What's that?' I'm learning in here!

> The searching after visits sickens you. Sometimes it's worse than others. You can be stripped any time and searched. You often are on your way back from work.

> Once in Borstal some money went missing. We all had to strip naked and bend forward, even those who had periods.

> After P.V.s you get strip searched – ears, nose, mouth, everything. It's really humiliating.

Random room searches were also made fairly often – they appeared to occur about once a month – and people's rooms would be left in chaos, their possessions, clothes, and bedding tipped into a heap on the floor. Obviously prisoners were not told when random body or room searches were going to occur and neither were they told beforehand about the general policy of searching. Unless they had already been warned by other prisoners, the first room search came as a great shock.

Finally, for one group of prisoners – the young – their relationships with their parents may be of crucial importance. A number of borstal girls said that their imprisonment had improved their relationship with their parents. Borstal training was almost always a first sentence and as such usually came as a great shock to parents. It may also provide a respite in a very hectic and disorganized life which means that parents' anxieties about physical and moral safety are for the moment allayed, and a breathing space created during which all parties may take stock. Two typical comments were

> I get on better with all my family now. It gave them all a shock and they've rallied round. My mother writes every single day – she doesn't like me to be left out in the dark. She tells me all the local news.

> I can really talk to my parents now. I couldn't before. My father's never missed a visit. My mother's agoraphobic but she came to visit me even so. They've said I'm to go back to them – it's proved to me that they care about me.

This being so, it seems a pity that more opportunites are not being created to take advantage of this, for example, in the form of extended visiting hours.

The way in which relationships within the prison and those between prisoners and their lives outside prison are dealt with provides further evidence of the ambivalence at the centre of the Cornton Vale regime. The small living units, set up ostensibly to foster relationships between prisoners, in fact provide the ideal mechanism for the constant surveillance, manipulation, and control of such relationships by prison staff. In such an atmosphere, certainly as far as adult prisoners were concerned, it was impossible for the staff to fulfil what was seen as a therapeutic role, for example by fostering relationships between themselves and prisoners. In addition, their training does little to fit them to take on such a role.

Some women enter prison with their relationship with family and friends outside already fragmented. All women will experience a severe testing of their outside relationships by the very fact of their imprisonment. Unfortunately, the experience of imprisonment will usually damage rather than maintain or build these relationships. The very artificial conditions under which visiting and letter-writing occur, and the total invasion of the privacy of the individual make the survival of outside relationships (if they do endure) a triumph against odds rather than the result of a regime designed to nurture the personal relationships of its inmates.

9

Turning Point

In this book, we have set out to understand and to analyse what happens to women in prison in terms of both the past and the present. We have considered the crimes of women and traced the development of punishment and prison regimes from the pre-industrial period to the present and have discussed the role of criminological theory in shaping those regimes. A principal concern has been to see women's prisons in the context of society in general, to see women prisoners as women who happen to be in prison rather than as a strange sub-species of humanity, and to see criminological theory relating to women in the context of general theories, ideas, and assumptions about the nature and role of women.

In the historical and contemporary accounts of women in prison, certain themes recur. We know, although these are not facts that have been sought for inclusion in prison statistics, that women in prison (like men) have been and are predominantly working-class, poor, and unskilled. They have been and are most commonly convicted for minor crimes against property. Prison was and is a different experience for women, at least partly because of the difference in penal responses to them. As soon as male and female prisoners were separated, differences in the sort of regime to which they were subjected became apparent, and have grown with time. It is clear that women in prison are more closely observed and controlled, more often punished, and punished for more trivial offences than are men in prison. The options that are open to women in prison are limited. Domestic work has been and still is the main work available to women in prison, whether its proposed aim has been to produce good servants, good wives, or most honestly, to keep the prison going.[1] The relationship with women's lives in the world outside is clear, if distorted.

We have shown how women offenders gradually came to be conceived as 'disordered' and 'abnormal', the yardstick of normality often being a stereotype of femininity. This thinking came to full fruition with the plans for Holloway and Cornton Vale in which two major women's prisons were to be virtually reconstituted as mental hospitals. In practice, they turned out to be just like prisons, oriented to surveillance, control and work but with an expanded vision of rehabilitation and reform meant to penetrate the emotions, psyche and personality through therapy. With this double form of control of both the body and the inner person, surveillance and control penetrated still deeper, and confinement for women became even closer. The issue of potential conflict between the goals of 'therapy' and 'discipline' was not considered at the planning stage, except glibly in terms of the supposed therapeutic benefits of tight security. When conflict broke out, the demands of discipline and security invariably won. Thus, the Health Centre at Cornton Vale, after some resistance, was staffed by officers and not nurses. 'Special programmes' for selected groups of inmates might be initiated but were inevitably sacrificed to the general demands of the prison. The drugs dependency unit at Holloway, known as the Therapeutic Unit, by the 1980s had seemingly been more or less absorbed back into the general prison system. The role of psychiatrists at both prisons turned out to be one of support for prison authority, rather than (as had been envisaged), one of initiation of policy and positive, more open innovative approaches to prisoners and prison life.

Meanwhile, the psychiatric experiment in women's prison reform that has evolved to what may be seen as its ultimate conclusion has reached its apotheosis in the situation in the psychiatric wing at Holloway. Confinement in cells throughout most of the day, inability to work and to use existing facilities, extensive use of solitary confinement and neglect of prisoners' needs are the most significant aspects of these deprivations. The regime in the psychiatric wing at Holloway has become a matter of national debate, the main tenor of which has been that there are women there who should not be there because they should be in 'secure units in mental hospitals' getting 'proper treament'. Thus, in a feature article in a national newspaper, it was stated that

> Both the Governor [of Holloway] and the head of the prison service say that people like these should never have been sent to prison in the first place. The Governor says she tries to get them transferred to hospital, but there are not enough places in secure units in mental hospitals. . , .[2]

Apart from the fact that psychiatrists themselves have described the sort of women in question as suffering from conditions not amenable to psychiatric treatment, this emphasis has meant that several important questions have been begged – have been only touched on or avoided altogether.

The publicity that Holloway's psychiatric wing has attracted has acted to reinforce the stereotype of women in prison as mad. In much of the treatment of the issue in the press, the women on the psychiatric wing have been described in almost subhuman terms, reminiscent both of Elizabeth Fry's early impressions of Newgate and Mary Carpenter's and Lombroso's descriptions of female convicts. An example is one journalist's description of a young woman

> . . . who had an odd shaped head with prominent bumps and a scar on her forehead. She is a head banger who repeatedly bashes her head against the wall when left alone for long periods. She had been banging her head the night before, and this morning had thrown a pot of urine over the officer who came to unlock her door. A few days ago, again left alone, she covered herself from top to toe in excrement.[3]

While it has been acknowledged that the regime is 'unsuitable' and produces its own reactions to extreme boredom and depression from the extreme isolation, alienation and lack of support experienced by those subjected to the regime, the implication is that it is unsuitable because deranged individuals have been subjected to it and not that its unsuitability may actually create the disturbance it was designed to 'cure'. Thus, an ex-art therapist, who resigned in disgust at the regime on the psychiatric wing bravely spoke publicly about it, saying:

> Women are sent to C1 [the psychiatric wing] because they are thought to need treatment. Instead, they find a regime aimed primarily at containment . . . C1 and the punishment block are very similar . . . They look the same and it's very much the same regime.[4]

Both in the recent controversy and discussion about Holloway, and in a less 'crisis-point' fashion in appraisals of Cornton Vale, it is often implied that the general prison regime is appropriate for most prisoners and it is only the really 'disturbed' few who should be getting different treatment, and that they, because prison regimes are inappropriate, incur the worst and most repressive responses of the institution in terms of solitary confinement and restriction of activities. However, punishment cells and punishment regimes as well as a 'psychiatric wing' (at Holloway) whose regime is more or less the same, if not more repressive, are in constant use in both prisons. Indeed there are frequent calls from staff for yet more punishment cells at Cornton Vale. And, as has been described, they are used in response to a very wide range of behaviour.

The whole question of the role of 'punishment' and the existence of punishment blocks in what were supposedly set up as therapeutic establishments, and their implications for women in prison whether or not labelled 'disturbed', need to be aired. No official policy was ever stated regarding discipline for either Cornton Vale or Holloway. In the case of the former it was simply not mentioned at all. In the case of the latter, it was suggested that

> the normal conception of a punishment block is regarded as incompatible with the ethos of the new establishment. It is proposed that, instead of a separate punishment block, one of the prison units will be specially designed and equipped as a unit for the prisoners who for one reason or another need to be separated from the others, but are not transferred to the hospital . . .[5]

Significantly, the sister in charge of the Health Centre at Cornton Vale would not allow its residential wing to be used if it were to be staffed by prison officers, on the assumption that it would inevitably become another punishment block.

It has been acknowledged that the extreme boredom of the regime on C1 itself encourages behaviour that may be labelled as 'mad' – such as the woman who tried to cut off her breast and said she'd done it 'to get out of my cell for a few minutes.'[6] However, this point should be strengthened. In conditions of extreme sensory deprivation, such as those experienced by women in solitary confinement in strip cells, whether in a 'psychiatric' block or a 'punishment' block, almost all avenues of expression and of resistance are cut off. Stevenson (the art therapist) vividly describes the predicament of women on the psychiatric wing

> . . . gradually deprived of furniture and clothes – either as punishment or in an attempt to control them – women can be left with just a blanket, crouched naked in a corner, refusing to wear the stripdress in protest. . . . These women rarely get out of their cells because they are causing problems for the staff.[7]

An important result of the public concern about Holloway has been the publication of a report on its future, suggesting that women in prison today are not, like those of yesterday, all mad, and that the new Holloway may have been horribly misconceived. By the end of the seventies though, there was beginning to be official dissension from the view of all female prisoners as mentally disturbed. In

1978/79 a Parliamentary Committee conducted an extensive inquiry into women and the penal system. One of their particular concerns was 'mentally disordered' women in the prison system, of which it was clear from the bias of their questioning they assumed there were many. However, there was little agreement between witnesses. An assistant secretary to the Home Office insisted that

> Our general impression is that the female population is depressingly normal and that a very large number of the women are normal women who happen to have committed criminal offences and happen to have been sentenced to a custodial sentence by the court . . .[8]

One of the members of the Committee expressed himself as 'disappointed' with this answer, and with the replies of the Assistant Director of Medical Services at the Home Office who claimed that

> . . . over the years there has been a shift, a change of type of person and that there are fewer who are psychiatrically disturbed in relationship to the total number than there were before. There are normal but difficult people in the system.[9]

In an apparent attempt both to justify the past basis of policy and to explain his own opinion about the nature of the female prison population, the Assistant Director claimed that women in prison used to be mad but were now bad.

The Holloway Project Committee Report, while prompted by events in the psychiatric wing, began with a general statement echoing the opinions of some of the witnesses quoted above, that most women in prison were 'normal' people.

> The proposed development of Holloway had been based on the proposition that most women and girls in custody required some form of medical, psychiatric or remedial treatment. By 1980 the view was gaining ground that the prison service was receiving an increasing proportion of women whose crimes, circumstances and personalities did not call for such specialised help. It was considered that they possessed many characteristics which were similar to those of the male inmate population.[10]

While the authors of the report imply that the problems at Holloway are not due to any mistaken theories about the nature of women in prison, but to an actual change in the sort of women being admitted to prison from one decade to the next, they do go on to admit a loss of faith in the medical model of treatment for criminal behaviour occasioned by mounting evidence that it did little to reduce criminality.

This account amply illustrates the confusion endemic in policy and practice pertaining to women in prison. While on the one hand implicitly or explicitly maintaining that women who go to prison are mentally disturbed, on the other hand it is declared that prisons cannot really do anything for such cases. Without accepting the point that such large numbers of women are mentally disturbed before going into prison it is, nonetheless, possible to examine the orientation of the policy makers and practitioners concerned. To date, the HMI Inspectorate Report[11] for Cornton Vale has declared that prison is unable to cope with its 'disturbed inmates' and psychiatrists agree. In an otherwise anodyne report, HMI stressed as the one 'problem' at Cornton Vale its 'disturbed' inmates (supposedly those for whom the regime had been designed). It was implied that prison was not an appropriate place for them since they needed 'treament', although the psychiatrists added in evidence that their 'condition' was not treatable!

As has so often happened in the history of prisons, the Holloway Project Committee in its proposals for the future placed a lot of emphasis on architectue. Just as the old buildings had been regarded as an insuperable block to development of the regime in the 1970s, in the 1980s there was general agreement that the newly built prison was architecturally a disaster. A report submitted to the Committee from the All-Party Parliamentary Health Group felt that 'the move away from established prison design towards a hospital model has proved disastrous.'[12] One of the recommendations of the Holloway Project Committee has been to demolish and rebuild the psychiatric wing according to the latest theory of prison design – the 'new generation' concept. This sort of latter-day panopticon current now in parts of the United States has been developed with high-security-risk, long-term prisoners in mind. The report on Holloway follows a recent Home Office Report on the management of long-term male prisoners that recommended the serious consideration of the concentration of long-term high-security prisoners who are perceived as disrupting the whole prison system under the current policy of dispersal, in several small 'new generation' type prisons.[13] The essence of 'new generation' prison design is increased control, although as usual there is talk of this being achieved through staff/prison 'relationships'. 'New generation' prisons often do away with cell corridors and instead arrange the cells around a central multi-use area in each unit. Since each cell opens directly onto the central area, staff can observe all the cells without having to move about in a consciously patrolling manner. It is claimed that these

designs have been very successful in simultaneously improving surveillance and encouraging control of inmates through the development of good inter-personal relations. Such designs have an 'inbuilt
capacity to separate groups of prisoners.' In the summary to the
Home Office Report on male prisoners it is stated that

> . . . no previous English study has considered the possibility of
> high security prisons built on the 'new generation' lines current in
> the U.S.A., that is, made up of units that embody a high level of
> supervision and that can be operated separately.[14]

This may be so, but as we have seen in the Scottish system, aspects
of prison design at Cornton Vale seem to resemble closely 'new
generation' thinking, and small units, purporting to foster 'relationships' are in fact used effectively for the surveillance, control and
manipulation of prisoners. It is ironic, but perfectly in the tradition
of the treatment of women in prison, that designs developed for
high-security-risk, long-term male prisoners, should be suggested as
appropriate for women who are supposedly in need of psychiatric
assessment or treatment, most of whom, far from being long-term
prisoners, are actually on remand. Moreover, the ordinary prison
regime with its framework of prison rules, and in women's prisons
the particularly close surveillance and control exercised allow almost
no individuality or autonomy and ironically no scope for collective
expression.

In the context of such a regime, attempts to resist or rebel are made in
isolation and can be easily interpreted as the acts of a disordered and
deranged individual. This has indeed been seen over and over again in
the past as well as the present, in which the acts of women who attempt
to resist or defy the regime are given no validity or significance.

Trying to discover what women in prison in the past felt about their
situation, and women in Scotland feel now, has been a major aim of
this book. This objective has been a particularly important one, given
the way in which women in prison have been objectified both by
prison regimes and by criminological theorists. Some criminologists,
while reaching non-traditional conclusions about the nature of
women's crime, nevertheless have followed traditional paths in
proposing monothematic analyses that take little notice of the reality
of womens' lives, or of women's own account of themselves.[15]

The problems facing women who are or have been in prison who
wish their voices to be heard are immense. However, the significnace
of women themselves as a source of change is vital. With even a small
amount of support, an arena within which arguments may be

debated and the need for the prison system to account for itself may emerge. A relatively new organization 'Women in Prison' whose aims are firmly based on the actual experiences of women who are or have been in prison, and which have been largely initiated and staffed by ex-prisoners, has been instrumental in bringing to light conditions in Holloway's psychiatric wing. It has campaigned on other issues also, and the mere fact of its existence can only strengthen the very vulnerable position of women prisoners and ex-prisoners.

One sort of change in the prison system that relies (although obviously not without outside support) on prisoners themselves for initiation and represents one form of struggle by women in prison, is the sort of change achieved in some women's prisons in the United States on the basis of equal opportunities legislation. Such campaigns can achieve increased work, training, educational and recreational opportunities.[16] While this may obviously be of some value, such an approach does beg wider questions in setting up men's prisons as enviable institutions, and in implying that imprisonment can be a valuable experience. Historical and contemporary evidence suggests rather that imprisonment *per se* is both an irrelevant and a damaging response to women's crime.

Similarly, the sort of reforms of prison regimes that seek to make them as much like 'outside' as possible ('almost human') seem tortuously pointless when the virtual abolition of prison should seem an achievable goal for a prison population, the majority of whom are remanded for social and medical reports, and the majority of whom have committed relatively minor property or behavioural offences.

Some examples of such 'reforms' are the demand for mixed sex prisons, and calls for conjugal or extended family visiting. Proposals for the latter incidentally met with howls of hostility from virtually all the prison staff interviewed by a parliamentary committee in 1978. Where mixed sex prisons have been established, the women prisoners have claimed that they are doubly exploited by the men for both their sexual and 'nurturing' services.[17] This demonstrates the tendency of innovative programmes within prisons, often established in the face of hostility from prison staff, to backslide and suffer distortion in the path of the reactionary force of prison tradition. In this very tradition, while Holloway and Cornton Vale can be seen as therapeutic experiments that have failed, they are in fact experiments that have never been tried. Whether in fact they ever could have been is in itself doubtful.

Notes

Chapter 1: The Imprisonment of Women in Britain and the United States

1 Dorie Klein and June Kress, 'Any woman's blues: A critical overview of women, crime, and the criminal justice system,' *Crime and Social Justice* 5 (Spring–Summer 1976), pp. 34–49. L. Bowker, *Women, Crime and the Criminal Justice System* (Heath, Lexington, Mass., 1978). C. Smart, *Women, Crime and Criminology* (Routledge and Kegan Paul, London, 1977. E.B. Leonard, *Women and Crime* (Macmillan, London, 1985).

2 F. Adler, *Sisters in Crime: The Rise of the New Female Criminal* (McGraw-Hill, New York, 1975). F. Adler, ed, *The Incidence of Female Criminality in the Contemporary World* (New York University Press, New York, 1981). Adler's latest book is very contradictory. In the first chapter she reiterates her thesis that there has been a substantial increase in the criminality of women due to the women's movement. Yet almost all of the contributions to the book show no such increase and some reject her thesis on the importance of the movement.

3 Scottish prisons are administered separately from those in England and Wales and developed somewhat independently.

4 S. K. Datesman and F. R. Scarpitti, *Women, Crime and Justice* (Oxford University Press, Oxford, 1980).

5 *Holloway Project Committee Report* (HMSO, July 1985), Annex E.

6 Ibid.

7 Ibid., Annex E. See also S. Edwards, *Women on Trial* (Manchester University Press, London, 1984), pp. 188–99, for a good discussion of the pre-trial process and the role of social inquiry reports.

8 *Prisons Statistics, England and Wales, 1984* (HMSO, 1985), pp. 74, 90.

9 Cited in T. C. N. Gibbens, 'England and Wales,' in *The Incidence of Female Criminality in the Contemporary World*, ed. F. Adler.

10 R. R. Arditi, F. Goldberg, M. M. Hartle, J. H. Peters and W. R. Phelps, 'The sexual segregation of American prisons,' *Yale Law Journal* 82, 6 (1973), pp. 1229–73.

11 Datesman and Scarpitti, *Women, Crime and Justice*.

12 P. J. Baunach, 'The national jail census, 1983 is now available', *The Criminal Justice Archive and Information Network* (Winter 1985), p. 1.

13 Ibid.

14 L. Singer, 'Women and the correctional process', *American Criminal Law Review*, 11 (Winter 1973), pp. 295–308. Arditi *et al.*, 'Sexual segregation of American prisons'.

15 *Holloway Project Report*, Annex C.
16 Singer, 'Women and the correctional process'. Arditi *et al.*, 'Sexual segregation in American prisons'. M. L. Velimesis, 'The female offender', *Crime and Delinquency Literature* 7 (March 1975), pp. 94–112.
17 M. Velimesis, 'Criminal justice for the female offender', p. 105.
18 James C. Fox, 'Women's prison policy, prisoner activism, and the impact of the contemporary feminist movement: A case study', *The Prison Journal*, LXIV, 1 (Spring–Summer, 1984), pp. 15–36, p. 22.
19 D. Kassebaum and G. Ward, *Women's Prison: Sex and Social Structure* (Weidenfeld and Nicolson, London, 1966). R. Giallombardo, *Society of Women: A Study of a Women's Prison* (John Wiley, New York, 1966). E. Heffernan, *Making it in Prison: The Square, the Cool, and the Life* (Wiley–Interscience, London, 1972).
20 See, for example, N. Goodman, *Studies of Female Offenders*, Home Office Research Unit Report (HMSO, 1967). T. C. N. Gibbens, 'Female offenders', *British Journal of Hospital Medicine* 6 (September 1971), pp. 279–86.
21 S. Cohen and L. Taylor, *Prison Secrets* (Pluto Press, London, 1976).
22 T. C. N. Gibbens, 'England and Wales', in *The Incidence of Female Criminality*, ed. F. Adler, p. 107.
23 F. M. Heidensohn, 'The imprisonment of females' in *The Use of Imprisonment* (Routledge and Kegan Paul, London, 1975). F. M. Heidensohn, *Women and Crime*. P. Carlen, *Women's Imprisonment* (Routledge and Kegan Paul, London, 1983).
24 P. Carlen, ed., *Criminal Women: Autobiographical Accounts* (Polity Press, Cambridge, 1985). A. Peckham, *A Woman in Custody* (Fontana, Glasgow, 1985). For a recent fictional though obviously biographical account of American prisons, see A. F. Loewenstein, *This Place* (Pandora Press, London, 1984).
25 J. Irwin, *The Felon* (Prentice-Hall, Englewood Cliffs, New Jersey, 1970).
26 C. Thomas and D. Peterson, *Prison Organization and Inmate Subcultures* (Indianapolis, Bobbs-Merrill, 1977). L. Goodstein, D. L. MacKenzie, R. L. Shotland, 'Personal control and inmate adjustment to prison', *Criminology*, 22, 3 (1984), pp. 343–69. For similar work on women, see G. F. Jensen and D. Jones, 'Perspectives on inmate culture: A study of women in prison', *Social Forces*, 54, 3 (March 1976), pp. 591–603. T. F. Hartnagel and M. E. Gillan, 'Female prisoners and the inmate code', *Pacific Sociological Review*, 23, 1 (January, 1980), pp. 85–104.
27 A. D. Smith, *Women in Prison* (Stevens, London, 1962).
28 The classic statement of this position is G. Rusche and O. Kirchheimer, *Punishment and Social Structure* (Columbia University Press, New York, 1939). I. Jankovic, 'Labour market and imprisonment', in *Punishment and Penal Discipline*, eds. T. Platt and P. Takagi (Crime and Social Justice Associates, Berkeley, 1980).
29 Michel Foucault, *Madness and Civilization* (Social Science Paperbacks, London, 1967); *Discipline and Punish: The Birth of the Prison* tr. A. Sheridan (Allen Lane, London, 1977). M. Ignatieff, *A Just Measure of*

Pain: The Penitentiary in the Industrial Revolution, 1750–1850 (Macmillan, London, 1978). D. J. Rothman, *The Discovery of the Asylum* (Little, Brown, Boston, 1971).

30 E. B. Freedman, *Their Sisters' Keepers: Women's Prison Reform in America, 1830–1930* (University of Michigan Press, Ann Arbor, 1981). N. H. Rafter, 'Hard times: Custodial prisons for women and the example of the New York state prison for women at Auburn, 1893–1933', in *Judge, Lawyer, Victim, Thief*, eds. N. H. Rafter and E. A. Stanko (Northeastern University Press, Boston, 1982). N. H. Rafter, *Partial Justice: State Prisons and Their Inmates, 1800–1935*, (Northeastern University Press, Boston, 1985). C. Schweber, 'The government's unique experiment in salvaging women criminals': Cooperation and conflict in the Administration of a Women's Prison,' in Rafter and Stanko, eds, *Judge, Lawyer, Victim, Thief*.

31 J. Manton, *Mary Carpenter and the Children of the Streets.* (Heinemann, London, 1969). J. Rose, *Elizabeth Fry: A Biography* (St Martin, London, 1980). Smith, *Women in Prison.*

32 Heidensohn, *Women and Crime*, Chapter Four. M. Fitzgerald and J. Sim, *British Prisons* (Basil Blackwell, Oxford, 1982), one of the few books on the British penal system that includes a critical analysis of the position of women. J. Sim, 'Women in prison: A historical analysis', *The Abolitionist* 8 (Spring 1981), pp. 14–18.

33 Foucault rightly points out that every site of domination produces its resistances and stuggle, yet he provides few examples of these reactions.

34 M. Ignatieff, 'State and civil society, and total institutions: A critique of recent social histories of punishment', in *Crime and Justice: An Annual Review of Research*, eds. M. Tonry and N. Morris (University of Chicago Press, Chicago, 1981), p. 157.

35 We also conducted interviews with eleven members of the uniformed staff. We initially planned to interview more, but the constraints of time and the demands of the prison made this impossible.

36 It is significant that the only records we were not allowed to see were the medical records.

37 One of the best autobiographical accounts is F. E. Maybrick, *Mrs. Maybrick's Own Story: My Fifteen Lost Years* (Funk and Wagnall, New York, 1905). For an excellent list of such accounts, see J.A. Scheffler, 'Women's prison writing: An unexplored tradition in literature', *The Prison Journal* LXIV, 1 (Spring–Summer, 1984), pp. 57–67.

Chapter 2: The Physical and Symbolic Punishment of Women

1 J. Bellamy, *Crime and Public Order in the Later Middle Ages* (Routledge and Kegan Paul, London, 1973). J. Thorsten Sellin, *Slavery and the Penal System* (Elsevier, New York, 1976).

2   Bellamy, *Crime and Public Order*. Georg Rusche and Otto Kirchheimer, *Punishment and Social Structure* (Columbia University Press, New York, 1939).

3   Michel Foucault, *Discipline and Punish: The Birth of the Prison*, tr A. Sheriden (Allen Lane, London, 1977) p. 45.

4   J. Thorsten Sellin, *Pioneering in Penology. The Amsterdam Houses of Correction in the Sixteenth and Seventeenth Centuries* (University of Pennsylvania Press, Philadelphia, 1944) pp. 98–9.

5   Ibid. p. 101.

6   Carol Weiner, 'Sex roles and crime in late Elizabethan Hertfordshire', *Journal of Social History* (Summer 1978) pp. 39–60.

7   Keith Thomas, 'The double standard', *Journal of the History of Ideas*, 20 (1959), pp. 195–216. R. Emerson Dobash and Russell Dobash, *Violence Against Wives: The Case Against The Patriarchy* (Free Press, New York, 1979).

8   Christina Larner, *'Crimen exceptum?* The crime of witchcraft in Europe', in *Crime and the Law*, eds. V. A. C. Gatrell, B. Lenman and G. Parker (Europa, London, 1980) pp. 49–75.

9   B. Ehrenreich and D. English, *For Her Own Good* (Pluto, London, 1979).

10   Natalie Zemon Davis, 'The reasons of misrule: Youth groups and charivaris in sixteenth century France', *Past and Present*, 51 (February 1971), pp. 51–75. Edward Shorter, *The Making of the Modern Family* (Fontana, Glasgow, 1977). R. P. Dobash and R. Emerson Dobash, 'Community response to violence against wives: Charivari, abstract justice and patriarchy', *Social Problems*, 28, No 5 (June 1981) pp. 563–81.

11   Dobash and Dobash, 'Community response'.

12   William Andrews, *Old Time Punishments* (Andrews, Hull, 1880), pp. 8, 19.

13   L. Jewitt, 'Scolds and how they cured them in the good old times', *The Reliquary* (October 1860), p. 18.

14   Christopher Hill, *Puritanism and Revolutions* (Secker and Warburg, London, 1958). Samuel Mencher, *Poor Law to Poverty Program: Economic Security Policy in Britain and the United States* (University of Pittsburgh Press, Pittsburgh, 1967). Rusche and Kircheimer, *Punishment and Social Structure*.

15   Karl Marx, *Capital. A Critical Analysis of Capitalist Production*, Vol 1 (Lawrence and Wishart, London, 1970).

16   Max Weber, *The Protestant Ethic and The Spirit of Capitalism*, tr. Talcott Parsons (Allen and Unwin, London, 1930). R. H. Tawney, *Religion and the Rise of Capitalism* (Pelican, London, 1938). Mencher, *Poor Law to Poverty Program*.

17   There is much agreement on this point: see Thomas, Mencher and Rusche and Kirchheimer.

18   A. L. Beier, 'Vagrants and social order in Elizabethan England', *Past and Present*, 64 (August 1974), pp. 1–29. For a similar observation for the eighteenth century, see J. M. Beattie, 'The criminality of women in

eighteenth century England', *Journal of Social History*, 72 (1975), pp. 80–116, p. 115. Many of these vagrants were women and children deserted by husbands or fathers.

19　For a discussion of these negative and positive measures, see Rusche and Kirchheimer, *Punishment and Social Structure*. Mencher, *Poor Law to Poverty Program*. William J. Chambliss, 'The law of vagrancy' in *Crime and the Legal Process*, ed. W. J. Chambliss (McGraw-Hill, New York, 1969), pp. 51–62. Marx, *Capital* Vol 1, pp. 671–96.

20　Thomas More, *Utopia*, ed Paul Turner (Penguin, Harmondsworth, 1980).

21　Sellin, *Pioneering in Penology*. See also Valerie Pearl, 'Puritans and poor relief: The London workhouse, 1649–1660' in *Puritans and Revolutionaries*, eds D. Pennington and K. Thomas (Oxford University Press, Oxford, 1978).

22　Eileen Power, *Mediaeval English Nunneries* (Cambridge University Press, Cambridge, 1922). L. Eckenstein, *Women Under Monasticism* (Cambridge University Press, Cambridge, 1896).

23　Power, *Mediaeval English Nunneries*, p. 342.

24　Sellin, *Pioneering in Penology*. Mencher, *Poor Law to Poverty Program*. E.G. O'Donoghue, *Bridewell Hospital: Palace, Prison, School* (Lane, London, 1923). A. Van der Slice, 'Elizabethan houses of correction', *Journal of Criminal Law and Criminology*, 27 (May-June 1936) pp. 45–67. Pieter Spierenburgh (ed.), *The Emergence of Carceral Institutions: Prisons, Galleys and Lunatic Asylums: 1550–1900*, Volume 12, Centrum voor Maatschappijgeschiedenis (Department of the History of Society, Erasmus University, Rotterdam, 1985).

25　The name Bridewell derived from the location of the palace which was near the Bride's well.

26　Van der Slice, 'Elizabethan houses'.

27　O'Donoghue, *Bridewell Hospital*, p. 156.

28　Sellin, *Pioneering in Penology*, p. 30.

29　Ibid., p. 87.

30　Ibid., p. 88.

31　Ibid., p. 92.

32　Pearl, 'Puritans and relief', p. 212.

33　Our analysis of the materialist aspects of labour in prison relies upon Marx's conception of labour. He defines 'socially necessary' labour as the labour necessary for the maintenance of humankind. 'Useful labour' is labour that creates or modifies use values (anything that is demanded) which is usually produced collectively under capitalism. 'Productive labour' is defined as useful labour that is 'directly linked to capital'. Thus, the same labour process may be socially necessary and even produce use values, but it is only productive when linked to capital. See Karl Marx, *Theories of Surplus Value*, Part I (Lawrence and Wishart, London, 1969), esp. p. 329. Ian Gough, 'Productive and unproductive labour in Marx', *New Left Review*, 76 (November – December 1972), pp. 47–72.

34　O'Donoghue, *Bridewell Hospital*, p. 192.

35　Ibid., pp. 190–1.

36 Michel Foucault, *Madness and Civilization* (Social Science Paperback, London, 1967). Sellin, *Pioneering in Penology*, pp. 102–10.

37 For a discussion of the differences between these institutions, see Sellin, *Pioneering in Penology*, pp. 102–10. D. Melossi and M. Pavarini, *The Prison and the Factory: Origins of the Penitentiary System*, tr. G. Cousin (Macmillan, London, 1981).

38 R. P. Dobash, 'Labour and discipline in Scottish and English prisons: Moral correction, punishment and useful toil', *Sociology*, 17, No 1 (February 1983) pp. 1–27. R. Mitchison, 'The making of the old Scottish poor law', *Past and Present*, 63 (May 1974) pp. 58–92.

39 E. P. Thompson, *The Making of the English Working Class* (Pelican, Aylesbury, 1963). E. P. Thompson, 'The moral economy of the English crowd in the eighteenth century', *Past and Present*, 50 (February 1971), pp. 76–136. D. Hay, P. Linebough and E. P. Thompson, eds, *Albion's Fatal Tree* (Allen Lane, London, 1975).

40 Weiner, 'Sex roles and crime', p. 48.

41 J. M. Beattie, 'The criminality of women in eighteenth-century England', *Journal of Social History*, (1975) pp. 80–116.

42 Beattie, 'The criminality of women', J. M. Beattie, 'The pattern of crime in England, 1660–1800', *Past and Present*, 62 (1974) pp. 47–95. Thompson, 'The moral economy of the English crowd'.

43 Thompson, 'Moral economy', p. 116.

44 Ibid., p. 82.

45 E. Richards, 'Patterns of Highland discontent, 1790–1860', in *Popular Protest and Public Disorder*, eds. R. Quinault and J. Stevenson (Allen and Unwin, London), pp. 75–114.

46 Beattie, 'The criminality of women', 'The pattern of crime'.

47 Beattie, 'The pattern of crime', pp. 96–7.

48 D. Hay, 'Property, authority and the criminal law' in *Albion's Fatal Tree*, (eds) Hay, Linebough and Thompson, pp. 17–64.

49 Ibid,. p. 27.

50 Ibid.

51 Ibid., p. 29.

52 Ann Jones, *Women Who Kill* (Fawcett Columbine, New York, 1981), pp. 54–5.

53 Peter Linebough, 'The Tyburn riot against the surgeons' in *Albion's Fatal Tree*, (eds) Hay, Linebough and Thompson, pp. 65–117.

54 Foucault, *Discipline and Punish*, p. 44.

55 P. Linebough, 'The ordinary of Newgate and his Account' in *Crime in England, 1500–1800*, ed. J. S. Cockburn (Methuen, London, 1977), pp. 246–69. W. J. Sheeham, 'Finding solace in eighteenth century Newgate, in *Crime in England* ed. Cockburn, pp. 229–45.

56 Foucault, *Discipline and Punish*, p. 66.

57 See Deirdre Beddoe's excellent *Welsh Convict Women* (Stewart Williams, 1979).

58 A. G. L. Shaw, *Convicts and Colonies* (Faber and Faber, London, 1966), p. 100.

59 Henry Mayhew and John Binney, *The Criminal Prisons of London and Scenes of Prison Life* (London, Griffin, Bohn and Co, 1862), pp. 285–6.

Chapter 3: Penitentiaries For Women

1 J. Brewer and J. Styles, eds, *Ungovernable People? The English and Their People in the Seventeenth and Eighteenth Centuries* (Hutchinson, London, 1978). A.P. Donajgrodzki, ed, *Social Control in Nineteenth Century Britain* (Croom Helm, London, 1977). D. Jones, *Crime, Protest, Community and Police in Nineteenth Century Britain* (Routledge and Kegan Paul, London, 1982). T. Quinault and J. Stephenson, eds, *Popular Protest and Public Order, 1790–1820* (Allen and Unwin, London, 1974).

2 M. Ignatieff, *A Just Measure of Pain* (Macmillan, London, 1978). J. L. Lyman, 'The metropolitan police act of 1829', *Journal of Criminal Law, Criminology and Police Science* 55 (March 1964), pp. 141–59. Andrew T. Scull, 'Madness and segregative control: The rise of the insane asylum', *Social Problems* 24, 3 (February 1977), pp. 337–51. Allan Silver, 'The demand for order in civil society: A review of some themes in the history of urban crime, police and riot', in *The Police: Six Sociological Essays*, ed D. J. Bordua (Wiley, New York, 1967). Victor Bailey, *Policing and Punishment in Nineteenth Century Britain* (Croom Helm, London, 1981). Sean McConville, *A History of English Prison Administration, Vol 1, 1750–1877* (Routledge and Kegan Paul, London, 1981).

3 John Howard, *The State of the Prison*, third edition (London 1874). Jonas Hanway's two essays 'Solitude and imprisonment', and 'Distributive justice and mercy', on which, see Robin Evans, *The Fabrication of Virtue, English Prison Architecture, 1750–1840* (Cambridge University Press, Cambridge, 1981), esp Chapter 2. Ignatieff, *A Just Measure of Pain*, Chapter 2.

4 Jonas Hanway, 'Thoughts on a Magdalen House', in R. Evans, 'Bentham's Panopticon: An incident in the social history of architecture', *Architectural Association Quarterly* 3 (1971), pp. 21–37, p. 24. R. Evans, *The Fabrication of Virtue*, pp. 71–2.

5 C. C. Western, *Remarks Upon Prison Discipline* (Ridgeway, London, 1821), p. 8.

6 Ibid., p. 10.

7 Ibid., p. 60.

8 Sydney Smith, *The Works of the Reverend Sydney Smith, Including the Contributions to the Edinburgh Review* Vol II (Longman, London; Roberts and Green, London, 1865). Ernest Rhys, ed, *Selections from Sydney Smith* (Walter Scott, London, 1922). Some twentieth-century observers see Smith as a progressive reformer who proposed these views in an ironical fashion. We doubt this, since the overwhelming tone of his work on prisons was strongly reactionary.

9 Rhys, *Selections from Sydney Smith*, p. 56.

10 Ibid., p. 57.

11 Smith, 'Prisons', *Edinburgh Review* (1822), in *The Works of the Reverend Sydney Smith*, pp. 353–67, p. 357.

12 Ibid., p. 367.

13 J. Bowring, *The Works of Jeremy Bentham*, Vol I, XI (Tait, Edinburgh, 1843), especially Vol I and Part II, Chapter III, 'Panopticon Peni-

tentiary', pp. 498–503. For excellent discussions of the panopticon principle, see Evans, *The Fabrication of Virtue*, and 'Bentham's Panopticon', Foucault, *Discipline and Punish*. Thomas Markus, 'Buildings for the sad, the bad and the mad in urban Scotland', in T. A. Markus, ed, *Order in Space in Society: Architectural Form and its Content in Scottish Enlightenment* (Mainstream, Edinburgh, 1982), pp. 25–114.

14   Bentham, 'Panopticon Penitentiary', p. 501.

15   On panopticon architecture and modern examples, see Evans, *The Fabrication of Virtue*. Markus, *Order in Space and Society*. Norman Johnston, *A Brief History of Prison Architecture* (The American Foundation, New York, 1973).

16   Bentham, 'Panopticon Penitentiary', p. 501.

17   Ibid., p. 498.

18   Ibid., p. 499.

19   Elizabeth Fry, *A Memoir of the Life of Elizabeth Fry with Extracts from her Journal and Letters*, eds. K. Fry and E. Creswell, 2 Vols, (1847).

20   E. Isichei, *Victorian Quakers*, (Oxford University Press, London, 1970). Margaret Fox, *The Life of Margaret Fox, Wife of George Fox. Compiled from her own narrative, and other sources; with a selection from her epistles, etc.* (Association of Friends for the Diffusion of Religious and Useful Knowledge, Philadelphia, 1859).

21   Ignatieff, *A Just Measure of Pain*, especially Chapter 3. F. K. Prochaska, *Women and Philanthropy in Nineteenth Century England* (Clarendon Press, Oxford, 1980).

22   There were earlier Christian visitors such as Sarah Peters who began her work in 1748; see R. S. Hinde, *The British Penal System* (Duckworth, London, 1951). It is also important to note the tireless work of Sarah Martin in administering to the spiritual and physical needs of prisoners during the early nineteenth century. Sarah Martin, *A Brief Sketch of the life of the Late Sarah Martin* (Yarmouth, 1845).

23   J. Clay, *The Prison Chaplain: A Memoir of the Rev. John Clay B.D.* (Macmillan, Cambridge, 1861), p. 81.

24   Isichei, *Victorian Quakers*, p. 126.

25   Clay, *The Prison Chaplain*, p. 81.

26   Catherine Fraser, 'The origin and progress of the 'British Ladies' Society for Promoting the Reformation of Female Prisoners, established by Mrs Fry in 1821', *Transactions of the National Association for the Promotion of Sciences* 6 (1862), pp. 495–501, p. 495. A. Griffiths, *The Chronicles of Newgate* (London, Chapman and Hall, 1884), p. 347.

27   Samuel Buxton, *An Inquiry into Whether Crime and Misery are Produced or Prevented by Our Present System of Prison Discipline* (Arch, London, 1818), p. 122.

28   Ibid., p. 147.

29   Griffiths, *Chronicles of Newgate*, p. 347.

30   Joseph John Gurney, *Notes on a Visit made to Some of the Prisons in Scotland and the North of England in Company with Elizabeth Fry* (Longman, London, 1819), p. 152.

31   Gurney, *Notes on a Visit*, p. 153.

32 Ibid., p. 157.
33 Ibid., p. 154.
34 Buxton, *Our Present System of Prison Discipline*, p. 122.
35 Gurney, *Notes on a Visit*, pp. 151–2.
36 Buxton, *Our Present System of Prison Discipline*, p. 119.
37 Ibid., p. 129.
38 Elizabeth Fry, *Observations on the Siting, Superintendance, and Government, of Female Prisoners* (Arch, London, 1827), p. 15.
39 Gurney, *Notes on a Visit*, p. 164.
40 Ibid., p. 158.
41 Ibid., p. 154.
42 Joseph Kingsmill, *Chapters on Prison and Prisoners* (Longman, London, 1852), pp. 383–4.
43 Griffiths, *Chronicles of Newgate*, p. 383.
44 Gurney, *Notes on a Visit*. Squalor Carceris was the practice of keeping debtors under extremely depriving conditions in order to force them to pay creditors. See R. P. Dobash, 'Labour and discipline in Scottish and English prisons: Moral correction, punishment and useful toil', *Sociology* 27, 1 (February 1983), pp. 1–27, p. 21, n. 4.
45 Gurney, *Notes on a Visit*, p. 29.
46 Ibid., p. 45.
47 For the architectural plans, see Markus, 'Buildings for the sad', pp. 78–83.
48 Gurney, *Notes on a Visit*, pp. 44–5.
49 Ibid., p. 55, note.
50 Ibid., pp. 56–7.
51 Fry, *Observations on the Siting*, p. 11.
52 Ibid., p. 10.
53 Ibid., p. 15.
54 Ibid., p. 33.
55 Ibid., p. 50.
56 House of Lords, 'Appendix to Minutes of Evidence Taken Before the House of Lords', on *The Present State of the Several Gaols and Houses of Correction in England and Wales*, part II, pp. 387–43, P. 327.
57 House of Lords, *Present State of Several Gaols*, p. 327.
58 Mayhew and Binney, *The Criminal Prisons of London* (Griffin, Bohn, and Co., London, 1862), p. 285.
59 House of Lords, *Present State of Several Gaols*, p. 327.
60 Ibid.
61 Fry, *Observations on the Siting*, p. 46.
62 House of Lords, *Present State of Several Gaols*, p. 328.
63 Fry, *Observations on the Siting*, p. 42.
64 Ibid., p. 36.
65 Ibid., p. 64.
66 Ibid., p. 38.
67 Ibid., p. 37.
68 Ibid., p. 61.
69 Ibid., p. 27.

70 Gurney, *Notes on a Visit*, p. 163.
71 House of Lords, *Present State of Several Gaols*, p. 338.
72 Clay, *The Prison Chaplain*.
73 A. G. E. Griffiths, *Memorials of Millbank and Chapters in Prison History*, (Chapman and Hall, London, 1884). Ignatieff, *A Just Measure of Pain*. McConville, *English Prison Administration*.
74 U. R. W. Henriques, 'The rise and fall of the separate system of prison discipline', *Past and Present*, 54 (February 1972), pp. 61–93. W. J. Forsythe, 'New prisons for old gaols, Scottish penal reform, 1835–1842', *The Howard Journal for Penology and Crime Prevention*, 10, 3 (1981), pp. 138–49.
75 Parliamentary Papers, *Parliamentary Report on the Prisons of the United States*, Vol XLVI (1834).
76 Ignatieff, *A Just Measure of Pain*, p. 189. McConville, *English Prison Administration*, pp. 350–4.
77 Cited in *First Report of the General Board of Directors of Prisons in Scotland*, Appendix, pp. 67–8.
78 Ibid., p. 68.
79 For a discussion of Pentonville, see Henriques, 'The rise and fall of the separate system'. Ignatieff, *A Just Measure of Pain*. For Perth, see Dobash, 'Labour and discipline'. Forsythe, 'New prisons for old gaols'.
80 At the outset of the separate system prisoners were held in solitary confinement for twenty-four months; this was reduced to eighteen, then twelve, and finally 9 months.
81 Parliamentary Papers, *Report on the Discipline and Management of the Convict Prisons, and Disposal of Convicts*, 1852 (1853), p. 14.
82 In the early 1850s when Frederick Hill was transferred to the Inspectorate of Prisons in Northern England he noted that very few prisons enforced the separate system. E. Hill, *Frederick Hill: An Autobiography of Fifty Years in Times of Penal reform*, ed. Constance Hill (Bentley and Son, London, 1893), pp. 259–60.
83 There are numerous reports on penal servitude; see, for example, Parliamentary Papers, *Report on the Discipline and Management of the Convict Prisons, and the Disposal of Convicts, 1852* (1853). *Reports for Commissioners, Inspectors and Others: Vol 38* (1878). M. Heather Tomlinson, 'Penal servitude 1846–1865: A system in evolution', in V. Bailey, *Policing and Punishment* (Croom Helm, London, 1981) pp. 126–49.
84 See Nicole Hahn Rafter, *Partial Justice: State Prisons and Their Inmates 1790–1935* (North Eastern University Press, Boston, 1984), for a discussion of women in early American Prisons.

Chapter 4: Penal Regimes

1 Henry Mayhew and John Binney, *The Criminal Prisons of London and Scenes of Prison Life* (Griffin, Bohn, and Co., London, 1862). Although

both Mayhew and Binney are credited with the authorship of this book, the majority of the book, well over 500 pages, was written by Mayhew. Binney added the remaining observations after Mayhew's death. Prison Commissioners, *Annual Report on the Prison Commissioners for Scotland*, for the years 1901, (1902), pp. 13–14.

2 Ibid., pp. 460–1.
3 Ibid., pp. 13–14.
4 Mayhew and Binney, *The Criminal Prisons of London*.
5 It appears that some women served their entire sentence at Millbank. Later in the century women might also spend all or part of their sentence in Parkhurst or Woking prisons.
6 Mayhew and Binney, *The Criminal Prisons of London*, p. 177.
7 Ibid., p. 176.
8 Ibid., p. 273.
9 Ibid., p. 183.
10 Ibid., p. 580.
11 See Prison Matron (F. W. Robinson), *Female Life in Prison*, 2 vols, (Hurst and Blackett, London, 1862), esp. Chap. 3. William Sievwright, *Historical Sketch of the General Prison for Scotland at Perth* (Wright, Perth, 1894).
12 Mary Carpenter, *Our Convicts*, (Longman, London, 1864), Vol 2, p. 257.
13 J. Clay, *The Prison Chaplain: A Memoir of the Rev John Clay* (Macmillan, Cambridge, 1861), p. 192, n. 2.
14 J. Clay, *The Prison Chaplain*, p. 197.
15 *Eighth Report of the Inspectors, Prisons of Great Britain*, 'Volume IV, Scotland, Northumberland and Durham', (1843), p. 82.
16 F. K. Prochaska, *Women and Philanthropy in Nineteenth-Century England* (Clarendon, Oxford, 1980), p. 156.
17 *Seventh Report of the Inspectors of Prisons of Great Britain*, 'Volume III, Scotland, Northumberland and Durham', (1842), p. 7.
18 Ibid.
19 Mary Carpenter, *Our Convicts*, Vol 2, p. 226.
20 Ibid.
21 Ibid., Vol 2, p. 268.
22 Mayhew and Binney, *The Criminal Prisons of London*, p. 194, note.
23 Ibid., pp. 194–5.
24 Ibid., p. 481.
25 Ibid., p. 195.
26 Ibid,. p. 194.
27 Mary Carpenter, *Our Convicts*.
28 For details of American Prison Labour, see J. A. Conley, 'Prisons, production and profit. Reconsidering the importance of prison industries', *Journal of Social History* 14, 2 (Winter 1980), pp. 163–87. M. Miller, 'At hard labour: rediscovering the 19th century prison', *Issues in Criminology* 9, 1 (Spring 1974), pp. 91–114. For discussions of women's labour in US and French prisons, see N. Hahn Rafter, *Partial Justice: Women in State Prisons, 1800–1935* (Northeastern Univer-

sity Press, Boston, 1985). P. O'Brien, *The Promise of Punishment: Prisons in Nineteenth Century France* (Princeton University Press, Princeton, 1982).

29 *Seventh Report of the Inspectors*, p. 7.
30 Ibid., p. 78.
31 Mayhew and Binney, *The Criminal Prisons of London*, p. 530.
32 *Second Report of the General Board of Directors of Prison in Scotland*, Appendix, p. 53.
33 Mayhew and Binney, *The Criminal Prisons of London*, pp. 189–91, pp. 473–5.
34 Prochaska, *Women and Philanthropy*. O. Banks, *Faces of Feminism* (Martin Robertson, Oxford, 1981).
35 J. Armstrong, 'Female Penitentiaries', *Quarterly Review* (1848), pp. 359–76. William Tait, *Magdalenism. An Inquiry into the Extent, Causes and Consequences of Prostitution in Edinburgh* (Rickard, Edinburgh, 1842).
36 J. Armstrong, *Female Penitentiaries*, p. 367.
37 Ibid., p. 372.
38 W. Tait, *Magdalenism*, pp. 329–30.
39 Ibid., p. 332.
40 J. Armstong, *Female Penitentiaries*, p. 374.
41 W. Tait, *Magdalenism*, p. 340.
42 Ibid., p. 350.
43 Ibid., p. 342, Tait described the shaving of women's heads as 'unjustifiable'.
44 Ibid,. p. 331.
45 The 1861 census of the 2.7 million employed women in Britain revealed that 2.0 million were in domestic service. Domestic service was the largest category of employment until the Second World War. D. Beddoe, *Discovering Women's History* (Pandora, London, 1983), p. 112.
46 *Ninth Report of the Inspectors*, *Prisons of Great Britain*, IV, Scotland, Northumberland and Durham (1844), p. 12.
47 *Eighth Report of the Inspectors*, *Prisons of Great Britain*, IV, Scotland, Northumberland and Durham (1843), p. 5.
48 *Ninth Report of the Inspectors*, p. 12.
49 Carpenter, *Our Convicts*, Vol 2, pp. 272–3.
50 Francis Robinson, *Female Life in Prison*, Vol II, p. 208.
51 Ibid., Vol II, p. 216–17.
52 Carpenter, *Our Convicts*, Vol II, p. 212–13.
53 Ibid., p. 270.
54 Ibid.
55 E. C. Lekkerkerker, *Reformatories for Women in the United States* (J. B. Wolters' Unitgevers-Maatschappij, Batavia, The Netherlands, 1931). E. B. Freedman, *Their Sisters Keepers: Women's Prison Reform in America, 1830–1930* (University of Michigan Press, Ann Arbor, 1981). N. Hahn Rafter, *Partial Justice*. A. Platt, *The Child Savers: The*

Invention of Delinquency, 2nd edition (University of Chicago Press, Chicago, 1977). S. L. Schlossman, *Love and the American Delinquent: The Theory and Practice of 'Progressive' Juvenile Justice, 1825–1920* (University of Chicago Press, Chicago, 1977).

56 Carpenter, *Our Convicts*, Vol II, p. 273.
57 Mayhew and Binney, *Criminal Prisons of London*.
58 One of the few authentic first-hand accounts is Florence Elizabeth Maybrick, *My Fifteen Lost Years* (Funk and Wagnall, New York, 1905).
59 *Seventh Report of Inspectors*, Appendix, p. 53.
60 Ibid., p. 70.
61 *Eighth Report of Inspectors*, p. 29.
62 *Ninth Report of Inspectors*, p. 25.
63 Governor's Journal, 20 April, 1818, cited in A. G. Griffiths, *Memorials of Millbank and Chapters in Prison History*, (Chapman and Hall, London, 1884), p. 49.
64 Griffiths, *Memorials of Millbank*, p. 153.
65 Mayhew and Binney, *Criminal Prisons of London*, p.181.
66 Griffiths, *Memorials of Millbank*, p. 153.
67 Sievwright, *Perth Prison*. Evans, *The Fabrications of Virtue*, discusses the extraordinary concern of architects to prevent such communications.
68 Mayhew and Binney, *Criminal Prisons of London*, p. 515.
69 Ibid., p. 185.
70 Ibid., p. 467.
71 Griffiths, *Memorials of Millbank*, p. 217.
72 Ibid., p. 199.
73 Mayhew and Binney, *Criminal Prisons of London*, p. 188.
74 Ibid.
75 Ibid., 182.
76 Ibid.
77 Ibid.
78 Ibid., p. 271.
79 Griffiths, *Memorials of Millbank*, p. 200.
80 Mayhew and Binney, *Criminal Prisons of London*, p. 186.
81 Ibid., p. 273.
82 *Tenth Report of the Inspectors, Prisons of Great Britain*, IV, Scotland, Northumberland and Durham (1845). p. iv.
83 Carpenter, *Our Convicts*, Vol II, pp. 222–3.
84 Ibid., p. 222.
85 Ibid., p. 255.
86 G. L. Chesterton, *Revelations of Prison Life*, Vol II (Hurst and Blackwell, London, 1856), p. 134.
87 Carpenter, *Our Convicts*, Vol II, p. 218.
88 Ibid., p. 217.
89 Ibid., p. 218.
90 See Freedman, *Our Sisters Keepers* and Hahn Rafter, *Partial Justice* for descriptions of reformatories.

Chapter 5: Experts and the Female Criminal

1   Frederick Hill was a remarkable person who appears to have worked extremely hard to bring about better conditions in the prisons of England and Scotland – a man of genuine concern and compassion with an enlightened conception of crime.

2   *Seventh Report of the Inspectors Appointed to Visit the Different Prisons of Great Britain, Scotland, Northumberland and Durham* (HMSO, 1846), p. 72.

3   V. A. C. Gatrell and T. B. Hadden, 'The analysis of the statistics', in E.A. Wrigley (ed.), *Nineteenth Century Society: Essays in the Use of Quantitative Methods for the Study of Social Data* (Cambridge University Press, Cambridge, 1972). D. Jones, *Crime, Protest, Community and Police in Nineteenth Century Britain* (Routledge and Kegan Paul, London, 1982).

4   Jones, *Crime, Protest and Community.*

5   Mayhew and Binney, *The Criminal Prisons of London*, p. 268.

6   *Seventh Report of the Prison Inspectors*, p. 11.

7   Clay, cited in Carpenter, *Our Convicts, Vol I*, p. 67.

8   J. Kingsmill, *Chapters on Prisons and Prisoners* (Longman, London, 1852), p. 364.

9   Ibid., pp. 364–5.

10 G. L. Chesterton, *Revelations of Prison Life* (London, 1856), p. 175.

11 A. Silver, 'The demand for order in civil society: A review of some themes in the history of urban crime, police and riot', in *The Police: Six Sociological Essays* ed. D. J. Bordua (John Wiley, New York, 1967). R. D. Storch, 'The policeman as domestic missionary: Urban discipline and popular culture in northern England, 1850–1880', *Journal of Social History* 9, pp. 481–509.

12 N. Chadorow and S. Contratto, 'The fantasy of the perfect mother', in *Rethinking the Family* (Longman, London, 1982). A. Brittan and M. Maynard, *Sexism, Racism and Oppression* (Basil Blackwell, Oxford, 1984).

13 Ruskin, cited in G. Wright, *Moralism and the Model Home* (University of Chicago Press, Chicago, 1980).

14 *Annual Report of the Prison Commissioners for Scotland, for the Year 1901* (HMSO, London, 1902), pp. 13–14.

15 See Mayhew and Binney, *Criminal Prisons of London*. W. D. Morrison, *Crime and Its Causes* (Swan, London, 1891), pp. 154–5.

16 Presbytery of Glasgow, *Report of Commission on the Housing of the Poor in Relation to Their Social Condition* (1981), p. 31. We would like to thank Phillip Morgan Klein for this reference.

17 The prison chaplain, W. M. Morrison, made a similar observation when he noted that in no other country in Europe are women as economically independent as Scottish women, ' . . . leading what is called a more emancipated life . . .' Morrison, *Crime and Its Causes* (1891), p. 159.

18 J. W. Scott and L. A. Tilly, 'Women's work and the family in nineteenth century Europe', in *The Family in History*, ed. C. E.

Roseberg (University of Pennsylvania Press, Philadelphia, 1975). L. Davidoff, J. L'Esperance and H. Newby, 'Landscape with figures: Home and community in English society', in J. Mitchell and A. Oakley (eds.), *The Rights and Wrongs of Women* (Penguin, Harmondsworth, 1976).

19   R. D. Storch, 'Police control of street prostitution in Victorian London: A study in the contexts of police action', in D. H. Bayley (ed.), *Police and Society* (Sage, Beverley Hills, 1977), pp. 49–72.

20   Cited in Storch, *Police and Society*, from B. Scott, *A State Iniquity: Its Rise, Extension and Overthrow* (London, 1890).

21   Ibid., p. 63.

22   Ibid., p. 64.

23   Ibid.

24   *Tenth Report of the Inspectors Appointed to Visit Prisons of Great Britain, Scotland, Northumberland, and Durham* (HMSO, London, 1845), pp. 2–3.

25   It appears that women who committed infanticide were often treated leniently by juries and sometimes judges. Juries failed to convict, recommend leniency and found women not to be in 'their right minds'. See J. M. Beattie, 'The criminality of women in eighteenth-century England', *Past and Present*, 62, (1974), pp. 47–95, pp. 84–5.

26   *Seventh Report of the Prison Inspectors of Scotland*, p. 71.

27   *Eleventh Report of the Inspectors Appointed to Visit the Different Prisons of Great Britain, Scotland, Northumberland, and Durham* (HMSO, London, 1846), p. xxiii.

28   B. Ehrenreich and D. English, *For Her Own Good* (Pluto, London, 1979), p. 22. N. Smelser, 'The Victorian family', in *Families in Britain* (eds.), R. N. Rapoport, M. P. Fogarty and R. Rapoport (Routledge and Kegan Paul, London, 1982).

29   M. Foucault, *Discipline and Punish* (Allen Lane, London, 1977), pp. 180–94.

30   *Tenth Report of the Inspectors Appointed to Visit the Different Prisons of Great Britain, Scotland, Northumberland, and Durham* (HMSO, London, 1845), p. xii.

31   *Seventh Report of the Inspectors*, p. 70.

32   *Eighth Report of the Inspectors*, pp. 72–3.

33   Ibid., p. 73.

34   *Seventh Report of the Inspectors*, p. 14.

35   *Eleventh Report of the Inspectors*, p. xi.

36   Ibid., p. 11.

37   *Eighth Report of the Inspectors*, p. 63.

38   *Reports from Commissioners, Inspectors and Others: Appointed to Inquire Into the Working of the Penal Servitude Acts, Vol II*, (1876), p. 1170.

39   *Seventh Report of the Prison Inspectors*, Appendix V, p. 53.

40   Eleventh Report of the Prison Inspectors, p. 68.

41   See Prochaska, *Women and Philanthropy*, p. 170 on the early prison inspectors' reactions to the lady 'visitors' work. In the 1870s the prison governor Arthur Griffiths described lady visitors as 'amateurs'

who engage in imperfect work in which they place a 'premium on misconduct'. Griffiths, *Memorials of Millbank* (Chapman and Hall, London, 1884), pp. 204–5.

42 *Fourth Report on the Inspectors Appointed to Visit the Different Prisons of Great Britain, Scotland, Northumberland, and Durham* (HMSO, London, 1839), Appendix 7, p. 59.
43 E. Donzelot, *The Policing of the Family* (Pantheon, New York, 1979).
44 Eleventh Report of the Inspectors, p. xvii.
45 Ibid.
46 Ibid, p. xviii.
47 Ibid.
48 Cited in Beddoe, *Welsh Convict Women* (Stewart Williams, 1979).
49 Jo Manton, *Mary Carpenter and the Children of the Street* (Heinemann, London, 1969).
50 Henry Mayhew, *The Life and Labour of the London Poor.*
51 *Criminal Prisons of London* was written by both Mayhew and Binney but Binney contributed only the last 150 pages after Mayhew's death. Thus we consider the orientation of the work to be set by Mayhew.
52 M. Carpenter, *Our Convicts*, Vol. II, p. 246.
53 Ibid., p. 226. Henry Mayhew had rather different views of convict mothers and children. Upon entering the nursery at Tothill Fields prison he observed that the '. . . eyes of the sternest stranger must tingle with compassion to note the wretched mothers caressing and fondling the little things. . .' Motherhood absolved women of guilt, and set them apart from the pariah class, and proved that '. . .the hearts of the women that bore the babies were not utterly withered and corrupt.' Mayhew, *Criminal Prisons of London*, p. 475.
54 Female Matron (F. Robinson), *Female Life in Prison*, Vol. I (Hurst and Stockett, London, 1862), p. 178.
55 Ibid., p. 284.
56 Carpenter, *Our Convicts*, Vol. II, p. 202.
57 Ibid., p. 209.
58 Ibid., p. 208.
59 Mayhew and Binney, *The Criminal Prisons of London*, p. 383.
60 Ibid., p. 386.
61 Ibid., p. 384
62 Ibid., p. 357.
63 Ibid., p. 356.
64 Ibid., p. 462.
65 Ibid., p. 455.
66 Ibid., p. 466.
67 Ibid., p. 456.
68 Ibid., p. 466.
69 Ibid., p. 456.
70 Ibid., p. 386.
71 Ibid.
72 Ibid.
73 Ibid., p. 466.

74 Carpenter, *Our Convicts*, Vol. I, p. 31.
75 Carpenter, *Our Convicts*, Vol. II, p. 208.
76 Robinson, *Female Life*, Vol. I, p. 46.
77 Ibid,. p. 45.
78 Ibid.
79 Ibid., p.46.
80 Carpenter, *Our Convicts*, Vol. I, p. 31.
81 Inspector's Report Cited in Carpenter, *Our Convicts*, Vol. II, p. 216.
82 Cited in Robinson, *Female Life in Prison*, Vol. I, p. 124.
83 Carpenter, *Our Convicts*, Vol. I, p.31.
84 Ibid., p. 115.
85 Ibid., p. 149.
86 Ibid., p. 108.
87 Ibid., Vol. II, p. 254.
88 Ibid., Vol. I, pp. 81, 116.
89 Ibid., p. 81.
90 Ibid.
91 Ibid., p. 116.
92 For a good general discussion of these approaches, see C. S. Suchar, *Social Deviance, Perspectives and Prospects* (Holt, Rinehart and Winston, New York, 1978).
93 For a discussion of this movement in Britain and America, see S. Roe, L. Amin and R. C. Lewontin, *Not in Our Genes* (Penguin, Harmondsworth, 1984). J. Katz and C. F. Abel, 'The medicalization of repression: Eugenics and crime', *Contemporary Crises*, 8 (1984), pp. 227–41.
94 For good evidence of bio-psychological perspectives on the insanity of women, see B. Ehrenreich and D. English, *For Her Own Good* (Pluto Press, London, 1979). S. Edwards, *Female Sexuality and the Law* (Oxford, Martin Robertson, 1981).
95 C. Lombroso and W. Ferrero, *The Female Offender* (Unwin, London, 1895). For one of the earliest and best accounts of Lombroso's ideas on the criminality of women, see Dorie Klein, 'The etiology of female crime: A review of the literature', *Issues in Criminology*, 8, 2 (Fall 1973), pp. 3–30. C. Smart, *Women, Crime and Criminology* (Routledge and Kegan Paul, London, 1977). F. Heidensohn, *Women and Crime* (Macmillan, London, 1985).
96 The British were responsible for some of the most damning evidence on Lombroso's thesis. The comprehensive research of the prison doctor Charles Goring demonstrated through the use of a large sample of male prisoners that they did not have unique physical features. C. Goring, *The English Convict* (HMSO, London, 1913).
97 Cited in H. L. Adam, *Women and Crime* (Laurie, London, 1912), p. 22.
98 Ibid., p. 23.
99 Henry Maudsley, *Responsibility in Mental Disease*, fifth edition, (Kegan Paul, London, 1892), p. 60.
100 For an excellent discussion of the application of these conceptions to women in the United States, see Nicole F. Hahn, 'Too dumb to know

better: Cacogenci family studies and the criminology of women',
Criminology 18, 1 (May 1980), pp. 3–25.

101   Maudsley, *Responsibility in Mental Disease*, p. 29.

102   Ibid., p. 30.

103   Henry Maudsley, 'Review of female life in prison', *Journal of Mental Science*, 9 (1863), pp. 69–87.

104   S. Edwards, 'Henry Maudsley: His role in changing attitudes to mental health,' *British Journal of Sexual Medicine* (October 1982), pp. 32–8. For an extraordinary statement of the relationship between women's biology and behaviour, see W.R. Cooke, 'The differential psychology of the American woman', *American Journal of Obstetrics and Gynaecology*, 49 (1945), pp. 57–72.

105   S. Edwards, 'Henry Maudsley: His role in changing attitudes to mental health', *British Journal of Sexual Medicine* (October 1982), p. 34.

106   A.F. Tredgold, *Mental Deficiency* (Baillière, Tindall and Cox, London, 1914), p. 314.

107   Ibid., p. 315.

108   Ibid., p. 332.

109   Havelock Ellis, *The Criminal* (Scott, London, 1901, first published in 1891), p. x.

110   Ibid., p. 91.

111   Ibid., p. 140.

112   Ibid.

113   Ibid., p. 167.

114   Ibid., p. 79.

115   Ibid., p. 204.

116   Ibid., p. 116.

117   Ibid., p. 170.

118   Ibid., p. 188.

119   For a discussion of Burt's bogus research, see L. J. Kamin, *The Science and Politics of I.Q.* (John Wiley, New York, 1974). Rose, Kamin and Lewontin, *Not in Our Genes*.

120   C. Burt, *The Young Delinquent* (London, University of London Press, 1931, first published in 1919).

121   Ibid., p. 422.

122   Ibid., pp. 47–8.

123   Ibid., p. 443.

124   C. Burt, 'Facial expression as an index of mentality', *Child-Study* 12, 1 (June 1919), pp. 1–3, p. 1.

125   Burt, *Young Delinquent*, p. 413.

126   Ibid.

127   Ibid., p. 83.

128   Ibid., p. 242.

129   Ibid., p. 216.

130   Ibid., p. 217.

131   Ibid., p. 224.

132   Ibid., p. 132.

133 Ibid., pp. 227–8.
134 Ibid., p. 224.
135 Ibid., p. 237.
136 G. Pailthorpe, *Studies in the Psychology of Delinquency* (Medical Research Council, HMSO, 1932). G. Pailthorpe, *What We Put In Prison* (Williams and Norgate, London, 1933).
137 Pailthorpe, *Studies in the Psychology of Delinquency*, pp. 27–8.
138 Ibid., p. 99.
139 Pailthorpe, *Studies in the Psychology of Delinquency*, p. 144.
140 Ibid., p. 146.
141 Pailthorpe, *Studies in the Psychology of Delinquency*, p. 17.
142 Ibid., p. 23.
143 Ibid., p. 19.
144 Pailthorpe, *Studies in the Psychology of Delinquency*, p. 146.
145 The British do not seem to have practised compulsory sterilization though it certainly occurred in the United States. See Rose, Kamin, and Lewontin, *Not in Our Genes*.
146 Pailthorpe, *Studies in the Psychology of Delinquency*, p. 98.
147 Ibid., p. 99.
148 S. Glueck and E. T. Glueck, *Five Hundred Delinquent Women* (Knopf, New York, 1934). For a general discussion, see Rafter, *Too Dumb to Know Better*. For a late British example of this type of research, see P. Epps and R.W. Parnell, 'Physique and temperament of women delinquents compared with women undergraduates', *British Journal of Medical Psychology* VIXXV (1952), pp. 249–55.
149 Morrison, *Crime and Its Causes*, p. 154–9.
150 Mary Gordon, *Penal Discipline* (Routledge and Sons, London, 1922), p. 158.
151 Ibid., p. 235.
152 Ibid., p. 234.
153 Ibid,. p. 227.
154 Ann Smith, *Women in Prison* (Stevens, London, 1962), pp. 213–14.
155 Inebriate reformatories were intended for men and women in England, whereas in Scotland they were primarily aimed at women. However, no unique regime was created for women. See P. M. McLaughlin, 'Inebriate reformatories in Scotland: An institutional history,' in *A Social History of Drinking* (University of California Press, Berkeley, forthcoming.) For an overview of developments in England, see *Prisons and Prisoners: The Work of the Prison Service in England and Wales* (HMSO, London, 1977).

Chapter 6: Therapy and Discipline

1 M. Wolff, *Prisons* (Eyre and Spottiswoode, London, 1967), p. 141.
2 J. Camp, *Holloway Prison: The Place and the People* (David and Charles, London, 1974), p. 149.

3 J. Kelly, *When the Gates Shut* (Longman, London, 1967), pp. 75, 104.

4 Ibid., p. 149.

5 The Education, Arts and Home Office Sub-Committee of the Expenditure Committee took extensive evidence on 'Women and the Penal System' in the 1978–9 session. No report was published because of the general election in May 1979, but fourteen volumes of oral evidence and written submissions appeared. Expenditure Committee, Education, Arts and Home Office Sub-Committee of the Expenditure Committee: (1978–9).

6 *Report of the Working Party on the Treatment and Training of Female Inmates in Scotland* (Unpublished Report, N.D.), p.12.

7 Ibid., p. 9.

8 Ibid.

9 Ibid., p. 10.

10 Ibid., p. 11.

11 D. E. R. Faulkner, 'The redevelopment of Holloway Prison', *Howard Journal*, 8, 2, (1971), pp. 122–31.

12 C. Gibbs, 'The effect of imprisonment of women upon their children', *British Journal of Criminology* 6, (April 1971).

13 T. Gibbens, 'Female offenders', *British Journal of Hospital Medicine*, 6 (Sept. 1979), pp. 279–86.

14 R. H. Blythe, SMO of Holloway, 'New plans for treatment in the New Holloway' – paper given to the Howard League for Penal Reform, quoted in Radical Alternatives to Prison, *Alternatives to Holloway* (Christian Action, London, 1972).

15 J. Cowie, V. Cowie, E. Slater, *Delinquency in Girls* (Heinemann Educational, London, 1968).

16 Gibbens, 'Female offenders', p. 280.

17 S. Dell and T. C. N. Gibbens, 'Remands of women offenders for medical reports', *Medicine, Science and the Law* (July 1971).

18 Gibbens, 'Female offenders', p. 286.

19 Ibid.

20 *Alternatives to Holloway*, p. 14.

21 P. Chesler, *Women and Madness* (Allen Lane, London, 1974). A. Oakley, *Subject Women* (Martin Robertson, Oxford, 1981). A. Oakley, *Women Confined: Towards a Sociology of Childbirth* (Martin Robertson, Oxford, 1980). C. Smart, *Women, Crime and Criminology: A Feminist Critique* (Routledge and Kegan Paul, London, 1977).

22 C. Lombroso and W. Ferrero, *The Female Offender*, originally published by Unwin 1895 (Owen, London 1959). W. I. Thomas, *The Unadjusted Girl* (Little Brown & Co., Boston, 1923). O. Pollak, *The Criminality of Women* (University of Pennsylvania Press, New York, 1950). G. Konopka, *The Adolescent Girl in Conflict* (C. Prentice-Hall, New Jersey, 1966). J. Cowie, V. Cowie and E. Slater, *Delinquency in Girls* (Heinemann, London, 1968).

23 T. Gibbens, 'Female offenders'. M. Woodside, 'Women offenders and psychiatric reports', *Social Work Today*, 5, 11 (Sept. 1974). M. Woodside, 'Psychiatric referrals from Edinburgh courts', *British Journal*

of Criminology, 16, 1 (Jan. 1974). H. M. Cookson, 'A survey of self-injury in a closed prison for women', *British Journal of Criminology*, 17, 14 (Oct. 1977), pp. 332–47.

24 Gibbens, 'Female offenders'. Woodside, 'Women offenders and psychiatric reports'.

25 Gunn, Robertson *et al.*, *Psychiatric Aspects of Imprisonment* (Academic Press, London 1978).

26 R. Giallombardo, *Society of Women: A Study of a Women's Prison* (Wiley, 1966).

27 *Treatment and Training of Female Inmates.*

28 Faulkner, 'The redevelopment of Holloway Prison'.

29 M. Jones, 'The concept of a therapeutic community', *American Journal of Psychiatry*, (1956), p. 647.

30 *Report on H. M. Institution Corton Vale*, H. M. Inspectorate of Prisons for Scotland, 1982.

31 Ibid.

32 *Treatment and Training of Female Inmates.*

33 B. Zilbergeld, *The Shrinking of America: Myths of Psychological Change* (Little, Brown, Boston, 1983).

34 R. M. Harrison and F. C. Mueller, 'Clue hunting about group counselling and parole outcome', Department of Corrections; Youth and Adult Corrections Agency, California, Research Report No. 11, (May 1964). Referred to in *Alternatives to Holloway*.

35 'Cracking up' is described later, on pp. 156–7.

36 Medical services within Scottish prisons are run as part of the general National Health System, unlike in England and Wales, where there is a separate prison medical system. The latter system has been consistently and heavily criticized. In the recent Prior Report, incorporation of the prison medical system into the National Health Services has been recommended.

37 HMI Report, p. 26.

38 HMI Report, para 8.4.

39 *Offences Against Discipline in Women's Prisons* NACRO, London, 1986).

40 A. D. Smith, *Women in Prison.*

41 Faulkner, 'The redevelopment of Holloway Prison', p. 128.

42 'Marginally named' is the mode of referring to the prisoner on report, whose name appears in the margin of the report.

44 This is also true of Holloway, as stated in the *Holloway Project Committee Report* (Home Office, 1985), para 4.5. The committee was concerned that the average sick absence at Holloway was so high, ranging from 39 officers per day on average during one week in January 1984 to 21 in June 1984.

45 Cookson, 'A survey of self-injury in a closed prison for women.'

46 M. Benn and C. Ryder-Tchaikovsky, 'Women behind bars', *New Statesman*, 8–10, December 1983. *Observer* 16 December 1984.

47 *The Guardian* 23 May 1985.

48 The issue of what consistutes 'personality disorder' is discussed fruitfully in P. Carlen, *Alternatives to Holloway*.

49 Woodside, 'Women offenders and psychiatric reports.' Gibbens and Bell, 'Remands of women offenders for medical reports.'

Chapter 7: Work, Training and Education

1   G. Rusche and O. Kirchheimer, *Punishment and Social Structure*, (Columbia University Press, New York, 1939).
2   D. Melossi and M. Pavarini, *The Prison and the Factory: Origins of the Penitentiary System*, translated by Glynis Cousin, (Macmillan, London, 1981).
3   Pat Carlen, *Women's Imprisonment: A Study in Social Control* (Routledge and Kegan Paul, London, 1983).
4   D. Ward and G. Kassebaum, *Women's Prison: Sex and Social Structure*, (Weidenfeld and Nicolson, London, 1966). R. Giallombardo, *Society of Women: A Study of a Women's Prison* (John Wiley, New York, 1966). E. Heffernan, *Making it in Prison: The Square, the Cool, and the Life*, (Wiley–Interscience, London, 1972).
5   R. Giallombardo, *Society of Women*, p. vii.
6   Ibid., p. 59.
7   Ibid., p. 61.
8   Ibid., p. 63.
9   D. Clemmer, *The Prison Community* (Holt, Rinehart, Winston, New York, 1958). D. R. Cressey (ed.), *The Prison: Studies in Institutional Organisation and Change* (Holt, Rinehart and Winston, New York, 1961). D. Glaser, *The Effectiveness of a Prison and Parole System*, (Bobbs-Merrill, New York, 1964). G. M. Sykes, *The Society of Captives: A Study of a Maximum Security Prison* (Princeton University Press, Princeton, N.J., 1958). P. G. Garabedian, 'Social roles and processes of socialization in the prison community', *Social Problems* 11 (Fall 1963), pp. 139–52.
10 E. Heffernan, *Making it in Prison*, p. 59.
11 Carlen, *Women's Imprisonment*.
12 Radical Alternatives to Prison, *Alternatives to Holloway* (Christian Action Publications, 1972).
13 R. J. Wajsblum, *Women in Prison* (East London Women against Prison, 1981).
14 E. B. Leonard, 'Judicial decisions and prison reform: the impact of litigation on women prisoners', *Social Problems*, 31, 1 (October 1983), pp. 45–58. F. Heidensohn, 'Women and the penal system', in A. Morris (ed) with L. Gelsthorpe, *Women and Crime* (Cropwood Conference Series No. 123), University of Cambridge: Institute of Criminology, 1980), pp. 49–70.
15 M. Chesney-Lind, 'Judicial paternalism and the female status offender', *Crime and Delinquency*, 23 (2), pp. 121–30.
16 C. Smart, *Women, Crime and Criminology: A Feminist Critique* (Routledge and Kegan Paul, London, 1977).

17 *Report of the Working Party on the Treatment and Training of Female Inmates in Scotland* (Unpublished Report), p. 7.

18 D. E. R. Faulkner, 'The redevelopment of Holloway Prison', *Howard Journal*, 13, 2 (1971), pp. 122–31, p. 128.

19 Ibid., p. 130.

20 Ibid.

21 Advisory Council on the Employment of Prisoners, *The Organisation of Work for Prisoners*, (HMSO, London, 1964).

22 'The Redevelopment of Holloway Prison', p. 150.

23 K. Fitzherbert, p. 302.

24 Treatment and Training of Female Inmates in Scotland, p. 7.

25 Ibid., p. 15.

26 Ibid, p. 7.

27 *Report of Board of Directors* (1847) quoted in A.D. Smith, *Women in Prison* (Stevens, London, 1962), p. 153.

28 A.D. Smith, *Women in Prison*, p. 296.

29 Ibid., p. 297.

30 Ibid., p. 296.

31 Ibid., p. 299.

32 See *Annual Reports for Scotland*.

33 *Report on H.M. Institution, Corton Vale* (H.M. Inspectorate of Prisons for Scotland, 1982). M. Fitzgerald and J. Sim, *British Prisons* (Basil Blackwell, Oxford, 1975).

34 F. Adler, *Sisters in Crime: The Rise of the New Female Criminal* (McGraw-Hill, New York, 1975).

35 R. Simon, *Women and Crime* (D.C. Heath, London; Lexington, Mass., 1975).

36 Adler, *Sisters in Crime*.

37 S. Box and E. Hale, 'Liberation and female criminality in England and Wales', *British Journal of Criminology*, 21, 1 (January 1983), p. 35.

38 J.G. Weis, 'Liberation and crime: the invention of the new female criminal', *Crime and Social Justice*, 6 (1976), pp. 17–27. L. Crites (ed.), *The Female Offender* (Lexington Books, Lexington, 1976). S. K. Dates and F. R. Scarpitti, *Women, Crime and Justice* (Oxford University Press, Oxford, 1980). C. Feinman, 'Sex role stereotypes and justice for women', *Crime and Delinquency*, 25 (1979), pp. 87–94. D. Klein and J. Kress, 'Any woman's blues: a critical overview of women, crime and the criminal justice system' (1976). A. Morris and L. Gelsthorpe, 'False clues and female crime' in *Women and Crime*, pp. 49–70. C. Smart, *Women, Crime and Criminology*. C. Smart, 'The new female criminal: reality or myth', *British Journal of Criminology*, 19 (1979), pp. 50–9.

39 C. Lombroso and W. Ferrero, *The Female Offender* (originally published, Unwin, 1895; Owen, 1959). W.I. Thomas, *The Unadjusted Girl* (Little, Brown and Co., Boston, 1923). O. Pollak, *The Criminality of Women* (University of Pennsylvania Press, New York, 1950). G. Konopka, *The Adolescent Girl in Conflict* (Prentice-Hall, Englewood Cliffs, New Jersey, 1966). J. Cowie, V. Cowie, E. Slater, *Delinquency in Girls* (Heinemann Educational, London, 1968).

40   D. J. Steffensmeier, 'Sex differences in patterns of adult crime 1965–77: a review and assessment', *Social Forces*, 58 (1980), pp. 1080–1108. D. J. Steffensmeier, 'Crime and the contemporary woman: an analysis of changing levels of female property crime, 1960–75', *Social Forces*, 57, 2 (1978), pp. 566–84. D. J. and R. H. Steffensmeier, 'Trends in female delinquency', *Criminology*, 18 (1980), pp. 62–85. D. J. Steffensmeier, 'Assessing the impact of the women's movement on sex-based differences in the handling of adult criminal defendants', *Crime and Delinquency*, 76 (1980), pp. 344–57.

41   General Household Survey 1976 (Office of Population Censuses and Surveys, Social Survey Division, London, HMSO, 1978). *General Household Survey*, Preliminary Results No. 1 (OPCS Monitor, 1982).

42   C. Hakim, *Occupational Segregation*, Research paper No. 9, (Department of Employment HMSO, London, 1979).

43   Statistics Unit, Equal Opportunities Commission, 'The fact about women is', pamphlet, 1985.

44   E. Miller, 'International trends in the study of female criminality: an essay review', *Contemporary Crises*, 7 (1983), pp. 59–70.

45   M. Velimesis, 'Criminal justice for the female offender', *Journal of the American Association of University Women* (October 1969).

46   J. R. Chapman, *Economic Realities and Female Crime* (Lexington, Lexington, Mass., 1980).

47   V. Greenwood, 'The myth of female crime' in A. Morris and L. Gelsthorpe, *Women and Crime*, pp. 73–88.

48   Box and Hale, 'Liberation and female criminality,' p. 43. *Report on the work of the Prison Department* (1980), Cmnd 7965, para 81, HMSO, 1981, quoted by F. Heidensohn in A. Morris, *Women and Crime*.

49   Treatment and Training of Female Inmates, p.3.

50   This point is well made in H. Legge, 'Work in prison: the process of inversion', *British Journal of Criminology*, 18, 1 (January 1978), pp. 6–22.

Chapter 8: Relationships

1   P. T. d'Orban, 'Social and psychiatric aspects of female crime', *Medicine, Science and the Law* (July 1971). T. C. N. Gibbens, 'Female offenders', *British Journal of Hospital Medicine* 6 (Sept. 1971).

2   P. Carlen, *Women's Imprisonment – a study in social control* (Routledge and Kegan Paul, London, 1983), Chap. 2.

3   J. Rose, *Elizabeth Fry*, p. 89.

4   *Report of the Working Party on the Treatment and Training of Female Inmates in Scotland* (Unpublished Report, N.D.).

5   *Report on H. M. Institution*, Cornton Vale, 1982 (H.M. Inspectorate for Prisons for Scotland, 1982), p.5.

6   This is well documented by Carlen, *Women's Imprisonment*.

7   As in the following: R. Giallombardo, *Society of Women: A Study of a Women's Prison* (John Wiley, New York, 1966). E. Heffernan, *Making it in Prison: The Square, the Cool, and the Life* (Wiley–Interscience,

London, 1972). D. Ward and G. Kassebaum, *Women's Prison: Sex and Social Structure* (Weidenfeld and Nicolson, London, 1958). D. R. Cressey (ed.), *The Prison: Studies in Institutional Organisation and Change* (Holt, Rinehart and Winston, New York, 1961). D. Glaser, *The Effectiveness of a Prison and Parole System* (Bobbs-Merrill, New York, 1964). G. M. Sykes, *The Society of Captives: A Study of a Maximum Security Prison* (Princeton University Press, Princeton, NJ, 1958). P. G. Garabedian, 'Social roles and processes of socialization in the prison community', *Social Problems*, 11 (Fall 1963), pp. 139–52.

8 'Borstal training lasted for two years. However, most individuals were released before they served two years. The usual release date for girls was often about 15 months, for boys just under a year. Until the two years were up, they were 'on licence'. They were supposed to see a probation officer or social worker regularly and could be recalled to prison to complete their Borstal training if they broke the conditions of their licence, which included no communications with other ex Borstal girls.

9 'List D' schools are residential establishments run by Scottish Local Authority Social Work Departments to which are referred children deemed in need of care and protection.

10 *Working Party Report*, p.12.

11 *HMI Report*, p. 10.

12 Radical Alternatives to Prison, *Alternatives to Holloway*, (Christian Action, 1972).

13 P. Carlen, *Women's Imprisonment*, p. 67.

14 C. Gibbs, 'The effect of the imprisonment of women upon their children', *British Journal of Criminology*, 11 (1971).

15 J. R. Chapman, *Economic Realities and Female Crime* (Lexington, Lexington, Mass., 1980).

16 This means the signing over of parental rights to the local authority.

17 M. Fitzgerald and J. Sim, *British Prisons* (Basil Blackwell, Oxford, 1982).

18 Ibid., p. 84.

19 James Anderson of Styal, *The Guardian* 1984.

20 *Prisons and the Prisoner*.

Chapter 9: Turning Point

1 *Holloway Project Committee Report* (Home Office, 1985), paragraphs 2–12.

2 P. Toynbee in *The Guardian*, 15 August 1985.

3 Ibid.

4 P. Toynbee in *The Guardian*, 15 October 1984.

5 Radical Alternatives to Prison, *Alternatives to Holloway* (Christian Action Publications, 1972) quotes Holloway Redevelopment Timetable, an internal document circulated 1970/71.

6   Statement made to representatives of the campaigning organisation *Women in Prison* (WIP), in *New Statesman*, 9 November 1984.

7   *The Guardian*, 22 May 1985.

8   'Women and the penal system', Education, Arts and Home Office sub-committee of the expenditure Committee, Vol. I. para 80, 1978–9.

9   Ibid., Vol. I, para 89.

10   *Holloway Project Committee Report*, Vol. I, para 1.3.

11   *Report on H. M. Institution Cornton Vale*, H. M. Inspectorate of Prisons for Scotland, 1982.

12   *Holloway Project Committee Report*, Vol. I, para 3.8.

13   Control Review Committee, *Managing the Long-term Prison System* (Home Office, 1984).

14   Ibid.

15   For example, F. Adler, *Sisters in Crime: The Rise of the New Female Criminal* (D. C. Heath, London and Lexington, Mass., 1975).

16   E. B. Leonard, 'Judicial decisions and prison reform: The impact of litigation on women prisoners', *Social Problems*, 31, 1 October 1983.

17   In mixed sex prisons in Denmark, women are in a sense used to keep men more acquiescent. This takes the form of women serving men in various ways. Personal communication with Ida Koch about her research in Danish prisons. See also C. Schweber, 'Beauty marks and blemishes: The co-ed prison and a microcosm of integrated society', *The Prison Journal*, (Spring–Summer 1984), pp. 3–14.

Selected Bibliography

Adler F. (ed.), *The Incidence of Female Criminality in the Contemporary World*, New York University Press, New York, 1981.

Adler, F., *Sisters in Crime; The Rise of the New Female Criminal*, McGraw-Hill, New York, 1975.

Andrews, W., *Old Time Punishments*, Andrews, Hull, 1880.

Annual Report on The Prison Commissioners for Scotland, for the Year 1901, HMSO, 1902.

Beattie, J. M., 'The pattern of crime in England, 1660–1800', *Past and Present*, 62, 1974, pp. 47–95.

Beattie, J. M., 'The criminality of women in eighteenth century England', *Journal of Social History*, 72, 1975, pp. 80–116.

Beddoe, D., *Welsh Convict Women*, Stewart Williams, 1979.

Beddoe, D., *Discovering Women's History*, Pandora, London, 1983.

Box, S. and Hale, E., 'Liberation and female criminality in England and Wales', *British Journal of Criminology*, 23, 1 (January, 1983).

Burt, C., 'Facial expression as an index of mentality', *Child-Study* 12, 1 (June 1919).

Burt, C., *The Young Delinquent*, London, University of London Press, 1931, first published in 1919.

Carlen, P. (ed.), *Criminal Women: Autobiographical Accounts*, Polity Press, Cambridge, 1985.

Carlen, P., *Women's Imprisonment: A study in social control*, Routledge and Kegan Paul, London, 1983.

Carpenter, M., *Our Convicts*, Longman, London, 1864.

Chesterton, G. L., *Revelations of Prison Life*, Vol II, Hurst and Blackwell, London, 1856.

Dates, S. K. and Scarpitti, F. R., *Women, Crime and Justice*, Oxford University Press, Oxford, 1980.

Dell, S. and Gibbens, T. C. N., 'Remands of women offenders for medical reports', *Medicine, Science and the Law*, July 1971, pp. 117–26.

Dobash, R. Emerson, and Dobash, Russell P., *Violence Against Wives: The Case Against The Patriarchy*, Free Press, New York, 1979; Open Books, Shepton Mallet, England, 1980.

Dobash, R. P., 'Labour and discipline in Scottish and English prisons: Moral correction, punishment and useful toil', *Sociology*, 27, 1 (February, 1983), pp. 1–27.

Dobash, R. P., and Dobash, R. Emerson, 'Community response to violence against wives: Charivari, abstract justice and patriarchy, *Social Problems*, 28, 5 (June, 1981), pp. 563–81.

Donajgrodzki, A. P. (ed.), *Social Control in Nineteenth-Century Britain*, Croom Helm, London, 1977.

Education, Arts and Home Office Sub-Committee of the Expenditure Committee, *Expenditure Committee, Education, Arts and Home Office Sub-Committee of the Expenditure Committee: Fourteen Volumes of Evidence*, 1978–9.

Edwards, S., *Female Sexuality and the Law*, Oxford, Martin Robertson, 1981.

Ehrenreich, B. and English, D., *For Her Own Good*, Pluto Press, London, 1979.

Ellis, Havelock, *The Criminal*, Scott, London, 1901, first published in 1891.

Evans, R., *The Fabrication of Virtue, English Prison Architecture, 1750–1840*, Cambridge University Press, Cambridge, 1982.

Faulkner, D. E. R., 'The redevelopment of Holloway Prison', *The Howard Journal for Penology and Crime Prevention*, 8, 2 (1971), pp. 122–31.

Fitzgerald, M. and Sim, J., *British Prisons*, Basil Blackwell, Oxford, 1982.

Forsythe, W. J., 'New prisons for old gaols, Scottish penal reform, 1835–1842', *The Howard Journal for Penology and Crime Prevention* 10, 3 (1981), pp. 138–49.

Foucault, M., trs. A. Sheridan, *Discipline and Punish*, Allen Lane, London, 1977.

Foucault, M., *Madness and Civilization*, Social Science Paperbacks, London, 1967.

Fox, J. C., 'Women's prison policy, prisoner activism, and the impact of the contemporary feminist movement: A case study', *The Prison Journal*, LXIV, 1 (Spring–Summer 1984), pp. 15–36.

Fraser, Catherine, 'The origin and progress of the 'British Ladies' Society for Promoting the Reformation of Female Prisoners, established by Mrs Fry in 1821', *Transactions of the National Association for the Promotion of Sciences*, 6 (1862), pp. 495–501.

Freedman, E. B., *Their Sisters' Keepers: Women's Prison Reform in America, 1830–1930*, University of Michigan Press, Ann Arbor, 1981.

Fry, E., *A Memoir of the Life of Elizabeth Fry with Extracts from her Journal and Letters* (eds), K. Fry and E. Creswell, 1847.

Fry, E., *Observations on the Siting, Superintendance, and Government, of Female Prisoners*, Arch, London, 1827.

Giallombardo, R., *Society of Women: A Study of a Women's Prison*, John Wiley, New York, 1966.

Gibbens, T. C. N., 'Female offenders', *British Journal of Hospital Medicine* 6 (September 1971), pp. 279–86.

Goodman, N., *Studies of Female Offenders*, Home Office Research Unit Report, HMSO, 1967.

Gordon, M., *Penal Discipline*, Routledge and Sons, London, 1922.

Griffiths, A. G. F., *Memorials of Millbank and Chapters in Prison History*, Chapman and Hall, London, 1884.

Gurney, J. J., *Notes on a Visit Made to Some of the Prisons in Scotland and the North of England in Company with Elizabeth Fry*, Longman, London, 1819.

Hay, D., Linebough P. and Thompson, E. P. (eds.), *Albion's Fatal Tree*, Allen Lane, London, 1975.

Heffernan, E., *Making it in Prison: The Square, the Cool, and the Life*, Wiley – Interscience, London, 1972.

Heidensohn, F., 'The imprisonment of females', in S. McConville (ed.), *The Use of Imprisonment*, Routledge and Kegan Paul, London, 1975.

Heidensohn, F., 'Women and the penal system', in A. Morris (ed.), with L. Gelsthorpe, *Women and Crime*, Cropwood Conference Series No. 13, University of Cambridge: Institute of Criminology, 1981, pp. 49–70.

Heidensohn, F., *Women and Crime*, Macmillan, London, 1985.

Henriques, U. R. W., 'The rise and fall of the separate system of prison discipline', *Past and Present*, 54 (February 1972), pp. 61–93.

Hill, F. *Frederick Hill: An Autobiography of Fifty Years in Times of Penal Reform*, (ed.) Constance Hill, Bentley and Son, London, 1893.

Holloway Project Committee Report, HMSO, July, 1985.

Ignatieff, M., *A Just Measure of Pain: The Penitentiary in the Industrial Revolution, 1750–1850*, Macmillan, London, 1978.

Jewitt, L., 'Scolds and how they cured them in the good old times', *The Reliquary*, October 1860.

Kassebaum, D. and Ward, G., *Women's Prison: Sex and Social Structure*, Weidenfeld and Nicolson, London, 1966.

Kelly, J., *When the Gates Shut*, Longman, London, 1967.

Klein, D. and Kress, J., 'Any woman's blues: A critical overview of women, crime, and the criminal justice system,' *Crime and Social Justice* 5 (June 1976), pp. 34–49.

Klein, D., 'The etiology of female crime: a review of the literature', *Issues in Criminology*, 8, 2 (Fall 1973), pp. 3–30.

Lekkerkerker, E. C., *Reformatories for Women in the United States*, J. B. Wolters' Uitgevers-Maatschappij, Batavia, The Netherlands, 1931.

Leonard, E. B., *Women, Crime and Society*, Longman, London, 1982.

Leonard, E. B., 'Judicial decisions and prison reform: the impact of litigation on women prisoners', *Social Problems*, 31, 1 (October 1983), pp. 45–58.

Lombroso, C. and Ferrero, W., *The Female Offender*, originally published, Unwin, 1895, Owen, London, 1959.

Markus, T., *Order in Space and Society*, Mainstream, Edinburgh, 1982.

Maudsley, H., 'Review of female life in prison', *Journal of Mental Science*, 9 (1863), pp. 69–87.

Maybrick, F. E., *Mrs. Maybrick's Own Story: My Fifteen Lost Years*, Funk and Wagnall, New York, 1905.

Mayhew, H. and Binney, J., *The Criminal Prisons of London and Scenes of Prison Life*, Griffin, Bohn and Co., London, 1862, reprinted 1968 by Frank Cass, London.

Melossi, D. and Pavarini, M., *The Prison and the Factory: Origins of the Penitentiary System*, translated by Glynis Cousin, London, Macmillan, 1981.

Miller, E., 'International trends in the study of female criminality: an essay review', *Contemporary Crises* 7 (1983), pp. 59–70.

Morris, A. and Gelsthorpe, L., 'False clues and female crime', in *Women and Crime*, A. Morris (ed.), Cropwood Conference Series No. 13, University of Cambridge, Institute of Criminology, 1981, pp. 49–70.

Morrison, W. D., *Crime and Its Causes*, Swan, London, 1891.

O'Brien, P., *The Promise of Punishment: Prisons in Nineteenth Century France*, Princeton University Press, Princeton, 1982.

Oakley, A., *Subject Women*, Martin Robertson, Oxford, 1981.

d'Orban, P. T., 'Social and psychiatric aspects of female crime', *Medicine, Science and the Law* (July 1971).

Pailthorpe, G., *Studies in the Psychology of Delinquency*, Medical Research Council, HMSO, 1932.

Pailthorpe, G., *What We Put in Prison*, Williams and Norgate, London, 1933.

Peckham, A., *A Woman in Custody*, Fontana, Glasgow, 1985.

Prison Matron (F.W. Robinson), *Female Life in Prison*, Hurst and Blackett, London, 1862.

Prisons and Prisoners: The Work of the Prison Service in England and Wales, HMSO, 1977.

Radical Alternatives to Prison, *Alternatives to Holloway*, Christian Actions Publications, 1972.

Rafter, N. H. *Partial Justice: State Prisons and Their Inmates, 1800–1935*, Northeastern University Press, Boston, 1985.

Rafter, N. H., 'Hard times: Custodial prisons for women and the example of the New York state prison for women at Auburn, 1893–1933', in N. H. Rafter and E. A. Stanko (eds.), *Judge, Lawyer, Victim, Thief*, Northeastern University Press, Boston, 1982.

Rafter, N. H. 'Too dumb to know better: Cacogenci family studies and the criminology of women', *Criminology*, 18, 1 (May 1980), pp. 3–25.

Report of the Working Party on the Treatment and Training of Female Inmates in Scotland, Unpublished Report, N.D.

Report on H.M. Institution Cornton Vale, H. M. Inspectorate of Prisons for Scotland, 1982.

Report(s) of the Inspectors Appointed to Visit the Different Prisons of Great Britain, Scotland, Northumberland and Durham, HMSO, especially the 1st–11th, 1835–1846.

Rusche, G. and Kirchheimer, O., *Punishment and Social Structure*, Columbia University Press, New York, 1939.

Schweber, C., 'Beauty marks and blemishes: The co-ed prison as a microcosm of integrated society', *The Prison Journal*, LXIV (Spring–Summer 1984), pp. 3–14.

Sellin, T., *Pioneering in Penology, The Amsterdam Houses of Correction in the Sixteenth and Seventeenth Centuries*, University of Pennsylvania, Philadelphia, 1944.

Sievwright, W., *Historical Sketch of the General Prison for Scotland at Perth*, Wright, Perth, 1894.

Sim, J., 'Women in prison: A historical analysis', *The Abolitionist* 8, (Spring 1981), pp. 14–18.

Simon, R., *Women and Crime*, D. C. Heath, London and Lexington, Mass, 1975.

Singer, L., 'Women and the correctional process', *American Criminal Law Review*, 11 (Winter 1973), pp. 295–308.

Smart, C., *Women, Crime and Criminology: A Feminist Critique*, Routledge and Kegan Paul, London, 1977.

Smart, C., 'The new female criminal: Reality or myth', *British Journal of Criminology*, 19 (1979), pp. 50–9.

Smith, A. D., *Women in Prison*, Stevens, London, 1962.

Steffensmeier, D. J. and Steffensmeier, R. H. S., 'Trends in female delinquency', *Criminology*, 18 (1980), pp. 62–85.

Steffensmeier, D. J., 'Sex differences in patterns of adult crime 1965–77: A review and assessment', *Social Forces*, 58, (1980), pp. 1080–1108.

Steffensmeier, D. J., 'Assessing the impact of the women's movement on sex-based differences in the handling of adult criminal defendants', *Crime and Delinquency*, 76 (1980), pp. 344–57.

Storch, R. D., 'Police control of street prostitution in Victorian London: A study in the contexts of police action', in D. H. Bayley (ed.), *Police and Society*, Sage, Beverley Hills, 1977.

Tait, W., *Magdalenism. An Inquiry Into the Extent, Causes and Consequences of Prostitution in Edinburgh*, Rickard, Edinburgh, 1842.

Thomas, K., 'The double standard', *Journal of the History of Ideas*, 20 (1959), pp. 195–216.

Thompson, E. P., 'The moral economy of the English crowd in the eighteenth century', *Past and Present*, 50 (February 1971), pp. 76–136.

Weiner, C., 'Sex roles and crime in late Elizabethan Hertfordshire', *Journal of Social History* (Summer 1978), pp. 39–60.

Weis, J. G., 'Liberation and crime: The invention of the new female criminal', *Crime and Social Justice* 6, (1976), pp. 17–27.

Western, C. C., *Remarks Upon Prison Discipline*, Ridgeway, London, 1821.

Woodside, M., 'Psychiatric referrals from Edinburgh courts', *British Journal of Criminology*, 16, 1 (January 1974).

Woodside, M., 'Women offenders and psychiatric reports', *Social Work Today*, 11 (September, 1974).

Index